Dear Katie,
I have so enjoyed getting to know you! You are a blessing and I expect to hear great things about you! I hope you enjoy this book and that it inspires you to share your stories.
Much love,
Jane June 2017

The 50/60 Kid

A Palo Alto Dreamer

The 50 / 60 Kid

A Palo Alto Dreamer

First published in the United States 2008

Published by Lulu.com

For information contact Jane Horton

janehorton@earthlink.net

First Edition, January 2008

ISBN 978-1-4357-0817-4

So, we were sitting outside at Liz's house, and Patricia said, "Hey, I **love** pinball, the real games, with the real pinball machine!," and I said, "Like in the movie 'The Verdict' with Paul Newman," and Lynn said, "Oh the alcoholic lawyer?" and we went on to explain the movie to everyone else, and then I said, "Hey my Gramma loved pinball; she had a pinball machine at her house, plus we used to go to the horse races at Bay Meadows in San Mateo. Gramma Gigi just loved that and she would let me cut school and take me places like wineries and the beach instead of school," and Gretchen said, "I can't believe all the different stories of your childhood… you should just write a book about it."

Here is the beginning of my story; it is also the story of a generation growing up in the 1950s and 1960s.

Dedicated to my Gramma, my daddy, my family and to all my friends who I so love and who so love me, and to

"The 50/60 Kids."

Contents

*Louis Road in 1955, the corner of Ames Avenue to the right,
and a model home down the street.*

Judy 6 and me 4: Two cowgirls on Louis Road

Louis Road in 1955, the corner of Ames Avenue to the right, and a model home down the street.

Judy 6 and me 4: Two cowgirls on Louis Road

When Palo Alto was Rural – The Beginning

I was born in the time when everything was in between. Between WWII and the Vietnam War, between segregation and civil rights, between the time when girls had to wear skirts and dresses to school and the time when they could wear pants. I think that these were some of the shadows that formed us all: The leftover shadows of WWII; the stay-at-home-moms whose own mothers had worked in the WWII factories, and the shadows of segregation and oppressions that gave way to later explosions, the results of which no one could have foreseen.

I became in-between in another way as well, in between my older sister Judy and my younger sister Jennifer.

My parents bought the home where my father still lives 53 years ago. How could it be 53 years? Louis Road was a dirt road, and there was a farm house down on the corner of Loma Verde and Louis, a three-story farm house with old rusty farm equipment and rabbit hutches and a kitchen that was old and sturdy with sun shining inside so bright that the dust floating in air looked like glitter fairies, and everything was hand-made and sturdy and of wood.

The opposite corner had the one-story farm house that the witch lived in. We thought that she was a witch and that she had murdered her husband and buried him in her front yard. As time passed and sidewalks came in along with the paved roads, we children believed that if we stopped at the edge of her property on the sidewalk crack, took a deep breath and ran as fast as we could to the other side of her property, then nothing bad could happen, or at least the old witch could not get us.

I think now what really had happened was that the old lady who lived there was a widow, and the septic tank in her front yard had been redone, not that her husband was buried there. Most of the time the old lady had her dress on inside-out or backwards with an apron over it and had pretty wispy hair so that she looked a little crazy to us neighborhood kids.

When we first moved there our house was surrounded by fields. Across the dirt road was a sticker field, all the way from our road to Middlefield Road, and out of the back window were more fields, clear to the Old Bayshore Highway. On the other side of Bayshore was the dump, the Yacht Harbor, and the Pheasant Club. Later my knowledge of pheasants made the study of history and peasants rather confusing at times, especially when I imagined hoards of pheasants defying the leaders and forming violent revolutions.

Yes, there were new post-war homes popping up in the middle of the fields between Middlefield Road and Old Bayshore Highway, which was a three-laned highway with some stop lights. Our home was the first home in the Sterling housing tract. Sterling. How disappointed I was later to learn that it had nothing to do with high-quality metal, but only that it was named after a Mr. Sterling who had something to do with the housing development...stucco, thank God, not those crazy Eichler homes with radiant heat and atriums that were soon springing up all over the place.

Adventure School

Every Saturday we would go to Redwood City to grocery shop at the Penny Mayfair store on El Camino. There wasn't a grocery store around our neighborhood that my parents liked, and besides, after we went to the grocery store we would go to Gramma and Grandpa's house...Gramma Gigi and Grandpa Bob. They were my mom's parents; my mom called them "mother and dad," and so did my daddy, but they were really my mom's parents. We would have lunch there and spend the afternoon and some evenings and then go home. I loved going to Gramma Gigi's house; growing up I spent parts of summers and many weekends there.

When I was four, there was a television show on called "Adventure School," and I was enthralled watching Miss Nancy on *Adventure School*. It wasn't like *Ding-Dong School*, the other TV show, because it was more about adventure. My favorite parts were when a little girl would come out in her slip with a towel on her shoulders and they would wash her hair and even rub the suds in her eyes and she didn't cry because it was *No More Tears Johnson Baby Shampoo*. I didn't realize that it was an ad; I thought it was part of the show, and wished that my mom would buy *No More Tears Johnson Baby Shampoo*. We got our hair washed once a week, Saturday night, and had to kneel on the old grey metal kitchen stool, leaning over the sink while we had our hair washed, rinsed, washed, and then rinsed with vinegar water. The only part I liked was when the vinegar water ran close to my mouth and I could lick that flavor, imagining that it might be what whiskey tasted like. It really burned if it got in your eyes, plus your stomach hurt from leaning over the sink, and your head hurt from having your hair pulled, plus then there was all that wet tangled hair to comb out. Cream rinse had not been heard of, and even if it had, I don't think my family would have splurged on a fancy product like that!

The other part of *Adventure School* that I liked was at the very end. The four kids who had been on the show got to sit at a little table just the right size for kids and drink *Bosco*. "I love *Bosco*, chocolate flavored treat...." *Bosco* was like *Hershey's* syrup but thicker and it came in a jar; a person could spoon the *Bosco* out and add it to milk to make chocolate milk. We never had *Bosco* at home, but I could imagine how good it must taste, because all those kids on *Adventure School* looked really happy when they drank their *Bosco*-flavored milk.

Well, one day my Gramma Gigi said that I was going to be on *Adventure School!* I don't know how, but she had made it happen. *Adventure School* was filmed in Oakland, so Gramma Gigi was going to drive me there to the other side of the San Francisco Bay and I would be on TV!

I couldn't wait. That morning when it was still dark outside, I was scrubbed, ribboned, braided, polished, and cleaned; clothes were ironed and starched, layers put on (two pairs of underwear: Regular with the fancy pair over the regular pair, an undershirt, a slip, a petticoat, and then the dress.) Clean socks and church shoes. We drove to Oakland, and on the way there I was reminded to be on my best behavior, to sit with my legs together, not to pick my nose, to say "please" and "thank you" and to breathe through my nose, not my mouth. We got there and went into the studio, and it was all busy with bright lights and I met some other kids and we sat around the little table I had seen on TV and the grown-ups asked questions and I got to pet a real white rat and a real baby alligator and then my gramma came over to the table and got me and we went home.

The filming had been going on, and I was on TV all right, but I didn't get any *Bosco* nor did I see the little girl getting her hair washed with *No More Tears Johnson Baby Shampoo*. I guess the show had run out of time for the *Bosco*. It didn't really seem like anything special had happened.

The other claim-to-fame things besides Adventure School that Gramma Gigi did was send in my drawings to the *San Francisco Chronicle*. *The Chronicle* had a part of the comics' page where they would have a copy of a drawing that a kid had done and the kid would win three dollars. I had my drawing in the paper when I was three, "Mother Pushing Baby Carriage" and again when I was seven, "The Flood."

I remember the three dollars when I was seven, because we went to downtown Palo Alto so I could buy something with the money. Woolworth's was on University Avenue, and it had a lunch counter and an upstairs part, and the people who worked there were very polite and would ask if they could help you. The lady at the lunch counter was scary because she looked like a half-man-half-woman, and dressed like a nurse in all white with a black apron. She was really fat and wore a hair net but she had whiskers too. Upstairs they had the clothes. I don't think I had ever had store-bought clothes before. I bought a pair of lime green pedal pushers with little green ribbons that tied at the bottom of the leg. I was so excited! I got a sleeveless blouse to go with them, all for three dollars.

When I got home I was a fashion model, a store-bought clothes stylish girl! I was so excited with my new clothes. I went outside to model them, and Daddy was on the back porch doing some kind of repair on a bicycle. I wanted to watch and sat down…right on the lid of the can of axle grease. The lid stuck to my pants, the black grease soaked into my beautiful new pedal pushers, a big five-inch circle. "Oh, of all the places to sit down! Why in the hell did you choose that one place?" my dad asked, shaking his head. I was sobbing. The grease never did come out of the pants.

And Baby Jennifer made three!
Jane almost 4 - Judy 6 years old

Baby Jennifer

There was something wrong with my mom when I was three years old. I didn't know that she was going to have a baby, but I knew that she was lying down in my parent's room a lot. People didn't say "pregnant" or talk about having babies, and I hadn't noticed anything different about my mom except that she lay down more and was a lot quieter because she was taking naps in the afternoon. Then she wasn't at home and Gramma Gigi brought over some food, and I heard that my mom was in the hospital and that I had a sister named Jennifer. In those days new mothers stayed in the hospital for three or four days at least, sometimes a week or more. It was the only chance they ever had to rest.

Now I was in the middle. I had been the youngest; Judy was 2 ½ years older than I, and now I was 3 ½ years older than Baby Jennifer. Judy was sick because she had been born with something wrong with her kidneys. She didn't get to play the same way as I did and sometimes she had to go to the hospital. But now I had my own baby sister! I was Judy's baby sister and now Judy had two little sisters.

My mom was in the Hoover Pavilion Hospital, and we were driving down Embarcadero Road in Palo Alto, just my daddy and I, and I guess Daddy was thinking more about the new baby than his driving, because Daddy got his one and only speeding ticket. When the policeman pulled us over and I saw that policeman asking my daddy for his license, I started to cry because I thought my daddy was being arrested, and I knew that a girl who was almost four couldn't drive the car home if they arrested her daddy. It was a really big cop on a motorcycle. He gave my daddy a speeding ticket for going 32 miles per hour on a 25 mile per hour road, and I wanted to beat that old copper up for bothering my daddy.

It's different looking back at it now, but at the time this happened, my daddy was 27 years old and Jennifer was his third child and he had been married for eight years, and had been in the Navy and gone to college and was a supervisor of the loan department at The American Trust Company. Daddy had a mortgage on a new home in the suburbs, courtesy of a G.I. loan, so I guess he did have a lot on his mind.

I was pretty good at watching for cops when I was in Gramma Gigi's car. I would sit in the backseat on my knees and be the lookout for cops. It was my job to tell her if a cop was following us, because Gramma Gigi didn't want to get a speeding ticket. But when my daddy got his ticket I was in the front seat, and besides, Daddy didn't have us kids be lookouts. In those days kids could sit up on their knees in cars or switch from the front seat to the back seat, or even lie down in the car so long as they didn't bother the driver, and little kids were allowed to sit in the front seat of the car and no one had car seats or seat belts. If your car was big enough you could put a baby basket in the car with a sleeping baby in it, but most of the time people in cars just held onto their babies. Families traveled together so there was always someone to hold a baby.

Later that week my daddy was trying to cook, but all I remember was that he was using the *Mixmaster* electric mixer and lifted up the beaters, and food was flying everywhere! Maybe it was batter, maybe it was mashed potatoes, but it spattered the walls and the table and the stove; I was ducking down and everyone was yelling. It just was not how that *Mixmaster* was supposed to be used!

Then the big day came, and Jennifer came home from the hospital, but there really wasn't much to see. She was all wrapped up in a baby blanket and she was tiny and got put into her bassinet right away. The bassinet was like a woven basket fitting into a stand with wheels that was just the right size for a little baby to sleep in. It was like a baby buggy and a cradle combined. A baby buggy was a little bed with wheels and a handle to push it, plus there was a shade that could flip from one side to the other to keep the sun out of a baby's eyes. A baby could lie down flat like in a bed and go to sleep while the mom pushed the baby on the sidewalk to wherever they were going.

So Baby Jennifer was in her bassinet and we sat down to a dinner of chicken, green peas, and potatoes, when my mom looked at me and said, "Dammit, Wayne, Jane's got the chickenpox!" There I was, eating my chicken leg and minding my own business, and Whoosh! I was taken out to the car, chicken leg in hand, for Daddy to take me up to Gramma Gigi and Grandpa Bob's house, because little girls with chicken pox could not be around babies.

Grandpa Bob was there at the house in San Carlos, but Gramma Gigi and Auntie Jan, who was 22 at the time, were at the movies. Daddy put me in Gramma Gigi's bed, and when my gramma and Auntie Jan came home there I was, all chicken-poxy in bed, wearing in one of Grandpa Bob's pajama tops.

I spent the next two weeks there. It turned out that I was allergic to calamine lotion, which was what people put on chicken pox in those days. So not only did I have the chicken pox, I had allergic itchies all over on top of the chicken pox, except for in my mouth and ears where no one had put the Calamine. I just had regular chicken pox there. Somehow I related eating that chicken leg with getting the chicken pox, and wasn't real eager to eat chicken again. I spent a lot of time in lukewarm baths with bicarbonate of soda in the water, and got to stay at Gramma Gigi's. The bad thing was that I gave Auntie Jan the chicken pox, and she had one little scar on her shoulder for the rest of her life.

Staying at Gramma Gigi's house was the greatest, even though I had chicken pox. She had a television and we would sit together in the big green chair and watch cowboy shows. We watched *The Gabby Hayes Show*, which we called "Fuzzy" and we watched *Roy Rogers* and a daytime show, *As the World Turns*, which was not a cowboy show but was on every day at lunchtime. We would sit on the chair and eat ice cream and when the TV was over we might play double solitaire, which was a card game. If Gramma Gigi was busy, then I could play single solitaire or play with the pinball machine, or I could turn on the radio and rotate the knob until I found a station I liked. "The Yellow Rose of Texas" was on the radio a lot, and if I could find that song, then I would stop right there and listen to it.

I could color, and Gramma Gigi had a box of crayons with a lot of colors in it, and she had these really special color sheets that were on the cardboard that came inside shirts that had come back from the cleaners. Grandpa Bob had all his work-shirts washed and ironed at the cleaners, and the boy from the cleaners would deliver the shirts to their house. Then when Grandpa Bob wore a clean shirt, he would take out the straight pins and save the cardboard that the shirt was wrapped around, because the cardboard was really a coloring sheet! It might be a picture of a mountain and a lake, or a flower, or a gingerbread man, or maybe a car, or a cat or a dog, but you never could guess which sheet would be inside that shirt! They had so many different ones it seemed like we never got the same one twice!

At home my mother didn't send my daddy's shirts to the cleaners like Gramma Gigi sent Grandpa Bob's shirts. My mom washed the white work shirts in the washer we had in the garage. The washer was a Sears *Easy Washer* that had a spin dry cylinder! My mom washed all the clothes in that; the regular clothes and my daddy's shirts, and the cloth baby diapers, but the diapers were always washed separately in the hottest water possible.

Then all the clothes that had been wrung out got hung up outside on the clothesline. The clothesline was thin rope that was coated with a soft white, smooth rubber-like coating. Our clothesline was like a giant umbrella, and there was a hollow tube stuck into the back lawn, and the clothesline pole stuck into that tube, so that the clothesline pole stood up straight. There was a handle on the pole, and when it was turned, the clothesline opened up and there were a whole lot of clotheslines all going around and around the pole like an umbrella without the cover. There was a big bag of clothes pins that hung on the handle, not the old-fashioned pins that looked like people, but the new-fashioned ones that had a spring in them. When you squeezed them they would open up and when you let go they would hold tight to the clothes and the clothesline. My mom would hang my daddy's shirts on the clothesline. After that, before she ironed the shirts, she had to starch the cuffs and the collars.

To make the starch, my mom would add starch flakes to cold water, and slowly heat up the water to boiling, and then dip the collar and dip the cuffs into the starchy liquid. Then the starch actually had to dry before the shirt was ironed. That way when the shirt was ironed and hung up it looked as good as if it had gone to the cleaners, with nice stiff cuffs and collar.

One good thing about those starched cuffs, we always knew we could give Daddy cufflinks for Christmas, because he always wore cuff links to work with his nicely starched shirts.

Jennifer & me...I knew I could make Jennifer walk!

Jennifer from our front walkway with Ames Avenue in the background

The Christening and Church

Baby Jennifer and our family went to the Congregational Church on the corner of Embarcadero and Louis Road for Jennifer's christening. There were a whole lot of people there. Usually at church we kids had to go to the kid part. Church school was confusing. We went to Sunday School, and learned about naked people and apples, but then they showed movies of lava erupting in Hawaii, and Moses and the Baby Jesus. So I asked the teacher if the people were really naked and she got mad at me and said no more questions, but then I asked what in the heck was a Holy Grail anyway?

I didn't really like the kid part, because even though you got to draw, there was this awful boy who would sit at the table I was at and he would eat paste and eat crayons. There I was trying to do the Bible Story coloring book page, and this icky boy would look at me across the table and open the jar of paste and put in his fingers and get a big lump of white creamy paste out and put it in his mouth. It smelled like something not to eat and looked like something not to eat, and then he would open his mouth and show the kids how his mouth was full of paste and it was all stuck to his tongue. I would never talk to him and tried not to look at him. Who knew what he would do next?! And he ate all the orange crayons. The crayon boxes in those days had six fat crayons in a box, with one flattened side to keep them from rolling away, and losing one color had a pretty big impact on how my drawing looked. And that pasty-faced (and now I knew why!) little boy would put the orange crayon in his mouth, bite it off and chew until his teeth were all orange, and just stare at me while he did it. I was not learning anything about God or the Bible, I can tell you that.

I was glad to go into the big church, except everyone had to be really quiet. One time Daddy put on his holiest cotton T-shirt under his good church shirt, and said it was his "Holy Shirt!" And there was this weird thing that all the old ladies wore…they would have dead animals around their necks, long skinny furry animals that had the head and the eyes and the claws and the nose and the other end had the tail and the feet with all the claws. I think someone had sewed a bunch of animals together to make one long animal.

My gramma didn't wear a dead animal; I don't think I could have stood looking at her if she had worn one. I couldn't imagine sitting in the car having to look at that dead animal the whole time. It was bad enough having those little eyes stare at you from that dead animal and wondering why they didn't rot and weren't all stinky. I found out later that the dead animals had glass eyes not real eyes, and that people actually had jobs of taking out the insides of animals, sewing them shut again, and putting in fake eyes!

At church if you were really quiet and sneaky you could touch one of the dead animals, but it was creepy and besides, the old ladies always would sense that a kid was trying to touch their stole, or whatever it was called, and they would either turn around and glare at you or slowly pull the dead animal up until you could not reach it anymore. I thought that those animals were called mink stoles, but I wasn't sure if someone had stolen them or what had happened to make them be called mink stoles.

I was dressed up in my church shoes and dress and hat and white gloves, and so were those old ladies, but their hats had little veils in the front of their faces; maybe they didn't want anyone to see who was wearing a dead animal; over their coats they hung those dead animals. There was always one of those ladies in front of me in church, and we sat down on a long bench called a "pew."

I sat next to Gramma Gigi while they took Baby Jennifer up to the front of the church and threw water on her or something that made her cry. And then they passed around the collection plate and everyone put in money that was not the regular money in the donation envelopes but money that everyone could see. Usually every week each person, kid or grown-up, had their own envelope and they wrote their name on it or their parent wrote for them, and they wrote how much money was inside the envelope on the outside of the envelope, so that even though this was supposed to be between that person and God everyone else saw it, and because God was all knowing and all powerful why in the heck did people have to write it down because wouldn't God just know about it anyway? So I thought I was whispering, but apparently not when I said pretty loudly, "Gramma, you mean we have to **pay** to get out of this place?!" I found out that even whispering in church is not a good idea.

There was another part of the church down the street on Louis Road. It was a place for kids to go for Sunday School when the other Sunday Schools were full. It was called "Parent's Nursery School." It had a big playground with a slide and a wooden play house that had another slide on it. It was fun to go on the slide up and down, up and down. My parents would go to the big church and drop us off there at Sunday School, but I don't remember the Sunday School part, just the play part.

Well, there was one dramatic thing that happened there: I was half way up, climbing the play house, when a big fat nail went through the back of my knee, and came out the front. I could see it poking through, and I was stuck and couldn't move and was trying to balance, but there were no grown-ups around to help or to notice and the kids were all busy. So there I was hanging on to a board with a nail stick through my knee, and because it was at church I was thinking about Jesus and the pictures of him hanging from the cross, and it was horrible. Finally the kids went inside and a teacher stood in the doorway yelling at me to come inside, come inside or I would be in trouble, but I couldn't move, so I was yelling back, "I can't! I can't!" Then the teacher came outside all mad because she thought I was just being bad, but then she saw that the nail was through my knee and she helped me get down. After she pulled me away from the nail there was a hole on the front of my knee. I couldn't see the back of my knee, but it hurt.

The teacher took me into the bathroom and washed my knee and put some band aids on it. When my parents came to pick me up, the lady told them what happened. The next day my mom took me on the bus to the Palo Alto Clinic so that I could get a tetanus shot. If you didn't get that shot a person could get a horrible disease called lockjaw.

I lived in a world that had Jesus and Sunday School, sisters, parents and grandparents. There were Communists and Americans and I struggled at night as I drifted off to sleep, wondering if any other little girl in the world had so much to figure out, and if she had ever been at her Sunday School when a nail went through her knee.

Vacation

Family vacation. That's a whole other story. Even though my parents worked really hard, there was still the yearly vacation. It was all planned out. Some years we went to Kansas to visit all the relatives of my father, and some years to Southern California to visit all the relatives of my mother. I really liked Kansas the best because there were lighting bugs. Bugs that flashed light at night; it was really dark, but all over the fields as far as a person could see there was twinkling of these golden and greenish bugs, and in the sky the stars twinkled and it was as if a person was in a magical place with darkness and crickets and bugs and a whole world of fairies doing magic all around. I probably needed glasses even then, so I was lucky because all the twinkling lights were smeary and looked like the star in the Bible-story books with the light all spreading around. I really liked the bugs, and there were glow worms which were the lightning bugs only on the ground.

We would do the vacation trip in the car with our family of Mom, Daddy, and we three girls. It was always the same: The car was packed the night before, and we would get up at 4:00 in the morning, and head south down Old Bayshore Highway 101, past the military base of Moffett Field with the enormous hanger that had once housed big airships. Moffett Field had many colored lights so that the planes could land safely in the dark.

Daddy used to always say, "Well, we're off like a herd of turtles!" until one year he said, "Well, we're off like a turd of hurtles!" which is really funny, especially at four o'clock in the morning. So every year after that we always left like turds of hurtles.

We would get near the town of Gilroy and the garlic smell would inspire conversation about garlic and pickles, because Gilroy was known for both of those things in those days and it smelled wonderful for miles, except my sisters wanted the windows closed so they didn't have to smell it or to feel the cold air come in the window. Then on through Pacheco Pass, the "Blood Alley" of the time, with the twisty and steep three-laned road sporting billboards with the death toll of the year, which would lead to the grisly conversation of car wrecks and head-ons and highway carnage. Usually someone would get car sick, usually me, and then someone else would get car sick, and we would have to pull over and clean up. In the early vacation trips there was not a reservoir along that road between Gilroy and Los Banos, just lots of rolling hills.

Casa de Fruta was a little ways out of Gilroy. It was a big cherry stand under a lot of trees, and they sold dried fruit and some juices, plus prunes, walnuts, apricots, pears and cherries. The road went right next to it, but we did not stop because it was always too early in the morning The Pacheco Pass road was a two or three-lane road, and the road went up and down, up and down, over the rolling hills. Finally as it would begin to change from dark to dawn, we would arrive at Los Banos and stop at the park in the middle of town for breakfast at the picnic tables.

We were part of a very elite group eating their breakfast at 6:00 in the morning in Los Banos, drinking juice and eating fruit and the dreaded canned Vienna Sausages. Those sausages probably contributed to me becoming a vegetarian while still a teen-ager, never to return to the life of a carnivore!

Jennifer age 3, Daddy & me, age 7- The Grand Canyon

We would make it to Kansas in two and a half days, staying in motels on the way for two nights. We would stay in Barstow the first night, and always had a motel with a swimming pool. It was fun when we were almost there and then finally there, and could see the blue water of the swimming pool. Usually we were pretty hot by then, because the cars we had never had air conditioning. One year my parents put these metal screens inside the back seat windows. They were supposed to keep it cooler, but I didn't think it was cooler, besides we couldn't see out the windows for the whole trip! Another year my parents bought this little cooler. It plugged into the cigarette lighter, and had a compartment for ice cubes and a little fan. I think maybe my parents might have felt the cool air in the front seat, but we sure didn't in the back seat. Just having the windows open was the best, even if we were not allowed to put our hands outside the windows. So when we went into the swimming pool it was so much fun just to get in and cool off!

My daddy could swim and dive, but we girls were too little and stayed in the shallow end. Usually my mom would go in the motel room to unpack things because she didn't want to swim and it was too hot outside if you were not swimming.

At the motel we would all share one room and fill the bathroom sink with hot water to heat cans of stew and potatoes by letting the cans sit in the hot water. It didn't work very well and the food tasted awful, but it was different. Somehow the can opener was always either forgotten or broke the first day, and we had all these cans of food to eat, so half the meal time was spent trying to open the stubborn cans! Then the rest of the night was musical beds, with my parents in one bed and two girls sharing the other bed and one girl on a cot. It was hard to sleep in a different room in a different bed, " No wait, move over, you're hogging my part!" and then the bedtime kicking and dirty tricks would start until someone, hopefully me, would be punished by sleeping on the floor all by themselves!

We saw so many breathtakingly beautiful things on those trips. The deserts, the Grand Canyon, Taos, Mesa Verde, and the miles and miles of American landscape. Shiprock Peak and the vast open places, the prairies and the farmlands. We never stopped at the two-headed snake pits or the alligator farms or the world's largest cockroach shack. I think my parents held those things in the category of trashy tabloids or ...gasp...comic books, a waste of time and resources, and for us the resources were always quite scarce. Still, I could pout silently for hours, internally discussing how unfair it was that everyone else in the world got to stop and see the flea circus or the two-headed sheep or the albino alligator. Those were the days before Lady Bird Johnson started the highway beautification program, and there were hundreds of billboards. The signs were often so close together you couldn't possibly read them all! They told us about the next great attraction...the only jackalope in the world! And then there were the *Burma Shave* signs....always read aloud, the poetic jingles of the American Highway. "Don't lose / your head / to gain a minute / you need your head / your brains are in it / *Burma-Shave.*"

Me and Jennifer in Taos, New Mexico

With no air-conditioning and some very, very hot places, we looked forward to stopping and getting out and stretching our legs. Usually by the time we stopped I was sitting in a puddle of sweat and my legs were stuck to the hot seat of the car. Then when we would get out, two things would happen: My mom would make us go to the bathroom, and then she would make us drink water. I was not good at either on-demand function, going to the bathroom when commanded, or drinking water when told.

Of course going to the bathroom meant that if the bathroom had tissue paper seat covers then we had to use those. The tissue seat covers were in a packet that hung inside the bathroom door and you would pull one out and put it on the seat before you sat down, but it was icky because if you really had to go bad then you spent a lot of time positioning the tissue paper and usually there was some liquid on the seat that you would not have noticed at all, but the tissue paper would stick to it, and then you would sit on the paper, and it would stick to your butt, and when you stood up then you had to pull it off your butt, and then you pushed the whole thing down the toilet anyway. If there was no seat cover, then you had to do this weird balancing act and try to stand over the toilet and not sit down while you went to the bathroom, because somehow you could catch all sorts of diseases from toilet seats unless there was tissue paper on them. Then we were supposed to wash our hands with faucets that you pushed down and then the faucet top slowly rose up, and when it rose high enough the water turned off, so you had to keep starting it over and over again, and the water was always cold and there might be soap but it was the powdery kind, and there was never any paper towels, but sometimes there was a cloth towel roller.

Sometimes you had to wait in line to go anyway, because it might be the only gas station for hundreds of miles, so lots of cars would be stopped there. It was just such a big production to go the bathroom, and usually about 10 minutes after we left then I would have to go, and would have to hold it until the next gas station about forty million miles down the road.

There was something about the water on vacation that I hated. Well, several things actually. First of all, the water would be icy cold, because we had this stainless steel water jug left over from some war, and it would be filled up with ice cubes the night before, and all day they would slowly melt and there would be ice water in the jug. But it didn't taste good. I didn't really like drinking water that much, but at home I had my pinkish rubber water cup and only drank water from the bathroom faucet. On the trips the water tasted different, and it was too cold and I didn't like that feeling of drinking cold water, feeling the water going inside of me while it was cold was something I didn't like at all.

One hot vacation afternoon we pulled into a gas station, and for some reason my daddy said for us girls to each go get a soda from the soda refrigerator! We never drank soda at home. Soda wasn't good for people and was a waste of money. But not this day. The man from the gas station helped open the lid of this long, low soft-drink refrigerator that was outside at the gas station, under an overhang that made shade. Inside the refrigerator it was full to the rim with crushed ice and ice water, and with many, many bottles resting on and in the ice.

Well I leaned over and reached in. My hand and then my wrist sunk into the wonderfully cold crushed ice, and I slowly pulled up a perfect, beautiful glass bottle of orange soda. There were little pieces of ice stuck to the bottle's sides, but almost immediately those pieces of ice started sliding down the bottle as they melted in the heat. There was a bottle opener right on the side of the refrigerator, and the gas station man helped us open our bottles. A little fizz came out, and a bit of something that almost looked like smoke hovered over the open bottle for the blink of an eye and then was gone, and then the orange smell of the soda tickled my nose. It actually did tickle. What a feeling of wonderousness! I stood there at that gas station, in the heat under the shade of the gas sign, and tilted the ice-cold bottle up to my lips.

I didn't know how to drink out of a soda bottle; I had to push my lips together a certain way and then let the soda come out so that it all didn't pour out at once. Incredible orange soda filled my mouth and cooled my throat. Never in my life before or since has anything tasted so complete, so tingly, so orange. Orange soda...it sparkled in my mouth and the orangeness of it was so perfect that I felt like laughing. It was as if time stood still and there was nothing in the world but the cold wonder of an orange soda. My hand held the coldness of the bottle, and my thirst was quenched by orange perfection. At that moment orange soda became the life salve that I seldom drank, but in times when my very spirit was shattered by deaths, divorces, layoffs, car accidents....if I drank a cold orange soda it was a time stopper and a soul soother.

We returned our glass bottles back to the gas station man. He said a truck would come by and pick up the bottles and send them to be washed and filled again. That was why some bottles looked older than other bottles; some had already been refilled many times. He asked me if I had liked my pop; I thought he meant my father, because I never heard the phrase "soda pop" before, so I told him I **loved** my pop, which was true in both senses, even though Gramma Gigi said people could not love food, love was reserved for people.

We got in a car wreck just outside of Denver when I was five. The plains there were prone to dust storms; the wind would speed along the top of the soil, and low, dark, racing storms of dust would rush across the plains. We could see the dust storm coming just like a bank of fog, rolling across the land, low and dark and scary looking. Once we were in the storm, we could not see anything. It was worse than fog because it was brown and gritty and you could taste the dirt. We were on a two-lane road with shoulders that dropped steeply off to the sides so that in the winter the snow had a place to be shoveled, and then we smashed into the back of the car that had stopped on the road in front of us.

Jennifer was just a baby, and my mom had been holding Jennifer in her arms when we hit the back of the car in front of us. My mom was able to protect Jennifer, but my mom's forehead went into the windshield. All of the glass baby bottles, filled with formula that morning and sitting in the old metal ice chest, shattered. No one had ever heard of seat belts in those days, and people and things flew around, and there was a lot of glass, but we were okay. My mom had a cut on her forehead, and her shoulder hurt for years, but that was just how life was.

When the dust cleared we could see that we were part of a many-car pile-up, and how lucky we were! The big semi truck that was behind us had been high enough off the highway that the driver could see the cars in front of him, and had been able to stop his truck just inches away from the back of our 1940's Ford. The grill of his truck was all that we could see out of our back window. The truck driver could see the long string of smashed cars in front of him, cars and trucks that had all smashed into the stopped vehicle in front of them during the dust storm. In California we knew that people got into wrecks because of the fog, but now we also knew that in Colorado people got into wrecks because of the dust storms.

People helped each other, and we got a ride into Denver with some other people whose car was still working, and our Ford was towed and traded in on a Studebaker. We girls were excited, because at home our neighbors down the street had a blue Studebaker, and now we had a tan one just like theirs! So there! Good-bye to the old black Ford with the running boards and hello to the Studebaker with the soft fabric on the back of the front seats and the windows that were easier to see out.

Kansas had more than lightning bugs. It had cousins and aunts and uncles and people who knew who I was but I had no idea who they were. People who called my parents Wayne and Louise and laughed with them and talked and talked and had so much to say about so many people that my head would spin. These people liked us and each other and laughed and talked and told jokes, and pretty soon my parents were laughing too.

We spent a week visiting farm houses, two-story houses on acres and acres of land, land planted in corn and milo and wheat, with hard-working people who were the descendants of those immigrant farmers who came to this country to find a better life.

We ate! "Dinner" was at lunch time and there would be kitchens full of mashed potatoes and chicken and ham and green beans and tomatoes and pies and so much food, food that was all from the farm, and they had "supper" at dinner time and then everyone ate so much food again; potatoes, roast beef, peas and pies and ice cream for dessert!

Tractors and horses and dogs, pick-up trucks and water that came from pumps...the sound of the crickets and the smell of the earth, the lightning bugs and the starry sky with so much space and clean air and seeing forever....that was Kansas and I really liked it. When we went to Great Grandpa Richter's farm house they had a pump on their front porch for water, but they only used it for emergencies because now they had indoor water. I was determined to get that pump to work, and took it as a challenge. There I was, as tall as that pump in my plaid dress, and I grabbed onto that pump handle to push it down. Well, I was too little to push that pump handle. But I grabbed onto the handle with both hands and tucked my feet up and hung from the handle while I pulled, and slowly the handle lowered. When it got all the way down as far as it could with me hanging on it, I jumped up and pushed the handle down all the way and then let go, and the handle went up again. No water came. I went inside and Great Grandpa Richter asked me if I had gotten water. When I told him, "No," he said that was because the pump had to be primed and pumped a lot of times before the water came out. I didn't know that Great Grandpa Richter meant to pour water down the spout; that was what priming meant, so I just went on pumping that pump.

Me at my great grandparent's front porch, pumping water

I spent the next hour on that porch; hanging from the handle, jumping up and pushing, letting go, then doing it again. And guess what! I got the water to finally come out! The water came out with a gurgle and a rumble and a trickle, and then it filled up the bucket as I pumped. It was cold, clear, sweet water, and I had made the pump work. Everyone came out and saw what I had done, and they were all smiling. We went back inside and I heard Great Grandpa Richter say, "Wayne, that girl has perseverance, I'll give you that." Whatever that word "perseverance" meant, I liked the sound. I rolled it over and over in my head: "Perseverance...perseverance." I liked having perseverance, and I heard in Great Grandpa Richter's voice that he was proud of me.

I didn't really know Great Grandpa Richter; we only went to Kansas for nine days every several years. He was my daddy's grandfather, but during the week we would be in Kansas we visited a lot of relatives, so even though he was my grandpa I had only spent a few days of my life with him and Great Grandma Richter. Great Grandpa Richter was very tall and wore overalls and had gray hair that was kind of wild and a lot of lines in his tan face. He was born a farmer and would die a farmer, and I liked that house and the porch and the big trees in the dirt front yard, and the tire swing hanging from one of the big old shade trees.

My California grandpa wore a suit to work every day and took the train to San Francisco. My Kansas great grandpa worked on the same farm all his life.

There was lightning in Kansas and Colorado and other places. My gramma in California was so afraid of lightning that she always said she would hide under the bed if lightning happened, but here in Kansas it was like they didn't even notice it. The grammas and aunties in Kansas had grey hair and wore old-lady shoes and long dresses and aprons. They were not like my California gramma, with black hair and makeup and face cream and fancy clothes; she drove a shiny new car with a factory-installed radio, an automatic transmission, and big fins on the back. These aunts and uncles wore overalls and flannel and jeans and the women could drive pick-up trucks and work with livestock. People even talked about swimming naked in the creek. Whoa now....I just don't get it, we can't swim naked at home and I have a new bathing suit and cap like a proper person! Plus swimming pools are for swimming in, not creeks, there might be leeches or snakes or something yucky.

Great Grandma and Grandpa Richter – The house with the pump. Jennifer age 1, Judy almost 8, and me, age 5

There were creeks on people's farms, creeks with catfish that got caught and cooked, and there were fields of corn taller than any person, and the corn tasted like heaven. After supper, at whatever house we were at, there was always a piano and someone would play the piano and everyone would sing. It was mostly Bible songs and I didn't know them, except for *Onward Christian Soldiers Marching as to War with the Cross of Jesus Going on Before....* sang with much gusto around the piano. Many years later our church in Palo Alto banned that song because there were so much anti-war feelings and it just didn't seem like a good song anymore, but there in Kansas it was the perfect song.

I had never seen anyone nurse a baby before, so when I saw a baby nursing in a room full of people to whom I was related, I whispered to another cousin, "What is that baby doing? Why is that baby biting her private parts and no one cares?" I couldn't believe the answer, and needed to be told over and over again. "What in the heck to you mean, and do you think I am stupid, people don't make milk, cows do, are you sure about all this? That baby is drinking milk from a woman who has a body that makes milk like a cow?!" And then I saw the nipple....that was forbidden territory and there we were in a room full of people and how come we could see breasts and nipples here at dinner time in the middle of the day, but back in California the only nipples and breasts that I had seen were on the back of matchbook covers that Auntie Jan brought back from some place called Las Vegas where people danced around naked, or maybe I had seen them in *National Geographic* or in my mom's art books. Auntie Jan had a lot of those matchbooks with topless ladies on the back of them, and they had the same surreptitious value as the *National Geographic*, but there in Kansas people acted like breasts (don't say that word you will get in trouble) and nipples (I am turning red from embarrassment) were something everyday and functional and necessary and natural.

It was weird and confusing...didn't they know that was nasty? Apparently I, the five-year-old that I was, was the only one shocked in the entire room. But I still did not believe it, babies drank from bottles, formula came from canned milk mixed with corn syrup and boiled and put in sterilized bottles and the bottles had nipples made from rubber that had to be boiled, and I had that head-shaking look of disbelief again.

My Grandma Ruth in Kansas had grey hair that was kind of bluish. I had never seen hair that color before. She was a nurse, and her house had an old-fashioned key that was long and black and only had one tooth on it. The inside of her house seemed dark; I think it was kept dark to keep it cool inside.

Grandma Ruth, my daddy and Uncle Jack had moved in with gramma Ruth's parents when my daddy and Uncle Jack were little boys. Grandma Ruth was divorced, and my daddy's father had married another woman in their same town, but the two sons never saw their father after that. In a small Kansas town of several hundred people this was a scandal; Grandma Ruth had to get a job and nursing was the only job there was. She wasn't Grandma Ruth then; she was just Ruth, the mother of Wayne and Jack. Uncle Vance lived at the farm also. Vance was only about a decade older than my daddy and Uncle Jack, so he was more like a cousin than an uncle.

When we visited Kansas, I heard about my daddy's boyhood. How they didn't have running water or indoor plumbing, but had the outhouse, and had a wood burning stove, and how Jack and Wayne had fought and Wayne hit Jack on the head with Jack's ukulele, and broke it, and how Jack pushed Wayne onto the stove and that my daddy still had a scar on his butt from the burn from that stove!! When my daddy was growing up his mom and grandma did all their cooking on a wood-burning stove; baked the bread and made the puddings, roasted the potatoes and cooked all the vegetables and desserts using a stove that burned wood.

Daddy and me in Kansas

I heard how they always waited for the new Sears-Roebuck's catalog to come, because they really did not have any toilet paper, and the old catalog would then be hung up in the outhouse as toilet paper! I had heard my daddy say that before, and I thought he had been joking, but in Kansas I heard that was really true. My daddy said they learned about all sorts of things while they were sitting in the outhouse; the catalog had just about everything in the world that a person could think of, and that they were happy to have such an interesting catalog to read. I was glad that wasn't me, I can tell you that! A few of the relatives still had outhouses, and I would try to hold it until we got to a house that had indoor plumbing. The outhouses were usually big enough that there were three seats inside them, and a wooden floor and a door that closed nicely and a few high-up windows. They were not really stinky, but I just didn't like the idea of going in an outhouse.

I heard how they all hated Roosevelt because he made the farmers kill their livestock during the Depression, and only gave them pennies on the dollar, and people lost everything. I heard of hardships and deaths and hard work, but listening about my daddy on horses, my daddy working at the gas station, and my daddy enlisting in the Navy at age 17 opened my eyes to a different world. At home in California we were always with my mother's relatives, but here in Kansas I heard during nine days every several years about who my father was and what his life had been like. I heard how he had worked, how he had been from the country, and how important family was. I heard of the country doctor, called an osteopath, who when removing the cast off my young father's broken arm had not rinsed the cast properly, so that when the cast was cut off my daddy's arm was burned from the acid, and much of the skin blistered off. My daddy still has scars on his arm from it. He had broken his arm when his horse had bolted, and my daddy fell off the horse and landed on a big salt block, the blocks they kept on the farms for the animals to have salt to lick.

When Daddy was in his late forties he got a phone call that his father had died, and it wasn't until years later that my daddy visited his father's gravesite. But Daddy and Uncle Jack did meet their half-brother; Uncle Jack and the half-brother, Charles, were pall-bearers at the funeral of their Grandma Richter. Uncle Jack and Daddy had a half-brother that looked like them and talked like them, and Daddy and Uncle Jack had 40 years of catching up to do. My daddy is still catching up with all the stories and things that happened in those years.

One of the greatest things about Kansas was home movies. Uncle Jack loved cameras, and always had the newest and the greatest in cameras. He had an 8 millimeter movie camera, and when we were in Kansas he took movies of us! He didn't live on a farm anymore, but lived in town, but the backyards there were really big and fences were short, so you could see into everyone's yard and people talked a lot over their fences to each other. One evening we played in the sprinkler in the backyard, and they had a slide in the yard and Uncle Jack took home movies of us playing on the slide in the sprinkler, I in my beautiful new bathing suit, up the ladder and down the slide with all the cousins and my sisters.

The next time we went to Kansas, we got to see those movies, and how much we had grown, but the best thing was that Uncle Jack could show the movie backwards, and I laughed until I almost wet my pants, because I slid up the slide backwards, climbed down the ladder backwards, and slid back up the slide again backwards, all in my bathing suit in the sprinkler! I could have watched that for hours!

Coming back from vacation came to signify that it was time for school to start. When we got home late Sunday night, the cat was mad and full of fleas, Daddy went to work the next day, and there was a whole lot of washing and ironing and cleaning up to do, and then getting ready for school. It also meant that for the next few weeks we got a lot of mail from

Kansas: The slippers I left under the bed at one relative's house; the hair ribbons left under the pillowcase somewhere else, the socks, the barrettes, and more little things that I had left at the different relative's houses.

The new Studebaker at the Continental Divide

Neighbors

The neighborhood was growing and expanding rapidly. By 1956 Louis Road was paved up to Barron Creek, although the street dead-ended at the creek; there was no bridge over the Barron Creek. The field full of sticker plants that had been between Louis Road and Middlefield Road had given way to a new street named "Ames Avenue" and now we had a model home just a few houses away from us and new houses being built across the street. A new elementary school was built right down the street from our house; Palo Verde was the school, and my sister Judy went there.

Judy was often sick, and had to see a kidney specialist. Judy sometimes was in the hospital, and she had to take medicine every day. But the boy down the street was really, really sick.

The neighbor's boy had gotten sick, and we kids were told by the boy's mom that he had polio, and all he did everyday was lay on a bed with a sheet over him and his mother fed him milk through a tube that went in his nose. He was blind and deaf and couldn't walk, and he lay there that way for many years. We knew that the boy was older than we were because his mom told us that, but he had stopped growing and looked very small. His mom still loved him so much; she would talk to him and gently stroke his forehead and the mom liked it when we neighborhood kids came into the room to visit her son. Even though the boy couldn't react, the mom felt that when we kids were in the room that her son felt our presence. It was sad about the boy who had to spend his life that way. Polio was a horrible, horrible disease.

When the series of polio shots came out, every kid was supposed to get them. I was pretty little when I got the shots, I think I was four or five; there were three shots and you had to get them spaced out over several weeks. I had my first and second shot, but then Judy told me that the third shot really hurt, that everyone who had the third shot said it hurt so bad that you couldn't even stand it! So we were on our way to the clinic in the car on a Saturday so that I would get my third polio shot. I was really afraid of the shot and didn't want to get it, plus they always gave it to people in their butt which was an added embarrassment.

We got to the clinic and I went into the room for the shot. My mom went with me into the room. There was green tile on the floor, and a lot of creepy doctor things hanging on the walls. The nurse came in and had me take off my shorts and panties and lean over and then she wiped the top part of my butt off with a really cold cotton ball. It was the part of my butt just below where my blouse stopped. And then the doctor came in with the biggest needle and biggest shot that I had ever seen, and suddenly in my mind I turned into a lion tamer! I ran and leaped bare-butted over to the corner of the room where there was a little kid's chair, and I picked up the chair by its back and aimed its legs at the doctor, just like a lion tamer! "Back, back!" I yelled, and I shoved the chair at him. The doctor was well over six feet tall; he was probably more dumbfounded than anything else, but it gave me the time to toss the chair at him and make my escape from the room, opening the door and running down the corridor into the waiting room, looking for the EXIT sign.

I guess my father and sisters were pretty shocked to see me streaking bare-butted through the waiting room and towards the emergency exit door. If only I could make it to that door and out of the clinic, they would not be able to give me that painful third shot! On my heels ran the nurse, my mother, and the doctor, and just before I reached freedom, they nabbed me! I think it took all three of them to wrestle this little bare-butted kid down, drag me kicking and screaming back into that room, and then hold me down for that shot.

The shot felt like fire going into me. I was furious that they had caught me so near to my freedom. I got my panties and my shorts back on, and my mother and I went back out to the waiting room. I think that a lot of people were staring at me, but all I could think about was how much that shot hurt. It felt like a big volcano was erupting where I had been shot, and I could visualize this enormous red volcano-like shape on my butt. I stood up in the back of the car all the way home because my butt hurt too much to sit down. Judy whispered at me, "I **told** you so! And are you ever going to get it when we get home!" But I wasn't talking to anyone; I was too mad.

When we got home I ran into the bathroom and pull my pants down and stood on the stool and look in the mirror. There was not even a mark! How could that stupid shot hurt so much when you couldn't even see it!

I had to go to bed as a punishment. I couldn't get a spanking because I had just had a shot. I sure wished that my lion-taming technique was better, because maybe I would have been able to hold off that doctor!

A new family had moved in next door to us, and their names were the Fritzwaters. Fritzwaters. What did that name mean? But my dad called Mr. Fritzwaters "Fritz." I really liked their garage; they had a girl that was all grown up, but they still had her childhood doll house and it was in their garage. Sometimes when I was over there with my daddy I was allowed to look in that doll house. It was a two-story doll house with stairs in it, but what I really liked was the tricycle! There was a little red tricycle that was made for a doll...just the size for a doll, and it had tiny pedals and pushing the pedals made the wheels turn. There was tiny furniture and tiny dolls to go inside the house and a little ice box that really opened.

One day when my daddy and I were walking up to their garage, I looked up at Mr. Fritzwaters and yelled, "Hiya Fritz!" Plus I waved my hand in a big sideways motion, like a movie star might do, and finished up with a glamour smile and a hand flourish. Well, in those days kids always called adults "Mister" or "Missus" and never used their first names. There was a stony silence all around, and Mr. Fritzwaters made a rather gruff sound in his throat. I waited expectantly for laughter or perhaps applause, but faded fast as I realized the world, and certainly the neighborhood, was not quite ready for such musical-like greetings.

On the way back to our house my daddy explained to me that even adults usually called other adults "Mister" or "Missus", and that he just called Mr. Fritzwaters "Fritz" because his name was so long; most adults called him that. Little girls and boys didn't call adults by their first names.

There were still some cows in the neighborhood, but not so many as when we first moved there. When we first moved there, there were a lot of cows. We were not allowed to go into their fields, but after the Jensens and their other side next-door-neighbor moved in, we used to sneak between the barbed wire fences and go into the field with the cows anyway. I would tell the big kids they had to take me or I would tattle on them, so I got to go too.

The Jensens were our new next-door neighbors. They had three girls too. The first time I met Sandy, the oldest girl, she asked me if I wanted to draw. I said, "Yes, sure!" and she said she would go inside and get a tablet to draw on. She went inside before I could tell her that I didn't know how to draw on a tablet, only on paper, because tablets were too small and you weren't supposed to draw on medicine, but she came out with paper anyway. Except she said, "Here's the tablet," when she handed me the paper, and I was looking all over for a little pill, and couldn't figure her out at all. Why would someone say they wanted you to draw on a pill and then bring you paper?

In the wintertime I loved to go over to the Jensen's house. Mrs. Jensen would stand right in front of the gas wall heater, and if I was cold she would say, "Come on over here next to me!" and I **loved** to feel that heat coming out of the heater right next to me and warming up even my clothes! We had the same heater at home, but my mother would not allow us to stand in front of it, because my mom was afraid that we would catch fire. I guess Mrs. Jensen thought it was okay because she would stand right next to us when we stood in front of the heater.

I liked to go visit the house where the boy with polio lived. The dad at that house collected bottle caps from sodas and beers, and he had made a curtain out of hanging bottle caps together, and it was in the door way of his garage. You could read all the different kinds of sodas and beers just from their bottle caps. In those days sodas and beers came in glass bottles, and people needed a bottle opener to get the cap off a bottle. There was no such thing as a "twist off" bottle cap. If you were going camping or to the beach for a picnic you always had to remember to bring your bottle opener. People called bottle openers "church keys," so they would say, "Did you remember your church key?"

To make the curtain our neighbor used a small nail to punch a hole on each side of the bottle cap, top and bottom, and then he threaded a wire through the holes and tied a small knot in the wire so the bottle caps wouldn't slide down the wire. When the breeze blew, the bottle caps would hit against each other and make a pleasant sound kind of like water splashing on rocks. Everyone in the neighborhood kept their eyes out for bottle caps, hoping we would find one that he didn't have so that it would be added to his curtain.

Judy almost 10 and Jennifer age 3
In front of Palo Verde Elementary School, Palo Alto

Kindergarten

I started kindergarten at Palo Verde Elementary School and got to paint. There were easels in the class, but you had to wait in line during painting time. When it was almost your turn the teacher would put the painting smock on you and give you the paint brush. Some of the kids must have known a secret about lining up, because there was always a line in front of me. I would watch the clock; that kind of telling time was easy, and we were allowed to line up to paint when the big hand was on the ten, but I never was the first in line. But oh boy! That year I painted the lightning bugs! First of all I had to paint the paper black. It was that newsprint that really didn't work very well because the paint kind of soaked all the way through, but I finally learned how to use the right amount of paint. Beautiful silky smooth black paint as black as the night, spread on the thin paper with a big brush, and the special paint smell, starting at the top of the paper and working my way down, with long smooth

strokes until the entire piece was black except for that part of the paper where the clip held it to the easel. Then I would pretend to keep painting while the paint set up so that I would not lose my turn, and I would take a smaller new brush and dip it in the yellow paint and paint on the lightning bugs. Yellow dots on the black paper. It was beautiful. I loved to paint, to smell the paint, to feel it as I spread it on the paper, to watch how it told a story.

We had snack in Kindergarten. Most of the kids in the class were like me, in that their mom made most of the food at home from scratch, so kids really thought store-bought cookies and crackers were a real treat, and all the kids liked graham crackers. There was a snack monitor and everyone got a turn to be monitor. One day I went in to the closet with all the other kids, because before the teacher came to the room everyone would go in the closet and eat snacks and sneak them when we weren't supposed to. Only then they all left before I did, and I was stuck in the dark closet by myself. I heard the teacher call roll call. Her name was Miss Livesay and she was the most beautiful teacher in the world. I heard her call my name, and there I was, still in the closet eating graham crackers. Only I couldn't say "here" because I wasn't really there.

I began to imagine that Miss Livesay would come in and find me, discovering that I was sneaky and had helped eat most of the crackers. She would probably go get the principal and call the police and I would have to go to reform school, where all the bad kids went. It was dark in the closet; I didn't know where the light switch was and anyway, I didn't want someone to see the light was on! So when the snack monitor finally came into the room to get the snacks after recess, well, they were mostly gone and I sneaked out, and Miss Livesay said that she was sorry she had not heard me say "here" and she better go to the office and

let them know that I was really there! My life of crime was not discovered. My pounding heart had been for nothing, my fear of discovery and the imagined prison sentence faded away.

I loved to read. I remember the very first book that I read from, a big red book with one word on each page, and one large black-and-white illustration next to the word. "Zoo." "Dog." "Cat." "Boy." "Girl." "Father." It was so exciting; did people realize that the shapes meant something? The same shapes that were letters and formed a word would always form that same word, and no one could trick you and say things had changed. The letters had power, so much power! I could read!

At home we had gotten a record player. It was from Santa Claus and was like a little suitcase, and when you opened it up there was an arm with the record player needle at the end of it. The arm stayed up unless you were listening to a record. You had to be really, really, careful with it, and the needle would wear out from all the playing and then we would go to the Sears- Roebuck store on San Antonio Road in Mountain View and get a new needle. I had records. I had a yellow plastic record that played the song "Davy Crockett." I would play it over and over, and knew all the words, and sometimes we would sing it at school. There was just one problem: "Born on a mountain top in Tennessee, greenest state in the land of the free....killed him a bar when he was only three! Davy, Davy Crockett, king of the wild frontier." I knew how to listen, and Davy Crockett killed him a BAR when he was only three. I wasn't quite sure what that meant, but it sure was not a bear, because if it had been a bear, then the song would have said "bear" not "bar."

Somewhere there were bars running around that needed killing, and Davy Crockett had been the man to do it!

Everyone knew the words to the Davy Crockett song, and all the boys had Davy Crockett hats. Here are the words to the Davy Crockett Song:

Born on a mountain top in Tennessee
The greenest state in the land of the free
Raised in the woods so's he knew ev'ry tree
Kilt him a b'ar when he was only three
Davy, Davy Crockett, king of the wild frontier

Fought single-handed through many a war
Till the enemy was whipped and peace was in store
And while he was handlin' this risky chore
He made himself a legend forever more
Davy, Davy Crockett, the man who knew no fear

He went off to Congress and served a spell
Fixin' up the Government and the laws as well
Took over Washington, so I heard tell
And he patched up the crack in the Liberty Bell
Davy, Davy Crockett, seeing his duty clear

When he came home his politic'ing was done
And the western march had just begun
So he packed his gear and his trusty gun
And lit out a-grinnin' to follow the sun
Davy, Davy Crockett, leading the pioneer

I had a boyfriend. His name was David. I liked him because he dressed like Davy Crockett. He had cowboy chaps and a coonskin hat, and he would come over to my house and we would sit on the picnic table benches in the back yard and hold hands, and look at each other. He had very thick blondish hair that stuck out every which way, and we just liked to sit there and hold hands.

David lived two houses down from us. He had an older brother Eddie, who was a bully. Eddie picked on everyone, younger or older, boy or girl. My mom went down to their house one time because Eddie was always beating me up, and told Eddie's mom that Eddie better stop. His mom asked Eddie if he had done anything bad, and Eddie said no, he hadn't, so that was the end of that. Their dad was in the Navy so the dad was never home, and that mom had her hands full with four kids and her mother-in-law all living there.

Sitting with David – he wore cowboy chaps – age 5

My mom told me that the next time Eddie hit me I was to yell, "I'm going to hit you **back**!" and then start chasing him back to his house. So I did, and Eddie ran screaming inside his house that he was going to get hit **back**! And then he got the spanking that he deserved!

Kids in those days got a lot of spankings; either the mom was the one who did all the spanking or the mom would tell the kids, "Just wait until your father comes home!" Most kids had moms that spanked, because the dad was at work all day. Kids would talk with each other and compare the things that happened at home; some moms just yelled, some moms used hairbrushes, some used wooden spoons, and others used belts. Kids were told things like, "I'm going to hit you clear into next week," or "I'm going to kill you, you better run," or "I'm going to break every bone in your body." It was an age of physical punishment; moms were managing a lot of things to keep houses running and had no time to figure out what a problem was...they just punished as they saw fit.

David's family was from New Zealand, and his grandmother lived with them. Her name was Grandma Adine. Grandma Adine was always sewing or cutting out fabric or knitting, and she had a parakeet that was allowed to fly anywhere in the house, but the parakeet pretty much stayed with Grandma Adine. The really neat thing was that whenever Grandma Adine was cutting out material, she would call the bird, and that little parakeet would sit right on the top of her scissors! We kids would be really quiet so we wouldn't scare the bird, and that bird sat there and balanced right on top of those shiny scissors as they went up and down, up and down, cutting through the fabric! We couldn't believe our eyes!

One time my mother lent David's mom some money, and the amount that she paid back to my mom included one-half cent. My mom said forget about the half cent, but his mom took a regular penny and put some black tape on it to hide the other side so it looked like half a penny. We were all laughing at that because it was so clever!

On Christmas Eve when I was in Kindergarten there was a huge flood in Palo Alto. For a little kid it was pretty scary. Thousands of people had to leave their houses because the police were knocking on doors and telling people to go someplace higher. Some of the people who lived a few streets away from us, closer to the Old Bayshore Highway, had more than a foot of mud inside their houses and the flood was up to the tops of their beds. The storm drains were all flooding, and when we looked out our front door, the street was full of muddy water that looked like a river, and the water came over the sidewalk and up onto the driveway. Our house didn't get flooded; some people we knew had their houses flooded.

Santa Claus came to our house anyway, even though it flooded, so that was more proof that he was real. But I was pretty confused about how Santa knew Baby Jesus.

Daddy and a neighbor mixing cement for the back patio

Lots of Work

When my parents bought their house, there was the house, and the house was surrounded by dirt, and there was a short fence around the sides and the back. Period. That was all. So over the next several years my daddy did a lot of work to fix up the yard. Sometimes Grandpa Bob would come down from San Carlos and help Daddy.

Together they dug up the entire yard by hand and poured a concrete slab for a front porch and planted the front lawn. My daddy laid out the frame for the back patio and he and Grandpa Bob rented a small cement mixer and mixed and poured all the concrete themselves for the back porch. They used the extra cement to make stepping stones for a path all around one side and the back of the house. And after the porch was done, they built a patio cover that had big posts and lattice sides and a bamboo slat cover on top, so that when we went outside our kitchen door we had shade and a wind break on our patio. It was wonderful!

Daddy put planter boxes all along the edge of one fence, and planted a lawn in part of the backyard. The other part of the backyard was for the garden, and Daddy put wooden edging all around the garden, and dug that up again and added manure and gypsum and grass clippings to the dirt to make good garden soil. He planted fruit trees at the back of the yard along the back fence; plum, apricot, peach and nectarine. The peaches were the white kind, the best in the entire world, sweet with a little bit of pink around the seed.

He built a trellis about 20 feet long near the other side fence and planted boysenberries all along the trellis. Daddy planted two lemon trees and two cherry trees (a third one was added later, but that is a whole story in itself.) As the trees and berries grew we always had fresh fruit from our garden all summer long, and my mom would make jams and jellies and can the fruit, and when we girls were old enough to help, then we helped too.

After our back lawn had grown in all the way, my parents got us kids a swing set! Daddy and Grandpa Bob put the swing set together and dug holes in the lawn for the legs, and we had a great place to play, with a glider and two swings and a trapeze. I could spend hours on that swing set, swinging as high as I could. Judy said that it was possible to swing so high that a person could swing all the way around the whole swing set, but we tried and tried to do that anyway and we never could. We had just one trapeze, so we had to take turns on it; hanging upside down from our knees, and then learning to pump upside down so that we could swing, and then getting brave enough to let our arms hang down and use our arms to pump too!

Judy was still sick, but with the swing set in the yard she could play outside and then go inside to lay down when she got tired. It was good to have our own play equipment in our yard.

I only wished that the swing set was in the front yard. I had gotten so good at swinging that I just knew a Hollywood director would ask me to be in a movie about kids who were really good on a trapeze, but that was only if that director could see me! I could jump rope for hours in the driveway, hoping to be discovered as a great rope jumper, and star in a movie as a child athlete and trapeze artist, but with the swing set in the back yard my chances of discovery were pretty slim.

There were more houses being built all the time, so my daddy ended up building a high fence along the sides of the house and along the back. Now we did not have many visiting jack rabbits any more. We no longer could see far away because of the fence, but if we climbed to the top of the swing set we could look over the fences. We weren't allowed to climb to the top, but we did it anyway, because how else was a kid still going to see what was on the other side of the fence?

Daddy, Auntie Jan, and Grandpa Bob in the new backyard

Judy watching Daddy smooth the wet cement

The following year: Patio, stepping stones, and the clothesline

Judy and me on the back patio

Jams and Jellies

As the trees in the yard grew bigger, we always had our own homegrown fresh fruit. It was exciting when it was time to make the jams and jellies. My parents made sure that we had enough jars, and on the weekend they would go into the garage and get all the jars that had been saved throughout the year, and any paraffin that was left over from the previous year. For jams and jellies you didn't have to use *Mason* jars, because jams and jellies could have a layer of paraffin wax on the top to seal them; we didn't have to use a special lid and ring to seal in the food, therefore it was much easier than canning fruits and vegetables.

My parents would wash and boil all the jars, and make sure that there were no chips on the rims of the jars. The special canning funnel and all the utensils got boiled as well. The kitchen table and the counters would be covered with jars, and my parents would buy cubes of paraffin and bags of sugar and little boxes of pectin, and cheesecloth for straining out seeds and pulp to make jelly and syrup; if there was a big crop of boysenberries my mom would make boysenberry syrup, and we would have that on pancakes and waffles all year long!

If my mom was going to make apricot-pineapple jam then we had to buy cans of crushed pineapple, and for strawberry jam we went to Watsonville and bought cases of strawberries, but otherwise all the fruit came from our yard. My mom would make enough jam and jelly to last the whole year. We would never buy store-bought jelly except mint jelly that went with lamb at Easter time.

Daddy would pick the fruit from the top of the trees because only he could climb up on the ladder. We girls were not allowed to climb the ladder, but we helped by picking the fruit from the low branches and the fruit from the ground. Most of the fruit on the ground was still good, because our job in the summer was to pick up the fruit from the ground each day so that fruit didn't get wasted and so the yellow jackets and wasps wouldn't come around to eat rotten fruit. All the fruit off of a tree would get ripe at almost the same time, so there would be hundreds of apricots or peaches or plums or nectarines all at once. The peaches, apricots and nectarines would be cut in halves or slices and canned, and the apricots and plums, boysenberries and cherries were also used to make jams and jellies.

We would pick baskets and baskets of ripe fruit, and bring it inside to the kitchen where we would wash the fruit and cut it in half and trim it. I didn't really like that part because a lot of the apricots and peaches would have earwigs inside of them, and so the sink would have earwigs thrashing around in the water, trying to climb out and sometimes you would feel something crawling on your arm and look down and it would be an earwig or a spider trying to escape the water.

All of us except Jennifer would cut the fruit; my mom was always cutting herself because she went too fast. When all the fruit was picked and washed and trimmed then my mom would start measuring: For jams and jellies all the ingredients had to be measured perfectly or the jam or jelly would not turn out right. It was fun to watch the sugar being measured, how it poured out of the sugar bag like a big avalanche of pure white snow. The biggest pots we had would be filled up with the measured fruit and sugar, and then the burner on the stove would be lit, and the stirring would start.

Whatever was being stirred had to be stirred constantly, because if it burned even a little it would ruin the flavor of the whole batch and all of it would have to be thrown out, and no one wanted to waste all of those ingredients! Some of the jams and jellies had to have pectin added to them; pectin came from apples and was in little envelopes like *Jell-O*. Pectin would make the jam or jelly thick enough.

My mom always would almost chant when she stirred, saying the same thing over and over so that she kept track and stirred it properly: "Around and around and a figure eight...around and around and a figure eight..." That meant she would stir the fruit around to the right one time, then one more time, going around the edge of the pot, and then do a figure eight with the wooden spoon right through the middle of the pot, and then she would stir to the left two times and do another figure eight....over and over again, and the fruit and sugar would get hotter and hotter until all of a sudden the fruit was like liquid and shiny and bubbly and you had to be very, very careful because the fruit would try to boil over.

Once the jam or jelly had boiled like that, the foam had to be skimmed off, and then the big pot was moved over to the table next to all the jars.

At the same time that all the stirring was going on, the paraffin was melting. Paraffin is wax that comes in a whitish cube and can be used to make candles, and used to seal up the jam and jelly jars. To melt the paraffin we had a clean empty coffee can that was put inside a bigger pan of water, and the paraffin went into that can and as the water around it heated up the paraffin would melt. My daddy had bent the can so that the liquid paraffin would pour out really easily right where you wanted it to go, and he had made a coat hanger handle so the can was easy to hold. Paraffin is very easy to catch fire, so everyone had to be careful that it did not get near the gas flame from the stove, plus we had to be careful not to drip any water from the sides of the can into the liquid paraffin.

Next my mom would take the canning funnel and put it into the mouth of a jar, and then use a ladle to scoop the boiling hot jam or jelly into the jar, filling it almost up to the top, filling one jar and then the next as fast as she could. If any liquid was on the rim, then one of us would use a clean tea towel to wipe it off. The next part I really liked to watch: The paraffin would be clear and looked just like water, and my mom would pour liquid paraffin right on top of the jam or jelly! And it didn't soak in; it just floated on top in a clear shiny see-through layer. And after a minute went by the edges of the paraffin would start looking cloudy; as it cooled the whole layer of paraffin would become whitish once again, but even if I stared at it the whole time I couldn't actually see it turn white because it happened slowly. I would have to blink or turn my head and then when I looked back it seemed like all of a sudden the paraffin was white.

My mom would pour another layer of paraffin on top of the cooled-off layer. When the paraffin was all the way cool it became hard wax once again, and that guaranteed that no air could get into the jam or jelly. Without air bacteria could not grow, so we would have clean safe jam or jelly all year long.

We had a hallway closet that my daddy had built shelves in, shelves that were just the right size for all the canned food. We had jams and jellies and syrup; canned tomatoes and cucumber pickles and watermelon rind pickles, cherries, spiced peaches and regular peaches. My mom would make green-tomato mince meat, which had no meat it in, but a lot of raisins and sugar and cinnamon and other spices. That would be used to make mince-meat pies at Thanksgiving and Christmas.

Canning was much different that making the jams and jellies. For canning, the *Mason* jars had to be boiled in a water bath to sterilize them, and then the fruit would be put into the hot jars, not too much fruit, and the fruit had to be an inch from the top of the jar, and then boiling hot liquid got poured into the jar until all the fruit was covered and there were no air bubbles. It was fun to stick a long clean knife into the side of each jar right next to the glass and watch little air bubbles come up from where air had been trapped, and then more hot liquid would be added to the jar to fill up the space that had been taken up by the air pockets.

If we were canning fruit the liquid would be sugar syrup; not too much sugar, but enough to make it a bit sweet. For cherries my mom would add a little almond flavoring to the syrup, and for tomatoes she used tomato juice that she made.

The rims of the full jars would be wiped dry using a clean tea towel, and the *Mason* jar lids would be taken out of a pan of scalding hot water and carefully positioned on the mouth of the jar, using sterile tongs. Then a metal ring was taken from the scalding water and the ring was screwed on the jar to hold the lid down, and then the jars were put into the canning kettle. The canning kettle held ten large jars; the jars couldn't touch each other or they might break. Then the jars had to be completely covered with boiling water, and then boiled for a certain amount of time, usually ten minutes.

Afterwards canning tongs were used to lift the jars out of the water, and the next batch went in the kettle. The hot jars would be resting on clean tea towels, and we could see through the glass that the liquid inside was still boiling! We would wait, and as the liquid cooled each jar would make a loud clicky-snapping noise, which meant a vacuum seal had formed and the lid had snapped downward. If by the next day a lid hadn't snapped down then we had to eat the food inside the jar that day because it hadn't been sealed properly and would still be good to eat that day, but not longer. When a jar didn't seal that meant air was still in it, and that meant bacteria could start to grow. When the canning worked correctly the food would keep for the whole year and then next year we would do it all over again!

I loved the canned tomatoes. They didn't taste like store-bought ones, they were whole and not soggy and the tomato juice all around them was the right saltiness, pepper and a little bit of sugar. Judy hated them, but they were my favorite.

In our garden we grew corn, onions, bell peppers, cucumbers, carrots, zucchini and a lot of flowers. No matter how much zucchini we ate, there was always too much and by the end of summer I would be sick to death of zucchini! Our garden had little patty pan squash and yellow crookneck squash too, and sometimes we grew eggplant.

My parents had a funny story about eggplant. When they were first married and Judy hadn't been born my parents lived in Kansas in a house with Daddy's mom, Grandma Ruth, and Daddy's brother Jack and Jack's wife, Bernie. Uncle Jack was growing a garden and planted eggplant, and finally a teeny tiny eggplant started growing on the plant. Uncle Jack had to go away for a day, and while he was gone my parents went to the store and bought a big eggplant and then took a needle and thread and sewed the eggplant's stem onto Jack's plant.

The next day Jack went out to his garden and came running back inside all excited and asked everyone to come out right away! My parents kept straight faces while Jack showed them the big eggplant that had grown overnight while he was gone! I heard that it was even funnier when Jack finally looked close enough to see that a trick had been played on him, and he was chasing my daddy all over the yard!

In our backyard garden we had different kinds of tomatoes: Cherry tomatoes, little yellow pear tomatoes, Early Girl tomatoes and big red beefsteak tomatoes. I loved to pick the warm tomatoes right from the yard and run inside, cut them open and sprinkle some salt and pepper on them, eating them just minutes after they were picked!

My mom would order the seeds for the garden from the *Burpee* Seed Catalog, and the seeds would come in the mail. It was so much fun to look at the *Burpee* catalog, and when the seeds came my mom would open up the box and make sure that everything she had ordered was in the box, and then we would all talk about what would be planted in which part of the garden, and why it would go there. If you planted the tall corn or pole beans in the wrong place they would make too much shade on the other plants, so a garden had to be planned out carefully.

We grew pole beans, which meant that the green beans grew up bean poles, and we grew yellow wax bush beans, which didn't climb up a pole but stayed small. Each year Daddy would dig up the garden again, using only his shovel and adding manure, gypsum and grass clippings. Once all the seeds were planted I got to help with the watering. Watering had to be done just right; if you sprinkled water all around, there would be a lot of weeds, and it just wasted water. The hose had to be set down on the dirt really carefully and water allowed to run only where the seeds had been planted. Usually Daddy dug little trenches right next to where the seeds were planted, and my mom would write on a little wooden stick the name of what was planted, so the sticks would show us where to water.

It was really exciting to see the seeds come out of the ground! The beans grew like magic, pushing the big seed up through the dirt so that a person could see the place where the bean was coming out of the ground even before it cracked the dirt and appeared, bright green and shiny. Then the bean seed would split open because the leaves were pushing their way out, and the leaf would flatten out, and before you knew it there would be rows of beans with their leaves opened up, and their runners starting to climb up the bean poles.

The corn poked up out of the ground looking like a green spike, and lot of times all the corn plants came out of the ground on the same day! I might go to sleep at night when there was no corn, and then in the morning there would be rows of little tiny corn poking up in straight rows, along with the tiny feathery carrots and the big zucchini and cucumber plants.

There were so many butterflies in the yard...there were tiny golden butterflies that flitted around very quickly, and white cabbage months, yellow tiger swallowtails, the orange and black monarchs, the viceroy and the painted lady. I loved learning the names of the butterflies, and it was really exciting to find a cocoon or chrysalis in the yard.

When I found a chrysalis I would watch it each day. My favorite was the tiger swallowtail, because the chrysalis would start out light green, and as days went by it would change color, getting darker until it was brown. That was when I knew the butterfly inside was going to hatch. I would cut the part of the plant where the chrysalis was connected and put it in a jar so that I could take it inside and watch the butterfly come out. I would make sure to find a jar that was big enough so that when the butterfly unfolded its wings the wings would not smash into the sides of the jar, and I would punch holes in the lid with a hammer and a nail so that there would be fresh air in the jar.

It was like magic to see the butterfly come out of the chrysalis and unfold its wings and dry off. In a blink of an eye the wings would go from looking wrinkled up and soft to being stiff and shaped perfectly. I would always let the butterfly go, because even though I had a butterfly collection it was like cheating to catch a butterfly if it had never had a chance to fly.

First Grade

When I was in first grade I still went to Palo Verde Elementary School, but I was in a different classroom with a different teacher. My teacher, Mrs. Sprague, told us that we were going to make some things out of the kind of clay that went into a kiln and that when they came out of the kiln they would be "fired" and hard, just like dishes. But there were a whole bunch of rules: This was going to be a Christmas present that we made for our family, it would be nice if it had a duck on it, and the one thing we could not make was an ash tray! Mrs. Sprague had a pet duck, and she would bring the duck to school sometimes. The duck would come into the classroom; it was a very friendly duck with a ribbon around its neck, and I think that Mrs. Sprague wanted us to try and make a three-dimensional duck and include it in with our project. We would learn about the clay, and about glazes, and about firing in a kiln!

My daddy smoked. How could I convince Mrs. Sprague that the ash tray I was making was really a candy dish with a duck sitting on the edge of it? I think the little indents for the cigarettes may have given it away, but I smoothed them over. Every time we were working on our project, Mrs. Sprague would announce "No Ash Trays!" and I tried to camouflage my ash tray more and more by putting a family of ducks around the edge. I was going to make my daddy an ash tray for Christmas no matter what; I would just make it look like something else!

In the end the ash tray blew up in the kiln, or so Mrs. Sprague said. She gave me the pieces in a box, and the colors were more beautiful than I ever thought possible, iridescent blues and yellows and whites. I wondered if, in the tug-of-war between a first-grader and the teacher, she might have given the ash tray a little nudge off the kiln shelf.

Mrs. Sprague had a piano in the classroom and she could play it beautifully. We got to watch her play and got to sing songs while she played the piano. It was fun and pretty amazing that she could get both of her hands to work like that, each hand doing something different than the other hand, sometimes playing the black keys or the top keys and the bottom keys. I couldn't figure out how each hand knew what to do. And she could read music!

Reading music was a completely different kind of reading than the regular reading of a book, because there were five lines and then circles placed on those lines or between those lines, and where the circle sat on the line stood for the note that was played. And the circles might be filled in or not, and might have tails or lines that stood straight up along their sides. And at the very beginning of the lines of music there was a special symbol (not a cymbal, that was something else) that looked like this:

So I tried and tried to write music. I would draw the five straight lines that were called the "bar," and I would add in some up down lines, and then I would draw different circles on or between the lines. Then I would take it to Mrs. Sprague and ask her to play my music, but each time she would say that it wasn't music. I couldn't believe it; I knew it must mean something!

Then one day I told Mrs. Sprague that I had written a song. It was about one of the several dreams that I would have every night. This dream was about flying. In my dream I would be at school, running on the redtop. The redtop was the part of the school that was under the overhang and the cement was colored red. So in my dream I would be running down the redtop, but it was not a happy run, it was a scared run. I would look over my shoulder to see why I was scared, and there would be two enormous bears running on the redtop, running faster and faster trying to catch me and eat me. In my dream there was no one else around, the school was empty except for the bears and me, and as they got closer and closer I could see their big claws and hear their growls and feel their breath. I would be running slower and slower, the bears running faster and faster, until I would take a sudden turn to the right, which took me out to the blacktop. The bears got closer and closer until they were ready to bite big chunks from my legs, breathing their hot breath on the back of my legs, and just at that moment my feet would leave the ground and I would be flying!

Flying in my dream was feeling weightless and zooming up to above the clouds, with my arms outspread and controlling my direction. I flew above the clouds and would look down at the earth below, the green and brown fields with rows of trees separating them. I would float in one place, drifting slowing, with the warm sun on my skin and beautiful clear air above me and pillow-like clouds below me. In my dream I knew that the clouds were cold and that I could not land on them. I would see the shadows of the clouds, and lakes and rivers, and small towns, and sometimes the sparkle of a car windshield when the sun reflected from it. I would see tiny farm animals fenced inside their pastures, and barns with big painted roofs. It was peaceful and free and I could move my arms just a bit to fly over another part of the beautiful land.

I sung the song I had made up to Mrs. Sprague. And she had me go over to the piano with her, and I would sing and she would copy the sound with the finger on a key until the piano matched my sound, and then she wrote the music on special paper, and wrote the words to my song underneath the music! I was too little to know how to write all those words, so she did it for me. Mrs. Sprague had listened to me and liked my song! She sent it into *The Chronicle* and they published it as a poem in the same section of the paper where they printed the kid's drawings.

Here are some of the words to that song:

"I wish, I wish, that I could fly
Way up high, in the sky
And I'd look down upon the town
And see the people toys and things
Way up high in the sky
I wish, I wish, that I could fly
Way up high, in the sky
I'd see the horses and the cows
And I'd look down upon the clouds
Way up high in the sky…"

Linda Earskin was my best friend in first grade. It's funny how you get best friends when you are little. We just decided to play together and then we were best friends. I would go to her house a lot, and one day we found a potato bug in her yard! Potato bugs are almost as big as your hand when you are in first grade, and they are brown and kind of soft and very interesting to watch. We put the potato bug in a jar, and punched holes in the lid of the jar for air; I already knew how to take a hammer and nail to punch holes in a jar for a bug, plus to then turn the lid over and flatten down the holes on the inside with a hammer to make them smooth so the bug would not get hurt from the sharp metal where the nail had punched through.

We put in some leaves and some dirt into the jar, and then hid the jar in the closet that was in Linda's house that had the water heater inside of it. The closet was pretty warm, and we thought the potato bug would like it. Linda and I checked on the bug everyday and give it more leaves. One day we noticed that there was a bunch of whitish round things in the dirt that was inside the jar. We still kept checking the jar every day.

Then Linda went on vacation and I couldn't check the potato bug all by myself because their house was all locked up. I guess that the day before Linda and her family went on vacation we didn't put the lid on properly, because when their family came back from vacation their house was overrun by potato bugs! Those whitish things must have been eggs, but how were we to know that? Linda's dad was pretty darn mad that we had hidden that jar inside the house and that he had a house full of potato bugs!

In Gramma Gigi's backyard – Judy 5 & Jane almost 3

Judy 7, Jennifer 1 & Jane 5

Jane almost 7, Jennifer 3 & Judy 9

Easter

I was almost done with first grade, and it was Easter time again. Easter time was confusing, because I wasn't sure about how Baby Jesus and the Easter Bunny knew each other, and why we dyed eggs and how the Easter Bunny got those eggs and hid them, except he must have the same kind of powers as Santa Claus to go all over the world and take the eggs that kids had dyed and then hide them and add candy to a basket.

For Easter my mom made us all new dresses. Fancy dresses. Usually all three of us girls had the same style dress but in different colors, and my mom would make herself a new dress too. Everyone got new hats and gloves and shoes and socks, except Daddy, who might have a new shirt or new tie, or maybe even sometimes he might have a new suit! Our dresses would be out of fancy material that we would get at the Emporium department store, often two layers, so that each of us girls might have the same white see-through material on the top of an under dress that was shiny material. I was happy to get blue or green, but please not pink, yuck!

The night before Easter we girls would get our hair washed and set with foam curlers. There were no hair dryers that people used in their houses in those days, only hair dryers that were at beauty shops, and no one had seen a hand-held hair dryer. Some times you might go to bed with wet hair and wake up with your hair still wet. We would sleep with the curlers in our hair and wear a fabric hat that was like a shower cap to keep the curlers from falling out into bed. So not only was it hard to go to sleep anyway because the next day was Easter, but sleeping on curlers was not easy, and it was really hard to get comfortable. My mom would set her hair with pin curls, and use little bobby pins to hold the curls in. In the morning we all had curlers to take out and hair to brush and when we brushed it, it had to be done just right so that we would have ringlets.

Jane almost 9, Jennifer age 5, Judy almost 12

Our hats were wonderful! I got a straw hat that tied with a ribbon under my chin, and it had little tiny flowers woven into another ribbon that went around the brim. The tiny flowers were made from some kind of paper and cloth, and there were teeny tiny buds and leaves as well. I loved taking off the hat and looking at those flowers. My sisters and I would have our petticoats holding out our new dresses, our hair curled and ribboned, white gloves and brand new patent leather buckle shoes, and socks with lace around the edges. We would each get a new little purse to go with our new dresses. And when we went to church on Easter, Judy and I got to go into the big church with our parents, but Jennifer went to the babysitting part of the church.

The minister at the church had crutches. There was something wrong with his legs. After everyone sat down on the benches, then Reverend Cassidy would walk down the side aisle to the f ront of the church. He was very tall and I never saw him without his robe on. The robe covered him up all the way to his shoes, so I couldn't see what was the matter with his legs. But he used those crutches to move pretty quickly, and lifted his body off the ground so that his feet didn't drag. That is where I heard the word "paralyzed," because his legs were paralyzed.

Like many other words, hearing "paralyzed" and trying to understand what it was and what it meant occupied quite a deal of intense thinking. Did "paralyzed" mean that just his legs didn't work? Did it have to do with lying? Maybe because he was a minister he had told a pair of lies and then God had made his pair of legs not work any more as a punishment. I wondered what lies would be so big, but perhaps it was because he was a Reverend, which was another word that sounded like "river end." My brain would go around and around on new words and try to understand those words. I think that for every kid there should be a translator that explains more about what things mean, and that kids should be allowed to make up some of the words, because then I would have just said that he couldn't walk without crutches.

The assistant minister had something wrong with his arm! Reverend Riley's arm had been caught in part of a saw mill when he was a young man, so his arm just hung there and was useless, and he usually held his arm when he walked, I think to keep it from swaying around. And when he sat down somewhere, he would use his good arm to lift his bad arm up to the table. If you first saw the two ministers sitting down together, like at a pancake breakfast, you wouldn't see anything was different about them, and then if they stood up together, you could see that they both had parts of them paralyzed. So then I figured out that "paralyzed" must have something to do with ministers or reverends that lied twice at church, and their pair of lies was punishment. And maybe his arm hadn't really gotten caught, maybe God had just smote him; smote was like striking him with lightning, and that probably was what really happened to his arm. With all that praying that went on it seemed a bit baffling to me that there wasn't some miracle that could cure them both. What with Adam and Eve and Jesus and the magic star and the *Onward Christian Soldiers Marching as to War*, I figured that we should all get to see a miracle sometime too.

There we were all dressed up for Easter, and listening to the story about Jesus dying and then not dying and then going to Heaven to be with his father. I had a really good imagination, but somehow I just didn't quite see how the clouds could hold all those angels and Jesus and God up there without everyone falling down. But then, angels could fly, so they would just fly off, and God was mighty like *Mighty Mouse*, who could fly like God, so God could fly off too, and maybe he even had a cape like *Mighty Mouse*; that would just leave Jesus to fall out of the clouds, and he was coming back to earth anyway so I guessed they could all sit on any old cloud they wanted to after all!

Easter Sunday meant that there was a special paper program that got handed out to the grown-ups when the usher took the family to their seats. This Easter there was a sketching of some hands praying on the cover of the program. It was beautiful, just the hands, and the way they were drawn had the wrists kind of disappearing and there were no arms, just the hands, but it looked like someone had used very special pens or pencils to draw those hands. They looked like the hands of an old man.

We drove home from church, and as we pulled into the driveway, my mom said, "Wayne, they forgot the newspaper today, go to the liquor store and buy a paper." My mom went inside the house and all of us kids had to go to the liquor store with Daddy to get the Sunday paper. It never crossed my mind that my mom might be hiding the Easter Bunny's eggs while we went to the store.

Judy and I hunting for Easter eggs

Finding our Easter basket was fun, but finding the eggs was **not** fun for me. Judy would have found all of her eggs...we each had a certain amount that we were supposed to find....and there I was, looking for eggs. Usually the first one or two were easy, but I was always the last one to find those darn eggs, and everyone would be saying, "You're getting warm, you're getting warmer, you're hot, you're boiling...you're getting colder...you're freezing!" until I would finally find all those stupid eggs hidden in crooks of trees or under big leaves or on the fence or some other place that was really hard to see. Then we would have egg salad sandwiches for lunch, and we girls would look at our candy.

I don't think I ever ate a chocolate bunny. They were too beautiful, with shiny chocolate ears and little frosting clothes and orange carrots made from frosting. But the most beautiful candy there ever was, was a sugar egg! The sugar egg was actually made of sugar, and was sparkly and hollow, and there was a peep hole at one end, and fancy frosting around the edges of the peep hole. It came in a special box made of stiff paper and cellophane, so that you didn't even have to unwrap the egg to see it. The box had scenes of little bunnies printed on it. When you carefully held up the sugar egg and looked into the peep hole, there was a whole bunny scene inside the sugar egg, made all of tiny colored paper bunnies, with little houses and trees! Some other kids might wreck theirs and eat them, but it was so beautiful how could anyone eat it?

Later that Easter day, Daddy took his program that he had brought home from church and made a cardboard frame for it. Then he took *Saran Wrap* and stretched it really tight around the picture part, and taped the *Saran Wrap* to the back of the program, and then put the picture into the cardboard frame. The frame was one piece of cardboard that he had cut a square into, so that it went perfectly around the picture of the praying hands. Then he hung it up in my parent's bedroom.

After Easter, it didn't seem long until the last day of school. We had a party on the last day of school, with juice and cookies and then we got our report cards. The report card would tell us who our next year's teacher would be, plus our grades. I always got the best possible grades. And on the last day of school when we got home, we girls took buckets down to the creek to get frogs and toads.

Palo Alto Children's Library

The Library

The Palo Alto Children's Library is the oldest free-standing children's library in the country. It was designed by noted local architects Birge and David Clark; the original building was built and furnished through a donation from Lucie Stern in honor of her daughter, Ruth. When I was a child the Children's Library had a fireplace tiled with scenes from fairy tales, child-sized furnishings, and a brick-wall which enclosed a Secret Garden.

I got a library card. All that a kid had to do was to write their name and then they could get a card. The card had their name on it, and when I got mine I put in my wallet so that it would be safe.

When anyone checked out a book the library lady wrote their name down and then used a rubber stamp to stamp the date that their library book was due. The stamp was the kind of date stamp that was changed every day by the librarian. If you were the first person to check out a book that day and the librarian had not changed the date on the stamp, you got to watch her do it. She would turn a little gear to change the day, and then test it on a piece of paper to make sure it was lined up properly. Each time she stamped the due-date slip, she would press the date stamp into an ink pad. If there were a lot of books that were being checked out, the rhythm could be heard ...stamp pad, stamp paper, stamp pad, stamp paper, and she always got the date stamp to stamp right between the lines in the little rectangle where it was supposed to go.

The very first time I went to the library was both overwhelming and unbelievable. This was a kids' library, an entire children's library, a library for only kids' books, and there was a hidden room in it and when it was your first time there, after you had just gotten your library card, the librarian would tell you that there was a secret, and give you clues, and then let you find the room. It was so exciting, because it was a room so small that it was just for children! As I grew older, curled up in a chair at that library, surrounded by books, I experienced wonderful and magical escapes, adventures, and doorways to the world as I traveled through reading to other times, other places, and saw the world through the eyes of many different authors.

They let you take home as many books as you wanted. I came home that first time with so many books, and read them and devoured them, unable to believe that all you had to do was sign a card and you could take books and then just bring them back! Every other Saturday my daddy would drive us to the library and he would sit in the car with Baby Jennifer while my mom went in the library with Judy and me. We would turn in our books and then get new ones.

Except that one Saturday afternoon something awful happened: I went to put my new library books on my shelf next to my bed where the library books belonged, and there on the shelf there was still a library book. I had not turned in all my books; I had left one on the shelf at home by mistake. I was miserable. I knew that my days at the library were over, that at that very moment the librarian had probably figured out that I had not turned in the book...the book with the picture of the starry night sky and the shiny moon on the cover. She probably thought that I had stolen the book on purpose. So I hid the book so no one would know about it, because when the police came and knocked on the front door to take my sorry little seven-year old ass to jail, I did not want them to find the stolen book without having to search for it.

As the week went by I was at first afraid, then resigned that my fate would be that of a jailbird. I moved the book several times, each time making sure that no one was around to see what I was doing. My stomach hurt, and each time someone knocked at the door I shuddered with the knowledge that at least two, maybe three, Palo Alto policemen were there at the door to tell my parents about my thievery and take me away. I woke in the night with a dry mouth, wondering how long I had before my crime would be discovered.

Two weeks went by, and it was time to take back library books. I didn't want to go; I didn't want to see the librarian and the police waiting to punish me over the stolen book. I never wanted to check out another book. I pleaded sick, but it didn't work, and there I was in the back seat of the car, on the way to the library with my stack of books that were due and a very heavy heart. How would my parents feel when they heard that I was a book thief? I couldn't even talk or participate in the usual "Let's torture each other with stupidity" that my sister and I usually did while in the car.

I turned in my books, and waited. I didn't feel like getting any new ones. The librarian had saved a book for me, but I couldn't talk to her. When it was finally time to go, finally time to face my crime, she called my mother over to the desk. They had a whispered conversation. "Why is this taking so long, police are probably on their way now, can't we just get this over?!" my tortured mind screamed out.

And then we just left the library. What was going on? Were my parents taking me to the Police Department themselves? Part way home I was told that the librarian had said that I had an overdue book and that we needed to look at home to try to find it, and that when we found it we would take it back and that there would be a fine to pay, and if we didn't find it the librarian would just think that the library had made a mistake and not marked the book in last time. The fine was two cents a day so I already owed fourteen cents; the money would come out of my allowance.

Over due?!?! Over due??? I wasn't going to jail? No jail time for a stolen book? All I had to do was find the book and pay a fine and everything would be right in the world? How could that be true...was this a trick? I took the first deep breath in two weeks, and when we got home my parents were surprised at how fast I found that book! And the fine? Well, I got twenty five cents a week allowance, and fifteen cents had to go into the collection plate at church, so I still had a dime left each week. I could pay the fine, but if I waited two more weeks then the fine would be a whopping twenty-eight cents, so Daddy drove me to the library and I returned the book and paid the fine.

My habit over the years was to take out the due date slip from the front of the book to look at it. There were two sides to the slip; sometimes the dates would go back ten or fifteen years, and I would look at the dates stamped in the little date rectangles and see mine as the last one. I wondered about all the other people who had read the book. If the book had been overdue the librarian made little initials to show that the fine had been paid. You could really figure out a lot about the book by reading the due-date slip. We had a library at my school, Palo Verde, but compared to the Palo Alto Children's Library the school library was more for checking out books than for sitting and reading.

Weekends

Weekends were great because my daddy was home. During the weekdays we would see Daddy at breakfast, but often he might not be home yet when it was our bedtime, especially on Friday nights, because he had to stay at the bank where he worked until everything balanced, so many times he was home late. But one of the funny things that usually happened at breakfast on Saturday mornings would be that my daddy would say, "I got the label again yesterday."

That meant that when my mom made his sandwich in the morning and it was Friday, the last piece of lunch meat at the bottom of the package usually had a label stuck to it. My mom wouldn't notice it and would make the sandwich for my daddy's lunch and put in the slice of lunch meat with the label still on it. On Fridays my daddy would check to see if the label was in his sandwich, because after a while he pretty much knew the label would be there and it became kind of a family joke.

Often on the weekends we would go somewhere, usually on Sunday afternoon. We might go for a Sunday drive after church, and in the spring time we would go down El Camino Real near Los Altos and see all the orchards that were blooming with their light pink flowers. It looked like fairy land. Or we might go to Big Basin State Park in the Santa Cruz Mountains, but I kind of hated that because our car would often get vapor lock going up Page Mill Road, and we would have to pull over at a pull-off by the edge of the road. Page Mill Road went from Palo Alto all the way up to Skyline Road, which followed the crest of the Black Mountain Range. Page Mill Road was a very narrow and twisty road with a lot of hairpin curves. When we got vapor lock Daddy would put the hood up so the engine would cool off, but I would panic because the edge of the road was scary and I was afraid my daddy would forget to put on the emergency brake and that we would roll down the twisty road backwards and then off a cliff. And of course someone (usually me) would get car sick going up Page Mill Road or else going through La Honda, which was the downhill part of the road that headed to the coastline and the beaches. Either way the roads were narrow and twisty and winding with many hairpin turns.

The San Francisco Zoo had a part of it called "Storyland," a playground that had scenes from nursery rhymes and fairy tales. We liked to go to the zoo, and Storyland was a great part of the zoo. The zoo had keys that fit into a keyhole in speaker boxes next to each exhibit; people paid to rent the keys, but most people, including us, didn't rent a key because you could always hear the information when someone else put their key in the box. When I say we liked to go to the zoo, I mean some parts of it. I hated the tiger house because the poor tigers lived in cages and roared really loud like they were upset and it was smelly. Storyland had all sorts of fairy tale creatures, but I still liked the zoo's merry-go-round the best. Sometimes we had money to go on the merry-go-round, and it was the perfect way to end the afternoon at the zoo.

We liked to go to Golden Gate Park in San Francisco to look at all the things there, and sometimes we got to drink tea at the Japanese Tea Garden that was in the park. There was a special bridge near tea house, and it was scary to climb because it was so steep. Usually Daddy had to help us girls get down because it was really difficult to climb down. We loved looking at all the plants and trees and little gardens and the beautiful fish in the pond. Lots of times when we left Golden Gate Park we would drive out to look at the windmills along the coast. We would look at Seal Rock, and then go down the Coast Highway and Devil's Slide, and then come back home through La Honda.

Japanese Tea Garden Bridge in Golden Gate Park

The other place we might go on a Sunday afternoon was to Monterey, and we would go to Dennis the Menace Park and then to Fisherman's Wharf. We would feed the seals and get hot caramel corn and there would be an organ grinder with a monkey. The monkey wore a jacket and a hat and if you gave the monkey a penny then it would take its hat off and on for you, then give the penny to the organ grinder. People really loved to watch that monkey, and I wished that I had a monkey!

My daddy never had to work at his job on the weekends. Saturday morning we would always go to Redwood City to grocery shop. We kids never got tired of going in the car...it was fun, and because my mom never drove, we usually only went in the car on weekends. When we drove places, Baby Jennifer was in the front seat with my mom holding her until Jennifer was big enough to sit by herself, and then Jennifer got to sit in the backseat with Judy and me. We would drive down Alma Street until it crossed the railroad tracks near the famous "El Palo Alto" tree and then we would get onto El Camino Real.

I liked to play the dinosaur game in the car. I had assigned to certain vehicles the names of specific dinosaurs: Pick-up trucks would be Tyrannosaurus Rex, *Chevys* would be stegosauruses. *Fords* would be the big peaceful brontosaurus, and the other cars I didn't know would all be mean flesh-eating dinosaurs. I had read a book that had a sentence in it that told me the Tyrannosaurus Rex was as tall as a telephone pole, so that really was worrisome, because anything that tall was pretty scary. In my dinosaur game, I would be on my knees looking out the back window of the car, and as each vehicle got near to the car, I would tell Judy something like, "Oh no, it's a Tyrannosaurus Rex! It's getting closer and closer, it's going to get us! Duck and hide!" And I would imagine the street filled not with cars, but with roaming dinosaurs, and each time one went around us I would dramatically wipe my brow with the back of my hand and give a loud sigh of relief that we had escaped that bit of danger. I don't think Judy saw the world quite the same way as I did, but at least she was willing to play, to duck and hide and cover as the dinosaurs went by. This was a fun game that Judy could do in the car because she didn't really have to do anything but she could still play. Being sick a lot meant that Judy often didn't get to always run and play, but she could sure do games inside the car!

Alma Street crossed the railroad tracks and merged onto El Camino, and there were many more dinosaurs on the way to the Penny Mayfair store; often by the time we got there I was exhausted from all the up-and-downs and escaping.

Judy and I were old enough that we didn't have to go inside the grocery store anymore; just Baby Jennifer had to go inside the store with my parents. It was fun to stay inside the car in the parking lot, the windows part-way open, watching the people come in and out of the store and Judy and I talking. Daddy would park the car under a shade tree, and with the windows open we would be quite comfortable and free to move about the car, climbing from front seat to back seat, taking turns sitting in the driver's seat and pretending to drive.

I had made up this other game that we would play while just the two of us were in the car. It was called the "Rich Kid" game. One of us would be the rich kid and the other would be the regular kid, and because I had a vivid imagination, I usually got to be the rich kid. I might start off saying something like this (in a **very** refined and snobby voice), "Oh, my beautiful velvet dress with the diamond buttons and gold lace and pearl trim has a button missing on it. I was going to write you a note asking you if you wanted it, but my diamond pen with the gold ink is way over on the other side of the limousine and my servant went to get me a diamond studded tissue, so I can't possibly write you now, but would you like this old rag with the missing button?"

Then we would go on to describe the rich house and the rich clothes, imagining a world of gold and diamonds on everything, with servants and luxury and the ability to just give things away at a whim: "Yes, these gold and diamond shoes have been worn once, and I can't possibly wear them again. Would **you** like them? I have a swimming pool inside my bedroom, and my servant brings me fancy little cakes before I swim in my nice warm pool. Would **you** like to come over?" We would weave the "Rich Kid" story each week, and add onto it until we had a mental tapestry of opulence and personalities, and travel and fine foods. In my head I could see the notepaper with each sheet trimmed in gold and diamonds, and picture the mansion and the servants. Judy and I liked sharing that time together, just the two of us in the car. When we finished our latest episode of "Rich Kid" then we could talk about other kids that we both knew, or school, or just tell each other riddles.

Then my parents would come out from the store, the groceries would get put in the trunk of the car, and we would negotiate through the dinosaurs up to San Carlos and have lunch at Grandpa Bob and Gramma Gigi's, eating in the kitchen while my parents and grandparents and Auntie Jan ate in the dining room. My Auntie Jan had a Pekinese dog named Missy Dog, and after lunch we kids might swing in the backyard and throw a fetch toy for Missy Dog or take Missy Dog for a walk around the block. Missy Dog was small, but she could run really fast and loved to get loose from us when we walked her! We might play pinball or Scrabble or play Auntie Jan's piano, or maybe just lie around on the couch and listen to the grown-ups talk.

Because we girls ate lunch in the kitchen by ourselves, and a swinging door divided the kitchen from the dining room, I made up all sorts of games for us three girls to play, but the favorite was called "Sloppy Mother." We got to take turns playing the mother, and the mother's job was to tell her kids how to eat sloppy. When it was someone's turn to be the mom, they got to say, "Eat with your mouth open," and "Use your hands, not your fork," and "Don't say please!" and "Don't say thank you," and "How dare you use a napkin," and the rules were that we had to eat sloppy; if the mother said "Eat with your mouth open" then we had to eat that way. It was funny and sloppy and made us laugh. If we got too loud some adult from the other room would yell in and ask what we were doing, and we would just say, "Nothing!" but it was a pretty difficult game because eating sloppy was harder than you might think!

I liked listening to the grown-ups, because it seemed like with a week of catching up to do, I learned all about Grandpa Bob's job, my daddy's job, Auntie Jan's job, and heard about what Gramma Gigi and my mom had done during the week.

Grandpa Bob took the train to San Francisco every day to his job at Southern Pacific Railroad, where he was an accountant. Before my grandparents moved to San Carlos they had lived in Oakland, and when my mom was little her daddy, Grandpa Bob, had taken the ferry boat every day to work in San Francisco. But now he took the train to work, and Grandma Gigi would drive him every morning to the San Carlos Train Station. Unless it was raining he would always walk home from the train station; one and a half miles uphill every week day. He always got home at the same time, so in the summer if we girls were there on a week day, Gramma Gigi would look at the clock and say, "It's time, go meet your grandfather!" We would get to walk down the hill and meet Grandpa Bob and then walk back up to the house with him.

On Saturday afternoons when all of us were there after grocery shopping, Grandpa Bob might say, "I guess it must be tiddly time," and the grown-ups would have drinks like scotch or Drambuie, and maybe a neighbor might drop by. There was a girl up the street named Charlotte, and if she saw our car she would come over; then we had someone else to play with.

Sometimes we might stay for dinner, and get to drive home down El Camino Real in the dark. We couldn't stay for dinner if we had other shopping to do, because in those days stores were all closed on Sundays, so if we needed to go to Sears-Roebuck or to the Eyerly's Hardware Store in downtown Palo Alto we had to do that on Saturday. When Sears-Roebuck announced several years later that they were going to open up Sunday afternoon, people thought that no one would go shopping on Sunday at all. Sears-Roebuck thought people might like to be able to shop after church. But when I was little, no one went shopping on Sunday because liquor stores were the only kind of stores open on Sundays. Besides, people liked to go for a Sunday drive after church.

Driving home from San Carlos after dinner was magical. El Camino in the dark was like a fairy land, because there were so many neon signs, and a lot of the signs looked like they were moving. El Camino was really "El Camino Real, The King's

Highway," and along the road every few miles there was a historic marker of a hanging bell, because the Spanish missionaries had walked on that very path a long time ago. But now it was paved and went for hundreds of miles through California, and driving down it there was so much to see! There was a motel sign that had a woman diving into a pool, there were lots of cocktail signs that had the outline of drinking glasses with swizzle sticks, and there was an exterminator sign with a hammer smashing a bug. It seemed that each storefront had a neon sign, each one more interesting than the last one. I would see neon signs for cigars, eye glasses, of course the movie theatre in Menlo Park, but that had a lot of regular lights too going on and off in a pattern.

There was a neon sign for a palm reader, shaped like a crystal ball with a pair of hands hovering over it. The gas stations had lighted signs; there were flower shops and barber shops, so many lights and signs that I never got tired of going home down El Camino in the dark. In the daytime I hardly noticed those signs, and besides, I was busy playing the dinosaur game in the daytime.

We would be sleepy and ready for bed when we got home, but usually we would get a story read to us on Saturday night. I liked to sit in Daddy's lap and watch him blow smoke rings while my mom read a story. We had a big green chair just like Gramma Gigi's chair that held my daddy and one or two kids, and it felt snuggly and safe to rest there and hear a story.

President Eisenhower and the Republicans

One of the things that happened in Palo Alto in the 1950s was that educators had to contend with the after-effects of McCarthyism, which was sweeping through the country in a frenzied attempt to root out Communism. As a child I didn't know or understand what this meant, but all of us students were affected, as teachers throughout the country were required to teach anti-Communism and to take loyalty oaths. Local grade schools and universities, including Palo Verde Elementary School and Stanford University, were no exceptions.

What this meant to me and to all the students is that we were growing up in an atmosphere of suspicion and fear of the "reds" and the "commies" and the "pinkos." I only knew that these were people from far away in Russia that wanted to drop bombs on us and didn't want us to vote. We were hearing and learning about the threat of nuclear war and of being bombed. All through elementary school we would have fire drills, earthquake drills, and nuclear attack drills. The attack drills meant that when the bells and alarms sounded a certain way, all us kids did a "duck and cover" under our desks with our hands folded over the back of our necks to prevent falling debris from cutting our neck when the Communists attacked. How this was supposed to protect anyone in the midst of a nuclear explosion was hard to understand, but we practiced anyway. And the town also had air raid siren drills on the last Friday of every month, where a long, long, siren would shriek through the air, and if you turned on the radio it would tell you that this had been a drill but that in the case of a real emergency then the local radio would tell you what to do. The earthquake drills seemed more real; we would duck and cover in the same way as for the bomb drill, but I could understand those drills. One time when I was in the bathtub at home we had real earthquake and the can of cleanser that was on the window sill way above the bathtub fell down and hit me on the head, so I understood about going in a doorway or under a desk in an earthquake.

I didn't know what Communists were except that they wanted to bomb us. Down the street from my house, across from Palo Verde, there was a family that had a big back hoe dig up their entire front yard and then they brought in a big crane which

TEMPORARY BASEMENT FALLOUT SHELTER

held a fallout shelter and they put the shelter in the hole and covered it up. There were stairs to get to the shelter, and that family was prepared with food and water for when the Communists attacked. All throughout town there were buildings that were marked with a special sign that showed they had a bomb shelter, usually in the basement. I was taught to be afraid of the Russians and the Communists and their bombs. There was a slogan that everyone knew: "Better Dead than Red." It

was confusing, because who were all these red people and why did they want to kill us? We never saw television coverage of nuclear bombs, but on the radio there were a lot of messages and programs about the dangers of nuclear fallout.

In October of 1957 the Russians successfully launched *Sputnik*, a satellite that circled the world. This upset everybody, especially the kids, because all the adults were upset about it. Russia was going to start spying on us. I worried at night about this satellite. One night my parents got all of us kids up out of bed in the middle of the night, because we could see a satellite cross the night sky.

My parents were Republicans, but they would never tell who they voted for, like it was a big secret. My mom insisted that it was her right to keep it secret, and that no one ever had to tell anyone, not even their wife or their husband, how they voted, because the voting belonged only to them. My daddy was a Republican too, because when he was a boy that "damn FDR" had the sheriffs come out to the farm and kill all the livestock so that prices would go up, and my daddy's family barely had enough to eat. All of this was the federal government trying to raise prices and get the country out of the Depression. But my daddy could not forgive FDR for making them kill their animals and then grow corn instead. My daddy said they were often hungry as kids, and farmers should never have to be hungry!

During the 1950s the State of California passed a law requiring any group asking to use school property to sign a statement swearing it was neither a Communist organization nor a front for a Communist organization, and the Palo Alto School Board had to comply with this policy. Politically, Palo Alto was like the rest of Santa Clara County, a heavily Republican town. In the 1956 presidential election, 14,438 Palo Altans cast their votes for Republican Ike Eisenhower, whereas only 8,727 voted for the Democratic candidate, Adlai Stevenson.

When Eisenhower and his wife, Mamie, were traveling on the train from San Francisco southbound, it seemed like the entire town of Palo Alto was standing all along the railroad tracks to catch a glimpse of the President and his wife. I think that they were on vacation on their way to Southern California.

We were there too, amid the crowd, and a lot of kids were up on their father's shoulders to be able to see. Many people had put pennies on the train tracks because they wanted a penny that had been ran over by the train that carried the president. We weren't close enough to put pennies on the track, and anyway, that would have been a waste of money. People were waiting and then some started shouting that the train was coming, the train was coming, and it was, and the train was going slower than the regular train and it had some red, white and blue flags on it. At the end of the very last train car, Ike Eisenhower and his wife, Mamie, were standing and waving. Everyone was so excited!

People waved and yelled and clapped, and as the train disappeared out of sight the crowd started leaving and people were slapping each other on the back and talking about Ike, Mamie, and the Commies. Then a man asked Judy and me if we each wanted a penny that Ike's train had ran over. "Yes!" we said, and when he handed me my penny it was so flat that you couldn't even tell it was a penny, and it was hot from having been squished so flat by that heavy train!

Me age 7 with my Hula Hoop in the backyard

Second Grade

I loved school. I wanted to live there. It was warm and quiet and orderly. Judy and I walked home from Palo Verde for lunch everyday and the best lunch in the whole world was olive sandwiches, white bread with a filling of chopped black olives mixed with mayonnaise. My second favorite sandwich was when we had leftover roast beef and my mom would put it through the meat grinder and add mayonnaise and salt and pepper to make ground roast beef sandwiches.

The meat grinder was made from cast iron metal and fastened to the kitchen table with a big screw-on clamp that was part of it. My mom would put chunks of meat in the top part while she turned the big handle with her other hand. The ground up meat would come out the bottom of the grinder and fall into the bowl my mom had put there. We would have cooked meat ground up into sandwiches, or put into hash for weekend breakfasts, or my mom would grind raw meat herself,

Meat Grinder

because it was better that getting it already ground up at the grocery store.

At school they sold ice cream bars at lunch. There was a special door on a little room; the door was called a Dutch Door so that the person inside could talk to you while the top of the door was open and the bottom was closed. On the Tuesdays and Thursdays that ice cream for sale, my mom would give me enough money to buy four ice creams, usually fudgecicles, and I would go back to school after lunch at home and buy the ice cream through that Dutch Door and then go home to eat it with my mom and my sisters. We felt sorry for the kids that had to eat their lunch at school instead of going home. There was one picnic table of those kids. They ate lunch at school because their mother was not home and probably had to work because their dad was dead or that their parents were divorced.

In second grade my best friend was Kathy Ferguson. She lived down the street on Louis Road, and they had so many kids in their family that I don't think they noticed I was there. They were Catholic. I wasn't sure what Catholic was, but when they ate dinner they would make this cross pattern over their chest after they said grace. My other best friend, Marie Fangonello, was Filipino, and she was Catholic too. She slept on the top bunk bed, and they had four kids in one room and four kids in another room, but they always had food that tasted like honey and smelled like cinnamon. With two Catholic friends I practiced that cross thing quite a bit, standing in front of the bathroom mirror at night trying to make a cross like my Catholic friends. I think my parents would have died if they had known that I was practicing that gesture! I thought that it was like being in a club with a special signal to everyone else who was a member of the same club. Plus the in the Catholic Club they didn't eat meat on Friday, but could eat fish, and they said it was because Jesus was killed on Friday, but that didn't make any sense to me. But they always called Friday "Fishday."

There was another girl in the neighborhood, Jenny, who asked me if I was baptized. I didn't know what she was talking about, and she said she couldn't play with me unless I was baptized. So I told my mom, and she said all of us little bastards were baptized, so I told that very same thing to Jenny and her father, and then a few days later Jenny said she couldn't play with me because I was a bastard! And that was one of many, many words that made no sense in the dictionary, so I wasn't sure why she couldn't play with me.

I had scarlet fever when I was in second grade. I was very sick with it and missed school for three or four weeks. And the next year at school when they tested everybody's vision and hearing, the school nurse gave me a note to take home to have my ears checked by a hearing specialist, because it turned out that the scarlet fever had damaged the insides of my ears and I was 70% deaf in one ear and around 30% deaf in the other ear.

No one knew that I was having problems hearing what was being said to me. I had learned in a very short time that people did not like to repeat themselves, and that everyone got sick and tired of hearing a little girl say, "What? What? What?" all the time. People thought that I was just not paying attention, but I just didn't understand what they were saying. After a while I just gave up and said, "Yes" to pretty much whatever people seemed to be asking or telling, because everyone else was happier that way and didn't get mad at me for asking, "What?" Unfortunately it meant that most of the time I just didn't understand what was going on or what I was supposed to be doing. And I spent a lot of time being told that I had already been told something, and it was not going to be repeated because I should have been listening. I just became defeated over the whole thing, and figured that there was something wrong with me because the world was more confusing than ever. I didn't know what had happened to me, so it was as if the rules to the world had changed without anyone telling me, and that most people around me didn't talk loudly or clearly any more. But I also started looking at people's faces more to try and figure out what they were saying. Imagine how hard it is when people don't look at you or they mumble and then say, "Never mind" when you ask them to repeat what they said. It seemed like people we just not interested at all when I said, "What?"

There was a special room at school that was part of the office and it was called the "Avee Room." It really was the audio visual room, and was "A.V." for short, but we always said it and thought of it as if it was one special word...The Avee Room. That was where students went to go to watch slide

shows. Slide shows were film strips that went through a slide projector and showed on a screen, and the teacher would read words out loud that went with the film strip show. The film strip was different than a movie: It was a slide show and the teacher could control how fast or slow it went by showing each slide for as long as the teacher wanted, and just turning a knob to go to the next slide. If the slide show was about a farm, for example, the slide of the farm would project on the screen, and the teacher would read the caption out loud, or maybe pick a student to read the caption out loud. Often it didn't work very well and the film strip would get crooked or messed up somehow.

Sometimes we got to see movies instead of film strips, and having those movies to watch was great. What was great was that there was a movie projector to watch. If you ever got to go to the real movies, you couldn't see what the movie projector looked like because it was hidden in a room that was high up in the theatre. But in the Avee Room we could really see the projector. The movie projector had two big reels, and one was empty and one had the movie film on it. The person who was operating the projector would thread the film into a little slot, and then turn the reel around, and then feed the film through the movie projector and then put the film into the little slot on the other reel. If everything went well, when the projector was turned on it would spin one reel, the movie film would thread through the projector, and then the second reel would start having the film roll up on it! The light would shine through the film, and we would have a movie to watch. Like I said, it was really exciting to have movies at school!

One of the biggest reasons that the little girls liked to go to the Avee Room was that we would play with each other's hair. All the kids sat on the floor of the Avee Room; in the warm weather the floor was cool, and in the cold weather the floor was warm. Almost like magic, one little girl would start braiding or smoothing the hair of the girl who was in front of her, and then who ever was behind that little girl would start smoothing or fixing that girl's hair. It felt nice and while the film was going it kept hands busy and it made us all more like friends, because we were touching and feeling close to each other. The teachers seemed to know that there was no harm in this and that it promoted friendships and bonding and kept those little hands from being mischievous. So if some girl came out of the Avee Room with a new hair style, then it would be scrutinized and judged by her classmates to see if it stayed that way or not.

We could whisper in the Avee Room if we did it quietly. Little girls talked about each other's hair and clothes. My mom had made me skirts that year, but she had put suspenders on the skirts, and the suspenders crossed over in the back and came

over my shoulders and buttoned in the front.
None of the other little girls had suspender skirts,
so when I would get to school I would unbutton
the suspenders and stuff them inside my skirt so
no one could see them. Most of the time the
suspenders were so long they would dangle out
below the hem of my skirt, but I didn't care.
Suspenders were for babies or for people whose
clothes just might fall off, and I didn't think my skirt was just
going to fall off of me when I was walking down the street.

People's skirts falling off made me think of a funny story
Gramma Gigi had told me. When my mom and Auntie Jan were
little, Gramma Gigi had been shopping in downtown Oakland
and had her hands full of packages and was also holding onto
Auntie Jan's hand when Gramma Gigi felt her own half-slip
starting to slip down. A half-slip was what a lady wore under her
dress if she didn't wear a full slip, and it was made from very
slippery fabric. Gramma Gigi supposed that the elastic in her
half-slip had gotten old and once her slip started to slide down, it
was falling off pretty quickly. There were a lot of people on the
sidewalk, Gramma Gigi's hands were taken up with packages
and holding Jan, so when the slip fell down to her feet, she just
stepped out of it and kept on walking without even looking
back! She said that was the only thing she could do on a busy
street, and she wasn't going to stop and pick up a half-slip off
the sidewalk! Gramma Gigi said if anything like that ever
happened to any of us girls, either collapse in a heap and act
helpless, or pretend that you knew nothing about it.

Sometimes all the kids in the whole school would go to
the big multipurpose room. We did that if there was a talent
show or a fashion show, or on a rainy day instead of walking
home for lunch we brought lunch from home and we would all
go into the multipurpose room to sit on the floor and eat.
Maybe they would show a movie to the whole school then. But

when everyone went to the multipurpose room usually it was to tell the whole school something about safety. Every year there would be a big assembly, and when students walked into the multipurpose room there would be the principal and some policeman, and a train engineer, who was the man who drove the train. Everyone would get handed a little safety book and maybe a little police badge or a little train engineer badge.

Then the adults would talk about the same three or four things each time: "Don't throw rocks at the train, especially at the train engineer while he is driving the train, and don't play on the train tracks, and don't try to run across the tracks when the train is coming..." like every kid in the world just hung around the tracks waiting to throw rocks. The little book they passed out had a sketch of a train wreck caused by bad and stupid boys who threw rocks at the train, and the train engineer that was talking to everyone that day would have all the kids turn their pages to look at that sketch.

The second thing was to walk or ride your bike **towards** the traffic if you were in a place that still had no sidewalks. "Towards the traffic." A policeman would say that over and over again, and then we had to turn the page to the part of the booklet that showed a sketch of a kid getting run over because they were walking **with** the traffic on a road with no sidewalks.

Then a policeman would talk about riding bikes and how people had to stop at all intersections, and if there was a signal light people had to wait until it was green and then they had to walk their bikes across the intersection. "Never cross unless it is an intersection, and always walk your bike, and even if there is no signal light or stop sign, walk your bike, and look in all directions!" Then we had to look in the booklet at a sketch of a kid being hit by a car because he rode his bike instead of walking his bike. The sketches were kind of like comic book sketches because there were stars and the kind of sketched explosions over people's heads that made it fun to look at.

The last thing was to not accept candy from strangers or to go in a stranger's car even if they seemed really nice or even if it was a woman or a man and a woman because they would really just be trying to hurt you and you might get killed, and the sketch for that had a smiling lady holding out some candy to a kid that was walking down the street, and there was a man driving the car and the car door was opened.

Those big meetings in the multipurpose room where okay the first time, but they told us the same things every year, and I had never ever wanted to throw rocks at a train until they kept talking about it, and then it was a good thing that we lived far away from the train tracks, because each year it sounded more interesting.

I loved to make things, especially little things for my dolls and presents for my baby sister. But one of the problems with making most things was that I needed glue or tape, not the icky glue that was called mucilage and came in a glass bottle with a funny rubber stopper kind of like a baby bottle nipple with a slit in it; it didn't work very well. I wanted real glue, *Elmer's Glue*, and *Scotch Tape*. But glue and especially tape were expensive, so I never had enough to make what I wanted. It seemed like tape was rationed out like gold. I would ask for a piece of tape, and my mom would want to know why, and I would have to explain the reason that I wanted tape, and then finally she would tear off a few inches from the roll of tape and give it to me as if it was the most valuable thing in the world. I would take scissors and split that piece down the middle lengthwise and cut it into small pieces to get the most tape possible.

I made a little record player for my dolls: I took a cardboard scrap and made a box. I had learned how to make a box, how to cut out the corners of a square and then fold it just right, making hard creases in the exact right places. This was a very small box, only about 2" square, and before I taped it shut I poked a little hole in the top of it towards the side, and pushed a piece of a pipe cleaner through the hole. I had stripped the very end of the pipe cleaner clean so that the wire stuck out just like the needle of the record player, and the pipe cleaner became the arm with the needle at the end. I drew a record on the top, and then taped all corners shut to finish it off. My dolls really liked it, but it kept coming untaped.

When Gramma Gigi asked what I wanted for Christmas I told her tape. I told her I wanted a whole box of *Scotch Tape* for Christmas! And guess what? When Christmas came I got a shoebox that was all wrapped up, but instead of shoes, there were rolls of tape in it, about 20 rolls of tape, and they were all for me. My Gramma Gigi had listened to what I wanted and actually heard me and had gotten me tape. It was one of the best Christmas presents that I ever got.

Also for Christmas my dolls got some beautiful furniture that Daddy had made. There was a doll bed and a doll closet, and the closet had a tiny clothes rod for the doll clothes to hang on, and a tiny mirror. I guess my daddy had been working in the garage after our bedtime to make doll furniture for Judy and me. Jennifer was too little to use doll furniture properly, so she didn't get any. Judy's was painted shiny, glossy pale pink, just like our kitchen table. My furniture was painted shiny blue. Daddy had put tiny hinges on the closet doors, the tiniest hinges possible, and a tiny latch made with a whittled wooden peg and metal eye, both painted gold!

I also got a *Bobbsey Twin's* book which had been left on our front porch all wrapped up with a card with my name written on the card. It was from David Trainer. He was my second-grade boyfriend, and not only had Santa Claus come to our house, but my boyfriend had left me a present on the porch! David Trainer was the tallest boy in my class, and later would become the tallest boy in school. The other David wasn't my boyfriend any more; I had outgrown him. A few months later, there was a chocolate heart with "Jane – Be My Valentine" written in frosting on it left on the porch for Valentine's Day. I kept that heart from David Trainer for more than thirty years, until it melted in the trunk of my car when I was moving it from my parent's attic to my house.

Now that I had *Scotch Tape* I could make treasure balls. I had gotten a treasure ball at the Obon Festival as a prize. The Obon Festival took place every year at the Buddhist Temple which was on the same street as my house. Obon was like a carnival, and I had won a treasure ball. The ball was made of paper which was wound up like a ball of yarn, and the end of the long strip of paper that made up the ball was fastened to the ball with tape to get it all from unwinding. When you untaped the paper end and unwrapped the ball, there were little trinkets hidden throughout the ball, until you got to the very middle and the last treasure was there inside the middle.

To make my own treasure balls I would cut paper into one-inch wide strips and tape them together end-to-end to form long strips of paper. It could be any kind of paper combined together: Newspaper, wrapping paper, drawing paper, tissue paper...it didn't matter, in fact it made it more interesting! When I had a very long strip I would make the treasure ball for Jennifer. I could put a penny in the middle, and then wrap it up a bit, and then add something else small, like a toy ring or a little plastic dancer doll, a special rock or maybe another penny. It didn't really matter so much what the prizes were, because the fun part was unwrapping the ball.

Whenever I knew I was getting to go to Gramma Gigi's house for the weekend, I would make sure to make treasure balls for Jennifer, one for Friday night, one for Saturday, and one for Sunday. I helped her learn to count, because I would write the numbers on the strips of paper and tell her that she could unwrap the ball until she got to number ten, and that then when I got to Gramma Gigi's, I would call her. Gramma Gigi let me dial the phone my self, so I would call Davenport 54278, which was really DA 54278, and ask my mom to put Jennifer on the phone. Then I would ask Jennifer if she was okay, because I used to worry about her, and then Jennifer would tell me what treasures she had found, and I would say, "Okay, now unwrap it until you get to twenty," and I could hear her count. But we couldn't talk long on the phone because it cost a lot of money to talk on the phone. But that way Jennifer wouldn't get lonely for me and she knew I was thinking about her. Jennifer was also learning to count by playing cards. It was funny because she thought that counting was "ace, duex, three..." instead of "one, two, three!"

When I was in second grade a new park opened up in Palo Alto: Mitchell Park. It had the greatest things, and we loved to go there! On Sunday afternoons there was always time to go to the park, and we girls could play there for hours and hours while Daddy would either play with us or do something else. There were concrete above-ground gopher holes that were like a big maze and kids could crawl through the maze and then stick their heads up, and it was great because kids could hide from their parents in there. It was really funny, because kids would hear a parent calling a child's name and everyone would go "Shhhh"

and be really quiet and pretend that no kids were inside the maze. But pretty soon all the kids would be giggling and laughing, so the parents knew kids were in there.

The park had a miniature freeway, complete with pedal cars that kids could drive through little tunnels, and we could ride the pedal cars around the freeway. There was a giant chess set that had an enormous chess board on the ground, and life-size chess pieces and grown-ups would play chess on that board, and people would sit all around the edges and watch.

There was a large metal "Picasso" climbing horse, and a big wading pool, and a shuffle board game. The wading pool was made for little kids to wade in, and a little kid could even sit down and still be safe, because the water at the edge was very shallow. Parents liked it because they could go in with their kid while wearing shorts instead of a bathing suit. In the summer we went to Mitchell Park pretty often, and it was fun to climb up inside the metal tower that was scary and had a slide, and taking Jennifer up inside it and helping her go down the slide was something I really liked to do.

At the end of the school year the whole school would get together for an evening cake walk and a helium balloon release. The cake walk was when mothers would make cakes and bring them to school. People would pay money to walk around inside of a circle that had a lot of numbers painted around the edge. Music would play, people would walk around the circle, and when the music stopped, so would the people. Then the person who had the microphone would call out a number, and the person who was standing on that number got to go pick out a cake! Later if someone else wanted that cake they would go to the person who got that cake and try and buy it from them. It was fun, and all the money went to the school, and people got to show off their baking skills.

When the cakewalk was over each family got a postcard and wrote their name and address on the postcard, and then fastened their postcard to the string which hung from a helium balloon. The other side of the postcard asked whoever found the card to mail it back and to write who they were and when and where they found the postcard. People who had gotten their card mailed back to them the previous year would tell everyone how far their balloon had gone and who had mailed back their postcard. It was amazing to hear how many cards came back in the mail and how far away some of the balloons had traveled. Someone had even had their card mailed back to them all the way from Colorado!

As it was beginning to get dark, everyone would let go of their balloons at the same time. We watched the balloons until they disappeared and we all hoped the card would be mail back to us. And every year a lot of the cards were mailed back, and one time a truck driver from back east mailed our card back.

During the summer we only had Church School. I couldn't wait for regular school to start, and would watch to see when the teachers would be setting up their classrooms, because I would help them and then know that school would start soon. I loved to help them unroll the corrugated cardboard in all its colors, to pin the letters onto the boards, and to make the room look pretty. I loved to visit their rooms and spend the days there looking at the books they would be using, and helping them make their rooms ready for school to start.

I could go visit a teacher in any room, and usually there would also be a few other kids going around helping. Teachers liked to talk and explain, and one year I got to help a teacher put up a time line, and it was so interesting! We folded a long strip of corrugated cardboard, the kind that had a scalloped edge, and folded it in half, and the halfway fold became the year "0" and everything on the right side was "A.D." and everything on the left side was "B.C." but it was confusing because that teacher said that there was really no year "0."

At home I was old enough to do dishes. Judy and I would trade. One week I washed and she dried, and the next week I would dry and she would wash. If it was my turn to wash, I would hand the clean dish to Judy, who would be the inspector for the week. If she found any food on what ever I had washed, then she would reject it, and it had to be washed again. Then the next week we switched jobs, and I would be the inspector. Being the inspector of the other one's dishes was kind of tricky: If it was really dirty then you had to give it back to be washed again, but if you were mad at your sister you could kick every dish back with a "Wash again!" command, but the trouble with that was then the next week would be payback time and all your dishes would be rejected and returned back to you to be washed again. We had learned through trial and error to only reject the dishes that were really still dirty.

We had to wash all the dishes from the whole day, and we had one dish pan for washing and one for rinsing, and then we had a dish drainer where all the rinsed dishes went. But we would put the glasses into the dish drainer right-side-up. While we were washing, the kettle would be heating up on the stove. The kettle was like a tea kettle, except it was bigger and the spout was longer and it held more water than a regular tea kettle.

When we were all done washing and the inspector had put the all the dishes that passed inspection into the dish drainer, the dirty water and the rinse water went down the sink, the tubs were dried out, and the person who was the dish dryer for the week got the kettle off the stove to scald the clean dishes. The kettle was heavy, and had to be held with a potholder. While the dishes were being washed the kettle heated up until the water inside it was boiling hot.

Scalding the dishes meant that we slowly poured water from the kettle over all the plates and the bowls and the silverware, and around the rim of each glass; then we filled the glasses with the scalding hot water.

The kettle got put back on the stove, and we would hold the glasses with a tea towel and turn them over quickly, letting the water run down the sink. If you did it just right the dishes did not have to be dried at all, because they would dry instantly from the boiling hot water. This killed all the germs and we had to do it every time we washed dishes.

We tried to keep things clean so that we would not get sick, and killing the germs with boiling water was important. After the dishes were dry, the person who was the dish drier for the week would put everything away, all the silverware and plates and bowls and glasses and cups.

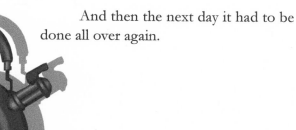

And then the next day it had to be done all over again.

My birthday present — 7 years old
I am in the front yard, in front of my mother's rose garden

Me almost 4, showing my new dress in
Gramma Gigi's back yard

Dresses and Shoes

My mother had a sewing machine, and sewed all of our clothes except for Daddy's. We would get one new school dress each year, and pick out the fabric (within reason and within the taste of my mother) so coming to a compromise on the choice of fabric and the acceptable pattern was a drawn out, lengthy process. Picking out the fabric meant a trip to the Emporium Department Store at Stanford Shopping Center. We would pile into the car and get there by nine o'clock in the morning, and the double glass doors would be opened by a formally-dressed employee, who strutted with the keeper-of-the-keys status, and then, miracle of miracles, a man dressed like a doorman would stand there right by the doors and blow a trumpet with the same sound as if you were at the horse races, then click his heels together and shout, "The Emporium is Now Open!" Wow! We always had to get there in time to see that, and usually there was a small crowd of people waiting to hear that trumpet and the shouted announcement.

I remember that the best new-school-dress fabric I ever got had green and orange in it. That I was allowed orange was a surprise and a treat because my mom wouldn't let me wear yellow or orange. She said they didn't look good on me, so to have the orange within the pattern was quite a concession. Then we spent time picking out the buttons, there were so many beautiful buttons to choose from, and the hair ribbons to match. I had braids, but had to wear the hair ribbons at the top of my braids instead of the bottom, because when I went to school in the morning with ribbons on the ends of my braids, I always lost my hair ribbons. They would just slide off or something, so I had to wear them right over my ears at the top of my braids. I had fat braids, and I wanted skinny braids with ribbons that would stay on the bottom and not come untied, because it is really hard to retie your own hair ribbons.

After the fabric, the pattern, the thread, buttons, interfacing (and maybe rickrack if you could be so lucky to have rickrack) were purchased, we would go new-school-shoes shopping. The Stanford Shopping Center had a Sommer and Kaufmann Shoe Store that was the best place in the world to buy shoes because of the monkeys.

Monkeys! You could see the monkeys from inside or outside the store; there was a glass cage that was four-sided, built into the wall of the store right next to the entrance, under an overhang so the sun would not shine directly on the cage, and the glass sides were very tall, maybe eight or ten feet tall, and about six feet long, and inside there was a imitation forest with four monkeys and their water and toys and they would play and jump around and you would watch them and they would watch you and there were always people on both sides of the glass cage watching those monkeys. If you came to the shoe store around lunch time, a store employee would unlock a secret part of the cage and go inside, and walking and standing in the cage he would feed the monkeys and make sure they were okay and most of the time a monkey would get on his shoulder. Sometimes the monkeys would be dressed up in little clothes, and then one time we went there and there was a baby monkey because the mama monkey had had a baby! Not only did you get a pair of new school shoes, you got to see the monkeys!

The monkeys lived there, that was their house, and sometimes at night I would lay in bed wishing that I could go out to the shopping center and see what the monkeys looked like when they were asleep and I wondered where they slept.

The shoe store had this machine to measure your foot that was like an x-ray machine, but for little kids their foot was too small to use it, so the shoe-store man would measure your foot for you. You stood up on the foot measurer, and he made sure your heel was all the way to the back, and then he slid a specially shaped piece right up next to your toe, and would carefully write down the measurement. Then he would do the same thing with the other foot. The new size would be determined, and it seemed so very important and exciting to see how much a kid's feet had grown over a year, like magic had happened and caused the change and it was always as if an achievement had been reached. "Oh, she is a size 5 now! Her old shoes are a size 4, she has grown a whole size since she last got shoes!" And come to think of it, it was magic because growing was amazing and magical.

We girls had three pairs of shoes: School shoes, play shoes and church shoes. We got new school shoes each September, new church shoes each Easter, and new play shoes at the end of school in June. Getting new school shoes involved the anticipation of the shopping, and then being there and seeing the new styles of shoes. I desperately wanted flats, or even buckle shoes, "Please let me have buckle shoes, maybe those red shoes with the shiny buckles..." I would try to send the telepathic thought to my mother about those shoes. She would look at all the shoes and the her eyes would find the ugliest saddle shoes to wear, not even the two-colored saddle shoes, but the clunky heavy tie shoes, and her finger would reach out, pointing to a shoe for the shoe man to check to see if he had my size. I would watch the end of the finger and try to will it, to manipulate her finger so that the finger would choose a pair of shoes like Kathy-down-the-street who had the cute girlish red shoes with buckles, but the finger would stop at the most clunky shoes and my mother would instruct the sales man to see if he had those shoes in my size. For many of the little girls this was an on-going fashion battle that went on between their mother and them. Little girls wanted fashionable shoes and moms wanted good sturdy shoes that would last all school year, and those were never the same pair of shoes!

I would wait, hoping and trying out those prayers to God, asking that there not be those ugly shoes back in the shoe place, or that the light would burn out, or that the shoe man needed glasses and couldn't find the shoes or that some other little girl had just taken the last one. I would try to send messages to the thoughts of the shoe man so that maybe he would come out and sadly shake his head and tell my mother that there were no more clunky tie shoes, and then from behind his back he would pull out a box of the most beautiful shoes in the store and with a smile and flourish ask me to try those on instead, and they would fit and my mother would say, "Yes" and I would have a great shoe year!

But that never happened. Sometimes the pair I hated most wouldn't be in my size, but there was always as pair that was a close runner up in ugly. On the first day of school I knew that my dress would be great and hoped that no one would notice my shoes, but of course all the little girls compared dresses and shoes. Some of them would even wear their buckle shoes without socks, and I would look at my clunky tie shoes with those thin anklet socks and know that I would probably not be walking down that fashion runway any time soon. But it became a ritual, I am not sure why, but little girls would often trade shoes for a school day. I would trade with someone who let me wear their pretty shoes and they would wear my shoes. Kathy Ferguson would trade the most, and I loved her for it, because her shoes were always the ones I wanted. I think we became best friends starting in kindergarten because of shoe trading. Little girls likes to trade shoes and sweaters, it was just part of what we did.

My favorite fourth grade dress

So when my mom would make our dresses and sew them, she would wash the material, and then we girls would iron it flat, then the fabric went on the living room floor, and the pattern was pinned onto the fabric. The pattern always said how much fabric to buy depending on how wide the fabric was, and at the Emporium my mom would open up the pattern and take out the layout sheet, and then buy less fabric than recommended, so that at home the challenge was to get all the pattern pieces on the fabric, because you couldn't follow the layout on the sheet. Usually there was hardly any fabric left over. There were special scissors to cut the fabric and those scissors couldn't be used on regular paper, just the tissue paper pattern and the material, because the paper would make them dull. That never made sense to me how paper could make scissors dull.

My mother would sit at her sewing machine, with the little light on the machine turned on, and the needle going up and down so fast that you couldn't see it, the fabric inside-out sliding under that needle, stitching backwards and forwards and snipping the threads. She knew how to sew perfectly and there was never a mistake on any of the clothes that she made us.

One day when we had only been at our house for a few years my mom was at her sewing machine and felt that prickle in the back of her neck that someone was watching her through the window. She looked up, and there was a big old jack rabbit standing on its hind legs with its paws on the window sill, just staring in the window, and my mom just stared back until he slowly lowered himself and hopped away, back across the fields towards the Old Bayshore Highway.

A lot of times there would be pheasants in the yard. My mom would be sewing and look up to see a ring-necked pheasant in the yard, and she would call us to come look. The pheasants would escape the hunters from the hunt club out by the Yacht Harbor, and fly to somewhere safe. Their feathers were like jewels, shimmering in the light. How could anyone shoot something so beautiful?

The Ruined Dress

My parents didn't have extra money or money for frivolous things. They would "go out" only a few times a year: Once to the bank Christmas Party and once for their wedding anniversary. Daddy worked at the bank. He had started out with the American Trust Company – "Americans Trust the American Trust Company" – and later worked for Wells Fargo when they purchased American Trust. Banks were a lot different in those days; a bank manager could loan money on a handshake and each bank branch had its own manager, and the managers knew everyone in their community. Each Christmas the bank had a big fancy Christmas party for everyone who worked there along with their husband or their wife. There would be an elegant dinner and then a dance, and my parents always looked forward to it, because that way my mom would get to meet a lot of the people that my dad worked with and who he always talked about. She could put faces with the names of the people that we heard my Daddy speak about when he would come home from work and tell about his day.

My mom would make a new party dress each year for the bank party; she couldn't wear the same dress each year. But one year she had to wear the same dress as the year before, and it was my fault.

I loved playing with my dolls, and using fabric scraps to make dresses for my dolls. By the time I was seven I knew how to embroider, and had my own sewing kit and embroidery hoop. I knew how to make simple clothes for my dolls; little skirts and shawls and simple dresses and sashes.

When I walked past my parent's bedroom one rainy day I saw the most beautiful material on the ironing board, and knew that my doll wanted a dress made from that material. It was blue like the ocean, with white and black swirls, and was the most smooth and shiny and silky material that I had ever felt. My mom's sewing scissors were right there on the sewing machine, so I took them and cut off a piece of the material big enough for my doll to have a new dress.

I put the scissors back, and went into my room with the material, and the weird thing was that it was already sewn into a perfect dress....I slid it right over my doll's head and down onto her body. It was a slinky soft tube that turned my doll into a fashion model. Well almost, anyway, as I had given all my dolls haircuts a few weeks earlier and the choppy semi-cropped look had not made the fashion magazines yet. But all in all, my doll was quite fashionable. Judy wasn't around and Jennifer was taking a nap, so I had no one to show the dress to, and went outside to play in the rain.

Well, that night our house was full of that tingly energy that happens when grown-up are going out. My parents had taken baths, my dad had on his white shirt and cuff links, and my mom had pin-curled her hair and had on her slip and nylon stockings. We kids were all excited because Grandpa Bob was spending the night. He would come down by himself from San Carlos and Daddy would unfold the hide-a-bed, and Grandpa Bob would sleep there. Some people called the couch a "divan" or a "davenport" and one family I knew called theirs the "chesterfield," but ours was the hide-a-bed. We kids would crawl into bed with Grandpa Bob, and then in the morning my mom would make waffles.

I went in my room to get my doll to show everyone my doll's new dress, when at the same time I heard my mom screaming, "...that little bastard! Dammit, someone cut the sleeve off of my dress!" My mom was screaming and crying, my dad was shouting, and there I was, standing there holding my doll, which was actually wearing the sleeve off of my mom's new dress that she had made for the Christmas Party and had put on, or tried to put on, and discovered that some little girl had cut off the sleeve.

I didn't know. It had been beautiful material, and now my mom's new dress was ruined, her beautiful new dress that she had been so excited about wearing, and she had no time to fix it, and even if there had been enough time she didn't have enough material left over to make another sleeve. I stood there holding my doll and I hated myself for being so stupid and I hated the doll's dress and I hated the doll.

After much crying and yelling and cajoling and consoling, my parents finally went to the Christmas Party, and my mom wore her last year's dress with her fancy coat over it. I think she wore her coat all night long.

After they left and it was just me, my sisters and Grandpa Bob, we didn't even talk about what I had done. I sat on the floor of the living room still stunned at the enormity of my transgression and of my sin. And I was the pariah, the traitor who had ruined my mom's dress. Judy said my mom was going to kill me, but the weird thing was that my mom didn't. I never really wanted to make a doll dress again.

It's made by Kodak...

It's the
Baby Brownie Special

Walking Around Town – The Photo Lab and the Market

My mom had an old "Box Brownie" camera. It was a small box camera that had an eyepiece that you looked down into and then to take the picture you pushed a little metal lever to the side, and it clicked back again. The roll of film had to be threaded just right on little pegs before the film could be wound over the picture-taking part, but when the whole roll of film had been used, then my sister or I, or both of us, got to walk to Willis Photo Lab to drop off the film.

Willis Photo Lab was a family-owned photography studio located on Loma Verde, a different street from my street. I think the Willis family lived in the back and had their studio in the front. There was a junk yard almost right next to Willis Photo Lab. In the junk yard there were toilets sitting in the dirt and bath tubs sitting on the dirt, and lots of piles of other junk. I used to look over at the toilets in a rather sneaky way, because I was not sure what to do if someone was going to the bathroom in one of the toilets in the middle of the field, but I was very interested in making sure that no one would ever have to see anyone using the field toilets for what they were intended in people's regular homes. After all, I had learned pretty early on that if you followed the rules, then people liked you, and it was pretty much a rule that you did not use a toilet in the middle of a junk yard.

Anyway, we would walk to Willis Photo Lab with the roll of film. And "…one each jumbo, one each jumbo" was the litany in my head. This was in the days when you took in a roll of film, and it was developed in the back of the shop by the owner or his wife. The prints were only black and white, and about two inches square. The kid who took in the film to be developed had to remember to say "one each jumbo!" That really was a secret code with no meaning, but somehow it had to be done to make sure that the snapshots were about three inches square and all developed with little scallops around the edges, instead of being about two inches square.

Once the memory test was over, and "one each jumbo" had been recited, then one could let out their breath. There was a market was on the corner of Middlefield Road and Loma Verde. There was a man who worked there who always tried to cheat the kids. If our mother sent us to the market for a loaf of bread, that man always would cheat us of some of the change. Then our mom would send us back to the store. "You tell him I sent you down there with a dollar, and I expected forty-eight cents back, not twenty-eight cents!" The man would always act like it was a mistake, and that he didn't mean to cheat us. But he did the same thing to all the kids. He was fat and old and stinky and had a bathroom at the back of the store. It seemed to me that every time I had to go to the store that he was in that bathroom, sitting on his toilet, with the door open, pretending that he didn't realize that the door was open. It was a good thing that he had on a big green apron. Somehow I learned to have that adult look of disgust, where I could cloud my eyes over, put my mouth in a straight line, and slowly shake my head. That old store man was not only a cheater and a liar; he was a stinky old slob.

By the time I was in second grade my walking area had expanded. I would turn right on Middlefield Road from Loma Verde and walk past the Winter Club, which was an ice-skating rink. If I had a dime I could stop at the A & W Root Beer stand that was on Middlefield Road before Bergman's, right after you crossed over the creek. The root beer stand had little tables outside, and you could get a root beet float for a dime. Usually I would only do that if I was with a friend, because buying a soft drink was quite a splurge. I did have a wallet and I kept the part of my allowance that I didn't have to donate to the church, but still, a dime was a dime!

Bergman's Department Store was on Middlefield Road, right after you crossed Colorado Avenue. The Variety Store was also near there, on Colorado Avenue near Middlefield. Bergman's was a fun store to go into, because there was a downstairs part with clothes and household things, but upstairs there were toys and fun stuff like wax lips and cinnamon toothpicks and Saint Christopher metals. There were a lot of knick-knacks, things that were interesting to look at that you didn't really need but were good to get for presents, like for my parents' birthdays or anniversaries, or for Mother's Day or Father's Day.

There were always other kids upstairs there, reading comic books or just looking at all the interesting things that were there to buy. One time I bought wax lips; they were big, bright red lips made from wax that covered a person's real lips, and the wax tasted sweet so that when you got tired of wearing them, you could chew on them like gum.

Smoking

I always wanted to smoke. My daddy smoked. Sometimes it was cigarettes, sometimes a pipe. Pipes were stinky, but my daddy looked like Dean Martin and Perry Como combined, only better looking, so smoking a pipe was more like a movie star's habit. Smoke rings. Beautiful smoke rings. It was magic to sit on my daddy's lap and watch him blow smoke rings, one ring attaching itself to the previous ring until it was a wispy smoke chain, the first link disappearing away as it spread apart and swirled up into the air and vanished. "Let me smoke, let me smoke. Let me smoke, I wanna try, please…"

Smoking was glamorous. The movie stars all smoked, and watching television showed us how smoking was sexy, was popular, and without a doubt was as much a part of adult life as eating or drinking. TV show hosts smoked, and contestants smoked, policemen, teachers, doctors, and ministers smoked. Not only were we accustomed to seeing adults smoking, it was unheard of to have a "No Smoking" area. The only time you saw a sign that smoking was prohibited was if there were a lot of "Danger" and "Flammable" signs around like at a gasoline pump or near some area that might explode if there was a spark. Also Smokey the Bear reminded people that "Only YOU can Prevent

Forest Fires!" so sometimes at camping places there would be "No Smoking" signs. Otherwise people smoked just about everywhere: Grocery stores, sporting events, parks, outside of church, in the doctor's waiting room, inside hotels and restaurants, and in bus and train stations.

There was smoking advertisements on the television, smoking ads in every magazine that we ever saw, and billboards about smoking. Inside of buses there were ads for smoking. It seemed that it was natural to smoke and very popular.

Grandpa Bob smoked five cigarettes a day. He would have one in the morning, one after lunch, one in the afternoon, one after dinner, and one just before he went to bed. He did that from the time he was a teenager until he died. Gramma Gigi hated the smell, so Grandpa Bob always smoked outside. He would sit on the back porch enjoying his cigarette, smoking it slowly and watching the smoke drift away.

People always had ashtrays inside their houses even if they didn't smoke so that their guests could smoke if they wanted to, and every store or shop gave out matchbooks with advertising on them so smokers always had matchbooks. People even collected matchbooks because there were so many different matchbooks and it was a fun way to remember where you had been. Kids could take free matchbooks from the counter next to a shop's cash register and no one thought anything about it.

I was seven and I think that my daddy was just tired of me nagging to smoke, so he finally said, "Here, smoke this, just put it in your mouth and breathe in..." so I did. A really big deep breath. Hooey! I thought that I was going to die. How could anyone do that horrible thing that made you feel like choking? The memory of that feeling kept me from smoking until I was fourteen years old!

A little while after he let me smoke, my daddy took on the task of painting our house. The paint brushes had to be cleaned off with turpentine, which is very flammable, so he quit smoking in order to be able to paint the house safely. Without him buying cigarettes, it meant that every day he could put a quarter in a really big jar, saving the amount that his pack of cigarettes would have cost that day.

Then pretty soon when he came home from work we girls were asking him where the quarter was. He would hand the quarter to one of us and we would put it in the jar. After a year or so we had one hundred and fifty dollars, which was enough to help go on vacation all because he quit smoking!

Santa Claus and cowboys smoked, twins smoked and so did couples.

Everyone smoked!

The Little Engine That Could

Life at Home

My mother had a lot of rules, but the tricky thing was that I didn't understand many of the rules and I was often confused about what was expected of me. Parents in those days didn't spend much time explaining things to kids. Time was a precious resource, and with all the work that moms had to do, the last thing moms had time for was to sit down and clarify things to kids. My mom was one of the moms that would yell and threaten us when she got mad, and when that happened I, for one, knew that it was a good idea to get out of her way.

As with many families of those times, our family relied on physical punishment to train children. I learned to respond to signals of anger, and was adept at escaping when my mom was mad. I was never sure what the triggers were, but like other kids, I learned to recognize the signs and tried to stay invisible when my mom was having a bad day, or better still, to escape the house until things were back to normal.

Kids would talk with each other about how their parents disciplined, and some kids spent a good amount of time evading their angry moms. We decided that it was even worse to have a mom who used the "Wait until your father gets home" strategy. That way the mom spent the day making the kid worry, and then the dad cam home to punish the kid without even having been around and knowing what had happened. Some kids would get locked out of the house until their father came home.

Kids talked and build their own communities; they lived in the same neighborhood, went to the same school and often to the same church. No one ever drove a kid to school...that was unheard of. Most families had only one car and the dad used that car during the week to go to work, so all the kids knew where each other lived and knew how to navigate around their neighborhoods by themselves.

We had never heard of the word "day care." None of us kids knew anyone that had both parents working outside of the home. Some times a mom might have a volunteer job or a sales clerk job for a few hours a day, but only if all the kids were grown up enough to go to school. Older kids might watch younger kids, or a grandmother might help out, but there was no building where a lot of parents left their kids for someone else to take care of except at the church where little kids went to Sunday School and grown-ups went to church.

Like mostly all of the families of the time, my mom was at home all day during the weekdays. She turned on the radio from the moment she started breakfast, and the radio was her constant companion all day of every weekday. The radio had a lot of news on it and talking; that's how people kept up with what was going on in politics and sports and science and also in their communities...that plus reading the newspaper every day.

There were no radio "talk shows" and the nearest thing to a woman's show was the TV show called *Queen for a Day*, where women would go on a stage and talk about why they should be the Queen, and the audience would vote among the contestants and the woman they pitied the most would win something. There were no Oprah-type shows, no Internet, no avenues for the young moms to exchange information or to discuss their feelings. I don't think topics like PMS were even known about and certainly never were discussed; in a neighborhood of stay-at-home moms there was no networking and only superficial interchanges. People minded their own business and expected their neighbors to mind their own business as well.

The families in our neighborhood were from all over the United States and from other countries as well. Most of our neighbors had left relatives behind; it was not the kind of neighborhood like those that still existed in San Jose, where a kid could walk next door to their grandparents' house and across the street to their aunts, and down the street to their cousins...it was a neighborhood of new, young families where people were making a post-war new life.

We had a phone at our house, but it was a party-line phone that several families shared, and phone calls were expensive. I don't think my mom ever talked to any friends on the phone; her life was taking care of the house and taking care of all the things that needed to be done every day while my daddy was at work. All the shopping was done on the weekends with my daddy, and the rest of the time she was at home with the radio on.

Physical punishment in schools was an accepted way of life; kids could get paddled with a paddle or hit with rulers. And physical punishment at home was part of most kid's life. In our neighborhood the only kids who didn't routinely get paddled, spanked, hit or some other physical punishment were our Jewish friends. We kids could never figure that one out. There was one girl down the street whose mom would punish her by making her eat food that she didn't like; that was horrible.

Some kids could make the leap of understanding that threats were an outlet for their parent; some kids, like me, believed the threats were real so that parts of my life were influenced and colored by that belief and fear.

That was how things were for many kids; we coped and figured things out the best we could, and we were resourceful and inventive. No one watched our every move or monitored where we were; kids were expected to be home at a certain time and that was how it was. It wasn't like today where children are monitored every moment and they have no time alone to just be themselves. We had time to ourselves to be creative, time to get in trouble, and times that we got punished.

Some kids heard that they were going to be "hit so hard they would end up in next week," other kids that they were "going to get the tar beat out of them." I heard, "I am going to break every bone in your body, get me that wooden spoon!" And then I knew it was time to get the heck out of the way!

Years later I heard my sisters yelling at their children the similar phrases that we had all heard growing up; I asked them if they remembered hearing them, and how could they even say those things to their children? Each sister laughed at me, and said that they didn't mean it; their kids knew they didn't mean it, it was no big deal and that they had known that my mother never meant it. I told them that I always had believed our mom's threats, and my sisters just shook their heads and told me that was my problem.

How could the world have been so different to children growing up in the same house?

My mother was intelligent. She was born in Riverside and grew up in Oakland during the time of war rationing and deprivation and black-market war goods. Her father, my Grandpa Bob, worked for Southern Pacific Railroad as an accountant but was a volunteer War Warden during WWII, plus he had been a soldier in WWI in France as a French-English translator. He had chased Poncho Villa around the Mexican countryside and had bleached his hair with peroxide as a bored and over-used soldier in WWI, along with the rest of his unit.

My mom painted a mural on a wall of her high school, and then went on to enroll in the University of California at Berkeley as chemistry major, knowing all the chemistry tables and how to use a slide rule. She lived in a boarding house in Berkeley and worked at Laguna Honda Hospital in San Francisco, did research for Shell Oil, and then did her duty as a patriotic young woman who went to the USO dances in Alameda, met my father and danced and fell in love and married.

She had gone to college, to Berkeley, when most women did not go to college and when they certainly didn't major in chemistry or do research for Shell Oil. But for me in my little-girl world I did not understand any of this, or understand what make my mom who she was.

My mother and I never learned to talk to each other. I have stories of Gramma Gigi growing up, of Grandpa Bob, of my daddy, but my mother shared very little of herself with me. Her childhood stories are those stories which were woven into Gramma Gigi's stories.

Baby Jennifer was supposed to take a nap every afternoon and I got really good at telling Jennifer stories so that she would be quiet. Then sometimes I would trick her by hiding under the covers and jumping up. But most of the time I just whispered her stories so she would be still and not make any noise. I would tell her about Candy Land and *The Big Rock Candy Mountain* and about Daniel Boone and about Davy Crockett. I told her the story of *The Little Engine that Could*. I had learned a lot of songs and stories from listening to records on our record player, so I would tell and retell them to Jennifer.

When I told her about *The Little Engine that Could*, I would make the story last a long, long time. I made sure that

Jennifer understood that she should not give up easily. I think that I understood the lesson from that story and what it meant, and therefore loved to tell it to Jennifer, changing my voice from despair, to hope, to achievement and happiness! I loved telling Jennifer stories and making them seem real to her

I told her all about *Babba Yaga*, the Russian witch who lived in a house that was mounted on huge chicken legs; a house that would lower and raise itself so Baba Yaga could go in and out easily. Sometimes I would hide under the covers and speak with a crackly voice like a witch and tell Jennifer that Jane was gone, and that I was a witch that had stolen Jane, and that I was going to steal Jennifer too! Then Jennifer would start to cry and I would pull the covers down and tell Jennifer that I had escaped the witch. Jennifer would crawl in bed with me and suck her thumb and I would tell her that I hadn't really been stolen and that I had played a trick on her.

I tried to make her walk by holding onto her hands and pulling her along, but that really didn't work. But she was tiny like a little elf, and would sit with her little legs sticking straight out and her back really straight. All she had to do was smile and my heart would melt. It was fun to teach her things, fun to put her in the wagon and pull her around. She had a very odd nose, because her nose would sweat. I never saw anyone else who had a nose like that. These tiny little droplets of sweat would cover her little nose, like clear droplets on a plant that had been watered too much.

We had a swing set with a glider on it, but Jennifer was too little for the glider. I would have her hold on to me and I would swing her. I liked to have her little arms holding me. We had a great backyard, great for a kid in the suburbs. We had a lawn, and a garden and fruit trees.

Every year Daddy would dig out the garden, dig several feet deep and add fertilizer and gypsum and turn over the soil because it was clay soil. One year when I was four or five, he was digging and called out, "Come and look at all the roots I've dug up." He had never seen so many roots in a clump in his life! He was standing there all sweaty in the hole he had dug, pointing to the clump of white thread-like things, leaning in his shovel, and I kept saying, "Where are the roots? Where are the roots? I don't see them!" And he would point at all those white threadlike things in the ground, like a ball of yarn almost. Well, in my mind, I knew what a rooster was, so when he said, "Look at all the roots!" my mind visualized a whole bunch of baby roosters, because roots must be roosters when they were little, that's what my brain told me. I couldn't get there fast enough to see a hole full of baby roosters, but all there was a bunch of dirty stringy things. I never did see the roots in the hole.

Our swing set was in the middle of the back yard, and each end was shaped like a capital letter "A." There were two swings, a trapeze, and then another "A" part with the glider. My mom didn't allow us to stand on the ends of the "A" parts, but after a while she gave up because we always would. And Judy and I would climb up there, one on each side of the swing set and then we would look through the long metal tube that held up the swings. You couldn't see anything if the kid on each end had their eye tight against the hole, because then all the light was blocked, but if your eye was almost to the hole, then you could see each other's eye. But what we really liked to do was this: We would take turns whispering into the end of the tube, one of us whispering and the other one listening. You could whisper really softly through that tube, and it would sound loud at the other end. We would whisper, "Can you hear me?" and the other person would whisper, "Yes" back into the tube, until we would get louder and louder and one of us would be bad and **yell** into the tube and the other one would yell back and then our ears would be ringing and we thought we were going deaf and my mom would come out in the yard and yell at us to stop our god damn yelling or we would get it, and then Judy and I usually said, "But **she** started it," and then we had to go to our rooms. But we called that game "Telegraph" and really liked playing it.

We were allowed to jump from the swings when we were swinging. We liked to take the hose and arrange it on the ground to make a circle, like a target to aim at, and I would try to land inside the hose circle. I would imagine that the area inside the hose was an island, and that all around it were alligators and piranhas so that I **had** to land there. Then each time I landed safely, I would move the hose a little farther away. We could do the same thing with a hula hoop, but it was a lot harder to land inside a hula hoop, because you usually bounced a bit when you first landed. I had learned about piranhas from *Reader's Digest*. I used to lay awake at night and worry about what I would do if I ever was in a river surrounded by piranhas.

Jane 6 & Judy 8 on the swing set glider – still a short fence but the trees are bigger!

In the part of our yard that wasn't grass, we had our garden and we grew tomatoes and corn and zucchini and apricots and white peaches and purple plums and boysenberries and onions. We had three different kinds of cherries: Royal

Anne, Bing, and some other kind that never did very well, and I got the blame for that:

I was five or six when my parents went to plant that third cherry tree. It was in a hole that Daddy dug in the lawn near the swing set. He dug this hole about a billion feet deep or maybe four feet deep, and filled it with water and fertilizer and planted the tree with a big stick to hold it up.

On the same day I happened to be walking across the backyard backwards. I liked to walk backwards, because somehow my feet looked different and so did everything else. And then my parents were yelling at me to stop and I was yelling back, "Why?" and they were yelling, **"Stop!"**…and then I fell backwards into the hole that had been dug, toppling over the tree and sinking into that fertilizer and water-filled hole. I was sinking pretty quickly, and hadn't hit bottom yet. There was probably a few long seconds that my parents seriously thought about leaving me there and letting my head go completely under. But my cries of help were pretty loud, and the neighbors were looking over the fence, and the stupid neighbor boys were laughing. They had no business looking over the fence like that.

Humph! Not only did I get pulled out by my arms; I got hosed off by the cold-water hose, then stripped down to my underpants, and then I was put in the laundry tray in the garage. The laundry tray was the big built-in sink on legs that was inside the garage next to the washing machine. It was most embarrassing, plus those neighbor boys saw it all. Then I got sent inside for a real bath, and of course got the spanking for not stopping when I was told to, even though I tried my best logic that if they had just told me why I would have stopped.

The cherry tree never did grow very well, and the cherry tree story was retold several times a year. But the caterpillar invasion story was much better, and I didn't think it was at all gross when I was a kid.

One year there was this absolute invasion of caterpillars. They were fuzzy and moved fast and were everywhere. You couldn't walk outside without stepping on them, and, in fact, my mom sent us outside to step on them because they were eating up the garden. My sister couldn't stomach the stepping on of the caterpillars, but for some reason, I took on the task with an obsession. And then I discovered the bare-footed stepping on of the caterpillars. I would stomp on them like there was no tomorrow, and then stick my feet in my sister's face just because it was so icky. My mom wouldn't let me back inside with those feet, but I didn't care, I liked to pop those caterpillars under my bare feet, because most of the time we were not allowed to go barefoot, but no one was going to tell me to put my shoes back on with all that gunk on my feet, so I ran around like a little maniac stomping those caterpillars with my bare feet, and then when my daddy came home he had to wash my feet in the laundry tray until they were clean.

My mother canned the tomatoes and peaches and made pickles. During the winter we would eat all the food she had canned in *Mason* jars. It was a lot of work and a lot of boiling water and doing things just right, but we didn't really want to buy store-bought things if we didn't have to. As we got older, we girls developed food-trading strategy. Judy hated canned tomatoes and liked *Spam. Spam* was disgusting. It was chopped up ham and fat in a can, all smooched together and slimy on the sides with jelled fat. I hated asparagus, shrimp and *Spam.* I could give or take canned peaches. If we ever had canned tomatoes and *Spam* at the same meal, we would eat so slowly that my parents would finally leave the table and then we would trade. I would get canned tomatoes and Judy would get *Spam*. When I couldn't trade, it was either fill my mouth really full and go spit it out in the toilet, or fill the table leg or feed it to the cat.

Filling the table leg didn't last really long, because pretty soon Daddy figured out where the smell was coming from and had to unscrew the foot on the bottom of the leg and out came all the liquefied food that I hadn't eaten.

I loved to play with my food. Everything in my head was always a story, and food was no exception. Our kitchen table was next to a window, and in the winter time it would be dark outside during dinner, and I could see my reflection in the window. I was a slow eater anyway, probably because I was always making stories with my food about mashed potato dams, dams bursting and the gravy rushing out and flooding the broccoli trees; I would play I was making mashed potato cookies, fantasize about food floods and construction....but seeing my reflection was magical because I could pretend to be the Queen and sit up with very fine manners and hold my cup with a finger pointing out and take quite small bites thank you, or I could watch my reflection eating like a slob.

Ever since I could remember, I would have the same nightmare over and over again. It was such a bad dream, and I dreamt it for years and years. This was my dream: I was me inside an amphitheatre, like inside of the Frost Amphitheatre at Stanford. I would be near the bottom of the amphitheater when boiling oil would start to pour down from the top, from all the parts of the top. It would get closer and closer, nearer and nearer, and I would move down lower and lower towards the middle trying to escape the boiling oil. It was hot, and getting hotter, and all around me there was boiling oil and I knew that I was going to get boiled alive. Then out of the awful-smelling smoke there would appear a woman dressed in a long dress and cape that covered her completely, and I could hear this incredibly sweet voice calling me to follow her. She would show me how to get out safely, and she would beckon me, but I could not see her face. I would follow her, but following her meant I got closer and closer to the boiling oil, not safer and farther away. And when the oil was about to swallow me up, and all I could see was the smoke, and smell the hot oil, and all the plants and benches were destroyed, the woman would turn around and remove the veil from her face, and I would see it was not a woman, but a man. The man would pull a long dagger from under his sleeve and stab me through the shoulder and completely through my upper arm. In my dream I could feel that knife going right into me. I could feel the pain, and it was all the way through me with excruciating clarity, and the smoke and the oil and the lack of air were all there. And then I would wake up completely afraid and gasping for air, feeling the unbearable pain in my arm. This dream went on night after night after night.

This was one of three dreams that I had so many times that it finally happened that when I was dreaming I would know that I was dreaming, but that still did not make it any better.

Jane 6, Judy 8, Jennifer 2, with Gramma Gigi on her back porch

Going to Gramma Gigi's House

I loved going to my Gramma Gigi's house; all of us girls loved going there. From the time I was little up through my teenage years I spent many weekends at Grandpa Bob and Gramma Gigi's house, and each summer many weeks at their house. Gramma Gigi and Grandpa Bob lived in San Carlos on Emerald Avenue, off of St. Francis. I never figured out how "St." could be both "Saint" and "Street."

Going to Gramma Gigi's meant so many things...she would ask me what I wanted to eat, and she would fix popovers for breakfast, tall toasty and hollow popovers that were eggy and we would fill with butter and jam. We would go to the beach or to the drive-in movie, or eat ice cream while we watched TV. But the best thing was listening about her life. I would beg her, "Tell me about when you were a little girl! Tell me about when you were a little girl!" And she would tell me stories as we snuggled together under her electric blanket. She probably had the first electric blanket in the whole world! She had her first of many heart attacks when she was 43 years old, and would easily get cold, so she had the electric blanket. The electric blanket was warm and snuggly and felt really good, with big heavy wires that would get very hot. No one was allowed to sit on the blanket, but that didn't matter, we had plenty of places to sit!

Grandpa Bob and Gramma Gigi's house was on a hill, and their driveway was so steep that a car could not be parked on it. The backyard had a beautiful big oak tree that shaded a large part of the yard, and Gramma Gigi's room had a plate glass window that took up almost one whole wall of her bedroom, and that window looked out onto the backyard. In the oak tree there was swing, a swing with thick rope handles and a wooden seat, and the rope went through holes at each end of the seat and there were big knots at the ends of the ropes to hold the seat there. When I would swing I could see my reflection in the window, and it was as if I was swinging with another little girl. I would try to swing so high that I would reach the window, but that wasn't possible. Even if I jumped out of the swing I was too far away to hit the window, but it was magical to swing in that swing under the big oak tree and see myself reflected in the window. A person could swing higher in that swing than any other swing I have ever known, and it was far enough from the ground that you could lean backwards all the way and not be afraid of hitting the ground with your head. There was no bar across the top like a playground swing, so if a kid wanted to stand up on the seat to swing, that was okay because there was no way that you would hit your head.

When we girls took baths at Gramma Gigi's house we got to stand up afterwards on the toilet lid and she would dust us off with dusting powder. Dusting powder smelled like perfume, in fact, people could buy dusting powder to match their favorite perfume. The powder might or might not come with a powder puff; most ladies had their own special powder puff and didn't want the cheap one that came with the box of powder. Gramma

Gigi had several powder puffs and two favorite perfumes, plus she had a pressed aluminum powder box that Grandpa Bob had given her as a wedding present. It was a musical powder box, but it also had a drawing on the inside of it that I had drawn with pencil when I was three years old and didn't know any better. It didn't really matter, because when it was full of powder and had the lid on no one could see my drawing anyway.

One time when I was at Gramma Gigi's house I noticed that her wedding-present powder box was not where it belonged. I thought it was missing, and ran to ask Gramma Gigi where it was. She told me she was mad at Grandpa Bob and that she had thrown it away! Well, I snuck into the trash can and looked, and sure enough, it was there! I rescued the powder box and put it back where it belonged, but when Gramma Gigi saw it she said she didn't want it; if I wanted it I could have it, because otherwise she would just throw it away again. I took it home with me that day and I still have the wedding present powder box that my Grandpa Bob gave Gramma Gigi as a present in when they got married in 1923.

Gramma Gigi's family could be traced back in this country to 1754, fighting with George Washington. I didn't know that when I was a little girl, but discovered it later when I was doing a family tree project when I was in eighth grade. Gramma Gigi's stories were about family and love and hate and hope, and hearing them from my gramma was one very important part of my life. Here is one of Gramma Gigi's stories, except in this story I did not call her Gramma Gigi, because this story is about when she was a little girl:

Gramma Gigi was born in Washington State in 1903 and she would always say "Washington State" because most people would assume Washington D.C. Her grandparents had the first "white man's" home between Walla Walla and Spokane Washington, an area of about 80 miles, and Gramma Gigi's grandma remembered going to the fort for safety when she was a little girl, because the Indians would attack the settlers. Gramma Gigi's own grandparents had come out to Washington State in the 1860's, one from the North and one from the South, and neither side of the families would accept a Yankee or a Rebel, so they came on their covered wagon all the way to Washington State to start a new life.

When Gramma Gigi was born her real name was Audrey Rae Emmert, and some of her family's roots went back to Emmert's Cove, Tennessee, and to people who broke the ground and farmed and explored the West. Little Audrey Rae was the first girl born in a family of many children, and she had four older brothers, so as the first girl she was expected to wait on those boys. Girls were not really encouraged to go to school or to learn things then; they were just supposed to be like servants. Their farm was isolated. There were no other farms for miles and miles, and little Audrey Rae's friends ended up being books and her horse. When she could get away she would take a book and ride her horse and go spend an afternoon some place on the farm where no one could find her. She was a little girl in a world that was at mercy of her bigger brothers and that required lots of thankless labor waiting on those brothers and on her parents.

One of her favorite books to read was about a girl who rode champion horses and jumped over hurdles and other obstacles. So Audrey Rae started practicing with her horse, trying to be just like the girl in the book. Audrey Rae and her horse were getting pretty good at jumping until one day when the horse decided the stream that Audrey Rae wanted him to jump over was too wide. The horse had been running, but came to an abrupt halt at the very edge of the stream, but Audrey Rae didn't! She kept going and landed head-first in the stream, and the water filled her nose and her mouth, and the muddy bottom of the stream was sucking her in! Just then she felt someone tugging her out of the stream, pulling on her dress, and Audrey Rae was able to free herself from the sticky stream bottom and crawl up to the bank. When she opened her eyes, spitting out water and mud, there was no one around but her horse! Little Audrey Rae looked at her filthy clothes, and could then see the teeth marks on her dress where the horse had grabbed her dress and rescued her from drowning in the mud and water.

Audrey Rae took off her clothes and rinsed them in the stream and set them in the sun to dry. Later she went back to the farmhouse but didn't tell anyone what had happened because she knew her parents would not let her ride her horse anymore if they found out what had happened.

While I was born in a time of in-betweens, my Gramma Gigi was born in a time of firsts and lasts. She remembered seeing the first car in the county, the first airplane that flew over their farm, hearing a radio for the first time, and living through the First World War. She remembered hiding in the ice house as a little girl and looking through the cracks in the walls and watching the Indians ride their horses in a single-file line on their way up to Canada to get berries for their pemmican. It was their last ride on horses because the world was changing so quickly. Gramma Gigi lived in a time which changed from horses to cars, from the telegraph to the radio, from silent women who were ordered about and treated like servants to women who supported a nation's economy while their husbands and brothers and sons went off to fight for freedom. The problem was that those men came back and expected things to be the same as when they left, and women like Gramma Gigi were not having any of that!

On that farm in Washington State little Audrey Rae didn't like waiting on her brothers; they were mean to her and expected her to do everything for them and nothing for herself. As a grown-up, Gramma Gigi was barely 5 foot 2 inches tall. She had been a tiny child, and she told me how one time her brothers thought it was funny to hold her down and rub moths on her...lifting up her blouse and rubbing moths on her until the moths were dead and little Audrey Rae was crying. There was no one there to help her. When she was 16 years old Audrey Rae left Washington and went to Southern California. That's where she met my Grandpa, at the Mission Inn in Riverside where Gramma Gigi was working as a waitress, and Grandpa Bob was a 21–year old soldier.

G randma Ruth's Visit

When I was seven our daddy's mother, Grandma Ruth, came from Kansas to visit us. She came on the train from Kansas, and we picked her up at the Oakland Train Station. She was in her fifties and had never seen the ocean! She stayed at our house for two weeks, and my daddy took vacation, and we went every where! We went to Muir Woods, to the Boardwalk at Santa Cruz and then to the beach, to Point Lobos and the 17-mile drive, to Monterey and to Golden Gate Park. We went to China Town in "The City," which was what everyone called San Francisco. If anybody said, "Let's go to The City," people knew automatically that they meant San Francisco. China Town had restaurants, and we ate at a restaurant. I had eaten one other time at a restaurant with my other gramma when Jennifer got christened, and I had gotten impatient (after asking if we had to pay to get out of church) and I had stood on the table at the restaurant and yelled to the waiter "Hey, man, bring the ice cream!" So perhaps my family was not too eager to take me out again. Besides, it was a real treat to eat out. We went to a restaurant in China Town with Grandma Ruth after we had walked and walked around China Town for hours.

When we walked we went into so many shops and there were so many beautiful and exciting things to see that I could not believe my eyes. Everything was different, and shiny and fancy, with embroidery and lacquered furniture and shells and things that smelled spicy and the people who worked there didn't speak English. Grandma Ruth bought us each a jewelry box. My box was black with a mountain scene made out of shells that were smooth and embedded into the surface of the box. And when you opened it played music, and there were two little doors inside the box that opened and then a shelf slid out. On the bottom was a key to wind up when the music ran down. I still have that musical jewelry box, and it still plays the music.

When we climbed up the stairs to the restaurant in China Town, we were tired and hungry. Most of the people inside were Chinese, and the table was round and there was another round thing on the table that spun around, called a "Lazy Susan," so that when the waiter brought a pot of tea and set in on the Lazy Susan, people could grab it and SLOWLY spin it around and everyone had a turn to get what was on that spinning small table in top of the bigger regular table. And you would not believe what the food was like! I never had that kind of rice, or noodles, or chicken, or soup as we had. We ate and ate and ate! My mother had grown up in Oakland, and knew about Chinese food, but my Grandma Ruth sure didn't and neither did I! And then we all got a special cookie that you were supposed to break in half and take out a paper that was inside to find your fortune. I didn't really want to break the cookie; I wanted to take it home to figure out how they had made a cookie with a piece of paper in it. Everyone one took a turn going around the table and carefully breaking open the cookie and reading their fortune, except Jennifer who was too little to read. The fortunes were things like "You will get great wealth," or "You are a person of great wisdom," or "Laughter is the medicine of the soul." I finally decided to open my cookie and wanted to save the pieces, but once it was broken open there were too many pieces to save.

My fortune was something like "Misery is the bane of mankind," which made no sense at all.

The other thing I got that day was a tiny tea set. Usually for our dolls we made our own things from scratch for them to play with. When we ate peanuts, we would save certain peanut shells, because the shells would be the right shape and size for doll cups and bowls. But at China Town I got a real miniature china tea set just the right size for my dolls! There was a tiny tea pot with a lid, and two tiny cups with saucers. They were white with pink flowers painted on them. When I got home after that magical day, I put that tea set on the tiny doll table that my daddy had made, and carefully, carefully only used it a few times, because I didn't want it to break and also, how many tea parties can dolls have without it becoming something that they are used to? I didn't want to spoil my dolls.

Grandma Ruth visited a few more times. When ever she would visit she would pay Jennifer to stop sucking her thumb. Jennifer sucked her thumb so much that the one thumb had a big callous on it; I thought that thumb was also slightly longer than the other thumb! Jennifer just loved to suck her thumb, and you would never see her without her thumb in her mouth. Grandma Ruth would say, "If you don't suck your thumb for a whole week, I'll give you fifty cents!" Even if Jennifer managed to not suck her thumb around Grandma Ruth so that she would get the fifty cents, as soon as Grandma Ruth left to go home, Jennifer still sucked her thumb all the time. I didn't know what the big deal was and why everyone told her to quit sucking her thumb. People would always look at her and ask stupid questions like, "Does that taste good? Can I try?" Jennifer learned that if she pulled out her thumb and nodded her head "yes" that people didn't really want to suck her thumb any way. I just wished that they would quit bothering her about her thumb. She liked it and that was it. Most of the time you didn't see big kids sucking their thumbs so I figured Jennifer would stop when she was damn good and ready. And besides, Jennifer was really shy and sucking her thumb gave her an excuse to not talk to people.

I had one doll named Cassadena. She was a baby doll, shaped like a real baby that was asleep. She had a rubber head, her eyes were always closed, and she had rubber hands with a thumb that would go in her little mouth. She was the size of a real baby, and her body and arms and legs were cloth stuffed with something like pillow stuffing. I hadn't named her on Christmas when I got her, but when we watched the New Year's Day parade on TV at my Gramma's Gigi's house, I heard the most beautiful name, "Cassadena," and named her that beautiful name. It was really Pasadena, where a New Year's Day Parade was held, but my doll was Cassadena. I also had a Jenny Doll. Jenny Doll was small and more fashionable and the right size for my tea set.

Grandma Ruth, Judy, my Mom and me on the ferry boat going across the San Francisco Bay

Jennifer's Accident

One night three-year-old Jennifer decided to very carefully move my tea set. She was carrying the set on the little table while she walked down the hall, but then she tripped. Our house had a concrete slab floor with asphalt tiles over the slab, and when Jennifer tripped with my tea set, she slipped and smashed her forehead into the door frame, cutting her forehead.

My mother didn't drive, so she ran over the Jensen's with Jennifer, and Mr. Jensen, whose name was Levi, drove my mom and Jennifer to the clinic for Jennifer to get stitches. Judy knew how to use the phone, so she carefully dialed Gramma Gigi's number, and Grandpa Bob said he would come down as fast as he could to our house.

When my daddy came home from work and found just Judy and me sitting on the couch in our nightgowns, plus saw the blood in the hallway, he went next door to find out what had happened. Grandpa Bob got to our house just a few minutes later, and there Judy and I still were, sitting on the couch, but this time with the front door wide open!

Then I found my tea set in the hallway. The tea pot was not broken and there was still one cup and one saucer not broken, but the rest of the tea set was smashed to smithereens. I wondered why Jennifer had decided to carry my tea set down the hall in the first place. I decided that Jennifer must have just wanted to play with it, and had been carrying it to go play it in the living room. Jennifer wasn't very good at explaining things; she would just get upset and put her thumb in her mouth and hold onto her blanket, so I never found out from her what she had been trying to do carrying that tiny table and tea set.

When she came home later that night, her stitched-up cut became her "Boom Boom." The Boom Boom was her scar in the middle of her forehead, but by the time she started kindergarten, the scar had moved much closer to her hairline, and as she grew the scar became hidden in her hairline so no one could see the Boom Boom any more.

Last Day of School & Summer

My mom wanted frogs and toads for the garden because they ate the bugs. The last day of school was apparently the day that pollywogs were done being pollywogs and had become frogs. So while other kids were going to after-school parties or to the beach, we went to get frogs. It was hard to convince your friends to go to the creek when they could go to the beach, but the truth was, I liked going to the creek and spent a lot of time there. These were little tiny frogs, about as big as an adult's thumb, even when they were full-grown. We would go to the creek and put creek water in our buckets and pick up frogs and toads with our hands until we had at least fifty each, and then we would go home and dump them in the yard. For the next few weeks when Daddy mowed the lawn we would go ahead of his mowing and look for frogs, because it was awful if a little frog got chopped up in the lawn mower.

We took swimming lessons in the summer. My mom had some kind of seat for Jennifer on my mom's bicycle, and Judy and I had bikes. I had gotten a new big bike for my seventh birthday, and it had three gears and a generator for a light on the front. When it was getting dark, I could get off my bike and flip the generator over so its wheel rubbed against the front wheel of my bicycle. The faster I pedaled, the brighter my headlight got! The three of us rode our bikes to Wilbur Junior High, which has since been renamed Jane Lathrop

Stanford Middle School. That's where the swimming lessons were held.

I hated swimming lessons. The teachers lied to the kids. We went there every morning for two weeks of half-hour lessons. We had to take a shower before getting in the pool, and we would be freezing on the cement next to the pool, teeth chattering while some teenager stood outside the pool dressed in warm clothes and told us how to kick or how to breathe. I figured this was just another way that teenagers were trying to kill little kids while the moms sat and watched. And usually in the Bay Area as soon as school was out for the summer, the weather got cold and foggy, especially on swimming lesson days!

My mom and Jennifer would sit on the bleachers on the other side of the chain link fence while I had lessons. I hated jumping into the pool. It was cold and the water would go inside my swimming cap and the cap would hold the cold water next to my head. My bathing suit would fill with air when I jumped in, and then little air bubbles would float up and it looked like I was farting in the pool. It was cold, and we had to do things like hold on to the edge and kick our feet and turn our heads and breathe, but with everyone kicking and splashing so much, how in the heck was a kid supposed to breathe anyway?! Then they gave us paddle boards and made us hold on to the boards and they would say things like, "I won't move, I'll stand right here, just paddle-kick out to me and I'll grab you," except then they would walk backwards farther and farther until I thought my lungs would burst; and when I finally would get there, the teenager would do something like pick me up, turn me around, and toss me back towards the edge. There were days that I thought I had drunk most of the water in the pool. And then if I or any of the kids was lucky enough to find the place in the pool where the warm water came it…ahhhh…it felt so good, but the teenagers would yell at you to get away from that part.

On the last day of the class we were supposed to jump off of the diving board. I kept going to the back of the line, because I was so scared to jump into the deep end. I was the last kid who had not jumped, and then the bell rang! Class was over! I bet the people on the bleachers had never seen a kid run as fast as I ran over to the gate to get out of that pool area! I was in the line to go through the gate, and then I heard everyone yelling my name, including my mom. "Get back over to the deep end and jump in! You are not done until you jump in, and the next class is already on their way into their lessons! Hurry up and jump, hurry and jump!" I got on the diving board. I was so scared and the water was so deep and it was a long way to the water. Oh well. My life was over, and everyone would be sorry they had yelled at me when I drowned.

I didn't drown, but I sure couldn't think of one good thing that jumping into that deep end had taught me. It was horrible and scary, and the water had gone in my nose and down my throat and I felt like I was going to throw up and my throat was burning. But on the bike ride home I started to feel happier, because swimming lessons were over until next year and I didn't have to do that again for a long time!

During the summer I spent a lot of time at Palo Verde School. It was right down the street from us, and they had a summer recreation program. Judy and I would take sandwiches and fruit, and put Jennifer in the wagon and spend the day at recreation. Most of the time Judy got to come to recreation. She still had a lot of kidney problems and infections, but when she was well she could pretty much do most things. I loved going to summer recreation. We made all sorts of things that we got to keep, and we didn't have to sign up, we could just go there. Plaster of Paris was amazing; we got to make three-dimensional things from it and I really looked forward to those. There were rubber molds that we rubbed *Vaseline* all over the outside, and then we would turn them inside out so the inside was what was all oily. There were molds shaped like seals, molds shaped like roosters, all sorts of shapes and they were three-dimensional molds. We would hang the molds between two sticks that hung between two picnic tables, and then the magic of Plaster of Paris would begin. The teenager who was in charge would measure out the plaster, and then measure out the water, and then add the water, and kids could help stir. At first it was really hard to stir, and then it got easier and easier, until the liquid plaster looked like milk, and I would be sure that it was too thin and watery. Then the leader would pour the plaster into the hanging molds. The molds had to be filled all the way to the very top, then shaken gently to remove air bubbles and then more plaster was added, because the plaster would shrink as it hardened. But what happened next was amazing: The plaster would get warm! If you touched the outside of the mold, you could feel the heat! And when it was done, it would be really cold, but it was never done the same day, or if it was, we kids didn't know.

The next day you would go to recreation and the leader would say to the kids to pick out their mold from the day before. All the kids would take their molds, and if everything went right, this is what happened: You would slowly peel the mold away, like peeling a banana or taking off a sock. And my favorite mold was the seal. It was like a barking seal in the circus, and as I slid the mold off of it slowly I would uncover the flippers, the head, the open mouth, the teeth and the whiskers pressing next to the face. The whole seal was about the size of my hand, but it was pure white and cold and exquisite in the detail. After it was unmolded we would gently sand off the seam line, where the mold had left a seam, until our little statue was smooth and perfect. Then we got to paint it. Roosters were a lot of colors, but the seal was pure black. The whole white Plaster of Paris seal got painted black, and the next day, when it was dry, we got to paint our statues with shellac! Shellac smelled to high heaven, and the brush could not be washed with water, but it made my black seal shiny and glossy and waterproof! It took about one or two days to dry, so you had to paint where it was not windy; sometimes we would even paint them in the bathroom!

The bathrooms at school were always cool inside, no matter how hot it was outside. They were big, with big sinks, and when you talked or yelled you could hear an echo. During recreation you could yell all you wanted to in the bathrooms, because there was no school. The recreation leaders didn't always have all the keys, so sometimes just the boy's bathroom was open. It was weird because there were these sink-like things hanging on the walls, and someone said the boys just peed in them without any doors or any privacy, but I couldn't really understand how that could be true. Why didn't boys have privacy? Then someone said they only had privacy when they went poop, and that didn't seem right either. What the heck was up with those crazy boys anyway?

We went on scavenger hunts during the summer, hunts that the recreation department would set up. The kids at recreation would get divided up into teams and each team of about 4 or 5 kids would stop by one of their houses and get their little red wagon, because everyone had a wagon, and each team would have a list from recreation, and the winning team would be the team who got everything on their list and made it back first. We would have things on the lists like glass coca-cola bottles, yarn, crayons, wax, old shirts, string, spools, foil, shoe boxes, coffee cans, buttons, nails, scraps of wood, old magazines or newspapers…. and you would go up to a person's door and knock, and when they answered you would tell them that you were on a scavenger hunt and ask if they had any of the things on the list. It was fun and people would be nice, and sometimes give us other things that they thought might be useful, or offer us some fruit from their tree to take back and share. Most houses had a mom at home with some younger kids, because the older kids would be some place else, not staying inside during the summer, and dads would all be at work. The mom usually would ask who we were and where we lived, because people wanted to know their neighbors. Some times we would be invited to come back to play with their kids.

The first team back with the most stuff from their list won a prize; maybe they got to make extra Plaster of Paris molds or some other special project. With all the things that the teams would get there would be lots of materials to make projects all summer long without having to spend much money for supplies. One project that I really liked was called "quilling." We twisted strips of crepe paper by taping one end of an inch-wide strip to a picnic table and then threading the other end through the hole of a spool, and then tying that end around a pencil and spinning the pencil, so that the paper twisted up until it looked like string. Then we would take a coffee can, the metal cans that coffee came in before there was instant coffee or coffee in bags, and glue those pieces of twisted-up crepe paper around the outside of the coffee can, decorating it all up beautifully. It would look like colored string wrapped all around the can. I gave a can I made to Gramma Gigi as a can to hold buttons.

Every woman sewed in those days, and had button collections. On rainy days I loved to go through Gramma Gigi's button can. She had buttons that were really old, and ones that looked like they were covered with diamonds; buttons shaped like flowers, and every color of button and size of button. It was fun to sort them by color, or by size, just to run your hands through the hundreds of buttons and watch them fall through your fingers back into the can. Gramma Gigi really liked the can I gave her for her buttons.

We got to make potholders at recreation. Potholders are the pads that a person uses to protect their hands when they pick up a hot pan or pot. My mom would say, "I need enough new potholders to last all year," so we would make many potholders at recreation. We wove the potholders on little looms that were usually made from square pieces of wood, about one-foot square, which had the kind of nails with no head pounded all around each of the four edges. The nails were only pounded in far enough to hold them in the wood, they didn't go through, and the nails were about one half inch apart and about one inch tall. Then we had these stretchy loops of fabric in all sorts of colors that we would weave with, putting down the first layer without any weaving, and then the next layer the opposite direction and over, under, over, under, until all the weaving was gone and we did the fancy weaving called "casting off" to finish the edges.

It was best to start the potholders at the beginning of the summer, because by the end of the summer there was pretty much only brown and black loops left, so whatever potholder got made then was pretty boring.

Also in the evenings during summer there would be a penny carnival at Palo Verde that the recreation department put on. The penny carnival was so much fun! Everything cost only a penny, and there would be tables set up and the tables would be made into booths for activities like a penny toss, or dart throwing, or bean-bag toss; a lot of different activities where people paid a penny and could win a prize. They also had candies you could buy for a penny.

The recreation department also sponsored a huge watermelon feast during the summer! The watermelon feasts were in the day time, and there would be a ton of icy cold watermelon on the grass field at Palo Verde, and the recreation leader would cut the watermelon into thick slices and everyone could eat as much as they wanted to. Families could all come, and then there would be watermelon-seed-spitting contests. By the time we got to the contests, pretty much everyone had the whole front of their shirt or blouse covered with watermelon juice, because we were eating and eating and the juice ran down our chins and onto our clothes. In those days the watermelons had lots of big shiny black seeds inside of them, and the seeds were slippery, so they were easy to swallow. They also had thick green rinds that faded to white and then faded to the pink of the melon. We would tease each other that when you swallowed a seed it would grow inside of you, but we had never seen a person with watermelon growing out of their body, and all the people, grown-ups and kids, had swallowed millions of seeds, so we didn't take that rumor seriously. Besides, *Reader's Digest* did **not** have a story about it, so I figured I was pretty safe.

There was a song about the watermelon that everyone would sing, and it went like this:

"You can plant a watermelon right above my grave
And let the juice run through
You can plant a watermelon right above my grave
That's all I ask of you
Now the chicken and the possum are mighty fine
But there ain't
Nuthin' sweeter than a watermelon vine!
You can plant a watermelon right above my grave
And let the

Juice ... Run ... Through!"

And people would sing that song over and over again, and laugh and eat watermelon. Singing the song, everyone's voice got deeper and deeper until at the end of the song everyone's voice was impossibly low, and slow, and it was hard to believe that people could make their voices sound so deep!

The seeds were fun to spit and we would have contests: Who could spit the farthest, who could spit the most seeds at one time, who could have their seed land inside a target. When you bit open a seed there was another little white seed inside the black seed and that seed was soft and tasted good.

At the end of the feast Judy and I had to take home as many watermelon rinds as we could carry so that my mom would make watermelon rind pickles. Those were really good pickles, and we always ran out of them before the watermelon feasts happened the next year. I stuffed my blouse full of the rinds; I shoved as many rinds as I could in my blouse, my pockets, and into my shorts. I was walking home all weird and holding rinds in both hands and pressing my arms against my chest to keep the rinds from falling out, but every step I took I would loose a rind. But I still got home with a fair amount, and then went back again and again to get more.

I kind of felt stupid getting those rinds, but my mom started the pickles right away. She would trim the rinds until there was no pink melon or green skin, just the rinds, and cut them into pieces about two inches long, and then soak them in salt water while she made a syrup that had sugar, vinegar, cinnamon, cloves, and other spices in it, and then she would boil up the pickle jars, and pack in the rinds, pour in the hot syrup, and then put on the canning jar lids and rings, put the jars into the boiling water of the canning kettle, and then time how long they were in there. When they were done, she would take them out with her special canning tongs that were made to fit perfectly around jars, and put the boiling hot jars on the table on top of clean towels, and let them cool off. When they got cool enough the lids would pop down and that is how you know they had been done right. Then the rinds would have to stay in the jars for several weeks before we could eat them. They were crunchy and kind of see-through, and tasted spicy and sour and sweet all at the same time.

My mother canned all sorts of things all summer long: Boysenberry syrup, peaches, tomatoes, apricots, and then made plum jam, apricot jam, boysenberry jam, and sometimes peach jam. She would make lemonade from the lemons in our yard by squeezing the lemon halves on the electric lemon juicer, and then straining out the seeds and boiling sugar in water and adding the sugar water to the lemon juice. It tasted really good.

The other thing that I got to do that summer between first and second grades was to go to Brownie Camp at Searsville Lake Camp, which was near Stanford University in the foothills. The Brownies and the Girl Scouts went on a bus to camp, and the camp was really exciting. There was a creek with crawdads and minnows, and there was clay in the ground that we could dig up and make things right from that clay...all that the clay needed was some water mixed into it, and then it was ready to use! There were a lot of oak trees and shade at this camp, so even if it was hot it didn't really matter. We got to go on hikes and eat outside. But I started coughing a lot and was having a hard time breathing, so my parents had to call the doctor and I couldn't go to camp any more. The doctor came out to the house and said I had asthma, and that the only thing I could do was lay down on my bed in a dark room until I could breathe better. It was bad because my mom pulled the drapes so I couldn't read, and the only thing I was allowed to do was lie down. I lay in the dark room for four days, not allowed to do any thing. In those days there weren't the kinds of medicines for asthma as there are today. It was a good thing that I had my teddy bear. My teddy bear had one glass eye and one eye made from two buttons, with black legs and a grey tummy. Probably his tummy was white when I first got him, but it turned grey pretty quickly.

When I would lie on my back and put my knees up, my bear could climb mountains and ski down. Sometimes when he got to the top of Knee Mountain there would be an earthquake and Teddy would crash down to Tummy Land. Up, up, up, down, down, down...at least with Teddy I had something to do. After about four days I could breathe again, but camp was over. The doctor said I couldn't go to camp that year again anyway.

Doctors came to people's homes in those days. Our doctor was Doctor Blair, and he was so tall he barely fit through the door. When he came to the house he would listen to your chest through his stethoscope. If you needed a shot, he would give it to you right then, in your own bed. Doctors didn't expect sick little kids to get on the bus and go to the doctors; they came out and took care of you in your own bed.

Judy got to finish camp even though I didn't. On the last day of camp she came home and threw her jacket on the floor of the living room. That was on Friday, and we always went grocery shopping on Saturday. When we all got home from shopping on Saturday, my mom came inside the house before my daddy, who was carrying groceries. My mom picked up Judy's jacket off the floor where it had been since the day before, and the tarantula that had been hiding in Judy's jacket pocket crawled out and my mom started screaming! If you have never seen a tarantula, the thing to know about them is that they are **big** spider and that they are hairy!

There were a lot of tarantulas in the foothills in the summer, and apparently one had snuck into Judy's pocket and hid there. My daddy dropped the groceries, breaking the eggs and some jars, and ran in, and the tarantula was pretty big and crawling around quickly, and then it went into the kitchen and hid under the refrigerator. We were all screaming and then my daddy went into the garage and got out the poison pump, which was a long skinny can with a spray nozzle on the end. Daddy pumped and pumped that poison under the refrigerator until finally that big spider staggered out from under the frig, and Daddy scooped it up into a paper lunch bag and took it outside! Judy was pretty scared to think that she had brought that spider home without even knowing it. I wanted to know what happened to the spider, but my daddy wouldn't tell me.

For Fourth of July everyone in Palo Alto drove out to the Palo Alto Yacht Harbor. In those days the channels were dredged and there was a marina where the boats moored and where they would go in and out, plus there was a Sea Scout Boat with their office that was separate and looked like a boat. There was a really big parking lot and everyone would park there and get out and put blankets on their cars and lie down on the blankets and watch the fireworks that the City of Palo Alto put on. Little kids just went to sleep inside the cars. It was really exciting, and people brought picnic dinners and everyone would go "Ahhhhh..." and "Whoa, look at that one!" all at the same time. I think that I might have needed glasses by summer after second grade, but needing glasses made the fire works look even more beautiful.

Near the Yacht Harbor was the duck pond, and near the duck pond was the dump. Whenever Daddy went to the dump we got to go too, if there was enough room, and we would bring stale bread to feed to the ducks. It was fun to feed the ducks, because they knew as soon as you got over to the edge of the pond that they would be fed, so all the beautiful ducks would swim over and if you were brave enough to let them eat from your hand, they would do that!

My mom said that when she was a little girl growing up in Oakland that all around the San Francisco Bay there were "outdoor plunges." These were big round cement-lined swimming pools that would fill with the sea water from the bay, because people then knew that the salt water was good to bathe in. When she was little so many kids and grown-ups had polio, and those people who suffered from the after-affects of polio would bathe in salt-water at Fleishhacker's Pool in San Francisco or one of the outdoor plunges around the Bay. All the regular public pools were closed during the "polio summers" but the outdoor salt-water pools stayed open. After several years the migratory birds like the geese and the ducks were taking over the pools, and they became too dirty for people to swim in. Palo Alto converted theirs to a duck pond, and each day the tide waters came in and out, and the migratory birds had a safe place to land and eat and the ducks and other birds would lay their eggs there and each year we could see the fluffy little ducklings and goslings in the pond.

When we got to go to the dump it was fun and scary, because there were a lot of bulldozers there, and with my dinosaur-in-the-car game, those bulldozers were double-scary. But when our family got a station wagon, our "Plymouth-two-toned-station-wagon-with-the-mustard-colored-sides-and-the-mayonnaise-colored-roof," well then, a lot of trash, usually prunings from the hedges, could go in the back of the station wagon. What was scary was that the spiders would be crawling all around and we all hated getting spiders on us, but my daddy couldn't just stop the car because we had a spider, so we would flick them off at each other, or worse, pretend that we had a spider and then flick the pretend spider and scream that it landed on each other. But once all the trash was out of the back and the canvas tarp that was leftover from some war was folded up, and the back seat put back up again, them our daddy would let us sit on the tail gate with it opened and our feet hanging out while we drove from the dump to the duck pond. That was fun and dangerous and we would beg and beg him to let us do that.

I would go to the creek during summer. We had Matadero Creek that looped next to and behind our neighborhood. The sides were paved with concrete that made a solid slanting sloping side, but the bottom was not paved, so a kid like me could easily get into the creek. If you had a wagon with you, then the wagon had to stay at the top of the creek, because the sides were so smooth that it was hard to get a wagon down and then back up those steep sides.

All sorts of plants grew in the creek, and pollywogs and frogs and toads filled the waterways. Dragonflies flew all around, with their big eyes and powerful wings. There were some people so stupid that they thought dragonflies could hurt you, but that made no sense to me because the dragonflies were afraid of people. When you sat in the creek you could hear the bugs singing and see minnows and frogs. I don't know if you ever looked at a dragonfly, but they really do look like a dragon or a monster. We used to have these rust-colored dragonflies, with hard bodies and big eyes and wings that looked like lace with iridescent skin held up by the hard red veins. The dragonflies were all over the creek, and so were the smaller damsel flies, which were blue, and not really related directly to the dragonfly, even though they looked like they were.

I knew all of this because I wanted to be an entomologist. That is a person who studies insects. I read all the books I could find about insects...it was so interesting, to find out that without insects we would not be alive, and that spiders were not insects, about the head, the thorax, the abdomen, and how there were moths in the Amazon jungle that were six inches across! Six inches across! I longed to see the Luna moth, and to go to the Amazon jungle and find an insect that no one had ever found before.

When we went on our family vacations I drove my sisters crazy. I would collect wallets during the year, old worn out wallets that no one else was using, and on vacation I used them to save bugs. Every time we stopped at the gas station, I would ask my daddy to lift up the hood of the car engine and then I would collect all the bugs off the radiator, and if there was a new bug that I hadn't seen before, then I would slide it into the part of the wallet that people usually put their photos in. This was before credit cards, so each wallet usually had about eight holders for photos, and that meant I could collect eight bugs per wallet. The wallet finished squishing them flat: I only saved the ones off the radiator that were in good shape, because after a few hundred miles a squished bug could look pretty bad!

Then I would spend the rest of the time until the next gas station reading about the insects and trying to identify them. I would bring my insect guide book with me on the trips, the book I bought with my Christmas money. It told all about bugs, where they lived, what they ate, how long they lived and how big they got. Most of the bugs were new to me, because once we were out of California there were locust, cicadas, lightning bugs, katydids, and a lot of different kinds of moths and butterflies. I couldn't believe that some people didn't know the difference between a moth and a butterfly! But when we were in Kansas I would never draw on my skin with the lightning bugs. I thought that was gross. Some of my cousins and their friends would trap the lightning bugs and then squish them onto their skin and draw with the squished bugs and they would have glowing drawings on their skin.

When I was nine and ten years old, I had my insect collections on display at the Palo Alto Junior Museum. My daddy helped me build the frames, and then I filled them with cotton and rested all my best bugs on the cotton, with their names next to them. I think I was the only kid to have such a big collection of insects! I would write the Latin name and the regular name. The Junior Museum was the first children's museum west of the Mississippi, and was a great place to learn about science.

Palo Alto Junior Museum

Down in the creek there were not only insects and pollywogs, but a lot of different kinds of plants. If you sat there really quietly, then you would begin to hear all sorts of things. You could hear people talking from a long ways away. You could hear the cars on the Bayshore Highway, and you could hear the insects and the birds. Most of the birds were on the other side of Bayshore Highway, but if you were very still you could hear and see the ducks and the herons and the egrets.

The mud was pretty tricky. One time I was looking in the creek, and thought I saw something, so I kept walking out farther and farther into the creek. Each time I took a step into the creek, I would sink deeper and deeper into the mud. Then I got stuck! The suction of the creek mud would not let me pull my feet up. I tried to remember anything from *Reader's Digest* that might help me get unstuck. I spent many weekends at Gramma Gigi's house, and read all of her *Reader's Digest* magazines. From *Reader's Digest* I heard about being on the ocean surrounded by sharks, holding on to a lifeboat and how to kick your legs to scare the sharks away. I learned that if you were stuck in quicksand, you did not panic; you did the breaststroke across the top of the quicksand. I read about every disaster that was ever known to mankind and how to handle it, so when I was there stuck in the creek, I went back in my head though my great repository of *Reader's Digest* articles and tried to figure out how to escape the mud in which I was stuck. I did not panic, and I looked around for something to hold on to, a branch from above to grab onto. Nada, zero, zilch. No branch. If I struggled I would be lost in a rather *Grimm's Fairy Tale* ending, sinking down like the girl that trod on a loaf.

Very slowly, without struggling, I tried pulling my feet up. And then I tried harder and harder. I was panicking, afraid that I would either be stuck forever or that I would sink into hell, when the suction released its hold on one foot and then the other. I was wearing beach walkers, and they were lost, stuck at the bottom of the suction hole, and I was never going to get them out of the creek. So I had to walk home with bare feet, and I had to think of a story as to why I didn't have my beach walkers. If it was too scary a story, like a bunch of kids stole my shoes, then I knew I couldn't go back to the creek. If it wasn't scary enough, then my mom would know that I was lying. I made a compromise story about some boys who thought that my shoes belonged to someone else, and I let them keep them, but it didn't matter because my mom was asleep when I got home anyway.

During the summer I would get books in the mail. Just before school ended, I had brought home a form for the "Weekly Reader Book Club," and my mom had given me the money to sign up for it. So every week I got mail! For three weeks I would get a weekly newsletter that had all sorts of interesting things, and on the fourth week I would get a book! I also got a magazine called *Jack and Jill*, and it had short stories and puzzles and riddles in it! What I loved to do was to take the card table out to the backyard and cover it with a sheet so that I had my own tent, and I would bring out a blanket to put on the grass inside my tent. I would eat my sandwich inside my tent and read my new book all day long. If Jennifer came into the tent with me then she could take her nap there, but I would not let Judy inside because she would just bother me and I couldn't read my book or magazine with her bothering me.

The other place that we would buy books was at the Emporium. They had a big section of books to buy there, and every year when I would get money at Christmas or money at my birthday I could pick out a book to buy at the Emporium, plus I would ask for books for Christmas and my birthday. I had started buying the *Little House in the Big Woods* series by Laura Ingalls Wilder, and also the *Anne of Green Gables* books by Lucy Maud Montgomery. In third grade I bought my own copy of *The Hobbit* by J. R. R. Tolkien. I loved to read, and most hard-backed books cost $3.00, so I could use my Christmas and birthday money to buy one or two books!

. The best book that I got that summer was called *Science in Your own Backyard.* This book was great! It was a Weekly Reader book and I got it in the mail. It had things that a kid could do every day of the summer, including experiments. Jennifer was three and a half, so she was a great student, and I was the teacher. One experiment that we did was this: **One**: Take three cotton scraps of cloth and rub them in the dirt until they are coated with dirt. Check, we did that. **Two**: Wash one scrap in cold water with no soap. **Three**: Wash the next one in cold water but add soap. Then it went on until the third scrap was washed in hot water while scrubbing with soap. It was pretty cool because a kid could actually see which one worked best, and then the book said to remember this not only for cloth, but for when you washed your hands! The most interesting lessons in the book were about erosion. I got to do a great experiment about erosion. One thing that we had in our back yard was a special sand box. My daddy had built the sand box, and it stood up on legs and had two benches on opposite sides. The bottom was metal and the rest was wood, except for the cover. There was a canvas cover, and during the day you lifted the cover by unscrewing a wing nut on each side, and then you slid the cover up between two boards that my daddy had put there, and the cover became the canvas shade. At night it was lowered again to keep the sandbox

My science book

clean so the damn cats didn't use it as a litter box. The metal bottom was great because if you were building roads or a lake, the metal shone through when you scraped away the sand.

My book had an experiment that would take one, two, then three weeks to do. It meant that I got one half of the sandbox and no one else could use it. In my half of the sandbox I built a big sand mountain, and on half the mountain I planted grass seeds. We always had grass seed in the garage because parts of the grass always needed redoing. I had Jennifer help me plant the grass seed on one half of the mountain. We had to water the seed every day, so we used the hand-held hose with the nozzle to water the mountain. Then after one week we got to do some fun part! We used the hand-held hose with the nozzle on the end to make it rain on our mountain, rain on the part with no grass, and then on some of the part with the grass. The part with no grass just washed away. Then we continued watering each day for a week, and made it rain again. Then we watered for one more week, and made it rain really hard! Jennifer and I could see from this experiment how much the grass keep erosion from happening, and also how as the grass got bigger that it held the sand even more.

The book had a little magnifying glass with it, and one experiment was to lie on your stomach on the grass and look through the magnifying glass. There was so much to see in science in **my** own backyard!

We could spend hours outside playing in the sandbox. The sand box was so much fun, even if it wasn't for experiments. We could build a town and a road and mountains, or we could cook. We had some little pots and pans and some little metal cars and trucks so we pretty much had everything that we needed, plus some old spoons. When you mixed the right amount of water into the sand inside a bowl and then poured it out just right you had a lot of little globs of sand that would form perfect sand drops. If you were making a castle or cooking, it didn't matter, because those sand droplets were good for a lot of beautiful decoration.

There was one thing that happened between first and second grade that had a good part and a bad part. Here is what happened: All three of us girls were at Gramma Gigi and Grandpa Bob's house for the weekend. My gramma had been taking an Ikebana class, Japanese flower arranging, and she was pretty excited about learning about the triangle shape and dried wood and fresh flowers and how to mix them in a whole different way of looking at nature, so she had started putting different arrangements all through her house.

Gramma Gigi had a marble coffee table in front of her couch, and the marble was beautiful light blown with pink streaks. She had made a flower arrangement on her coffee table; a low arrangement in a mauve ceramic vase that had a "spike frog" holding all the flower stems exactly where she wanted them. The spike frog was heavy and rested on the bottom of the vase,

and held all the flowers in the exact right place. This particular spike frog was about three inches across, and had spikes that were rigid and made of steel sticking up about an eighth of an inch apart from each other and about an inch tall. The name was strange, because it looked nothing like a frog. Spike frogs came in square or round shapes, and some were tiny and some were very large, depending on what size flower arrangement a person was making.

Well, my sisters and I were sitting on the couch and started fighting and pulling the pillows out from underneath each other, and when Judy pulled the pillow out from underneath me, my bare foot slammed down onto that flower arrangement and shattered the vase. I felt like I had been stabbed in my foot, the same feeling of being stabbed that was in my nightmare, and in fact I had, because my foot had broken the vase and cut me, and the spike frog was embedded completely into my heel! So then my sister was trying to grab me to pull the frog out of my heel, I was screaming and hopping around holding my foot and not seeing what had happened to it, Jennifer was crying, and Gramma Gigi, who had been on the garage landing, came into the midst of all that chaos!

The landing was the tiny back porch where you went out the back door of the kitchen. It was at the top of the stairs inside of the garage. When Gramma Gigi parked her car inside  the garage, there were steep wooden stairs inside the garage to climb up to go inside the kitchen, and at the top of the stairs was a little landing where the wash machine was. There was also a long clothesline on pulleys that started at the landing and went all the way across the garage. The pulleys meant that the same clothesline went around two pulleys, one at the landing and the other on the opposite side of the garage, and Gramma Gigi just had to pull the clothesline around the pulley to make the laundry get closer to her when she was ready to take it off the clothesline.

Gramma Gigi had been taking clothes off the clothesline when she heard all the ruckus and came back inside. Off I went with Gramma Gigi to the emergency room at Sequoia Hospital to get my heel fixed up and the spike frog pulled out. Then I had a bandage on my foot and on my heel.

The good thing that happened was that when it came time to buy new school shoes I got red sandals to wear to school! I couldn't wear any shoe that rubbed on my heel because my heel was healing...that was such a funny thing to say and hear: "My heel is healing, my heel is healing," or maybe it really was "My heal is heeling!" So I had red sandals with gold buckles to start second grade. I had to wear them with socks because of the bandage, but I really liked looking at those sandals and seeing them on my feet.

Gramma Gigi had to take me back to the doctor to have my heel checked and they put me on the table and said to think of the best treat I could imagine, because there was some skin that they had to cut off my heel, some skin had died and the doctor needed to cut it off and it shouldn't really hurt if I concentrated on something else. I thought of Disneyland, and of a strawberry float made of strawberry ice cream and *7-Up* as tall as the castle at Disneyland, and imagined that I was sitting on the top of that gigantic glass, drinking the strawberry float through the longest straw in the world. I could feel the weird sensation of the skin being cut, and it didn't hurt, and I concentrated on the strawberry float, but when the doctor got too close to the live skin and cut some of that by mistake that sure did hurt!

I liked the picture of the giant strawberry float so much that I kept it in my head all the way home from the doctor.

Auntie Jan and Missy Dog

Dress Up and Auntie Jan

One of the things that all the girls liked to play was "dress up." Practically everyone we knew, including us, had a box or a trunk of clothes that were there just for dress up. And the girls in the neighborhood could spend hours trying on those clothes and pretending, and critiquing each other's outfits and making new fashion combinations. At our house we had the best dress up box in the neighborhood, if not the town!

Auntie Jan loved fashion and she flew to Hong Kong and had some of her clothes made there. She had clothes that no one else had and that were made to fit her perfectly, and when she was done with them, we kids would get them for dress up! We would also get clothes that had been my mom's and that were from Gramma Gigi.

Most of the other girls would have one special outfit in their dress-up box, so when you went to their house kids had to take turns wearing the fancy outfit. But we had many beautiful outfits to try on and play "pretend." My favorite of all our dress ups was a burgundy-colored velvet skirt and blouse with a pale pink satin cummerbund. When I would put that on, I was glamour itself! The blouse was almost sleeveless, with a lot of extra fabric in the front so that the front hung down in beautiful folds, and the skirt was so long that I would have to daintily pick up the hem to keep it from dragging on the ground. The cummerbund was a wide satin belt, with material folded on purpose so that the lines of satin caught the light and shimmered when the girl wearing it moved. The cummerbund fastened with a row of hooks and eyes, and each one had beautiful stitching, because the hook part was made of thread that had been sewed into a tiny hook with even tinier knots all along its edges. There was a row of the hooks and eyes, about eight of them, so usually whoever was wearing it fastened those together by wearing the cummerbund backwards and then turning it around.

We also had accessories. Auntie Jan always wore high heels, very high heels, and we had many, many pairs of high heels in our dress up box. High heels, jewelry, hats, dresses and little jackets, gloves and purses. Each dress or skirt or blouse was fancy, with the skirts lined with smooth shiny material and zippers hidden in the seams. There were tiny buttons or very big buttons on the blouses and dresses, and so many fancy things that girls could spend hours and hours playing dress up and pretending. I don't remember any slacks in the dress ups, because this was a time when women did not wear slacks or long pants, except for horseback riding or special outdoor events. They might have a pair of pedal pushers or slacks to go to the beach or to ride a bike in, or a pair of shorts if it was hot and they were with their family, but those would be the only reasons.

Auntie Jan lived in a three-story apartment in San Carlos while she worked in San Carlos as an executive secretary. Auntie Jan had gone to business school in the East Bay, and was an executive secretary, which meant that she would do all the typing and preparation and behind-the scenes work for the executive at whatever company she worked. In those days the work was different; the secretary had to type without any mistakes and spell and punctuate perfectly, because there was no way to fix a typing mistake. To make copies of what was being typed the secretary would put a layer of carbon paper underneath the top piece of paper, and then a second piece of paper under the carbon paper. So if there was any mistake at all, it could not be corrected and would have to be redone!

There were no copy machines, no faxes, and no answering machines. Traveling on a plane was quite an adventure and not very common. So in Auntie Jan's world she got to be an important part of a company, because the executive really relied on the secretary doing everything perfectly.

She had worked at Wells Fargo Bank in San Francisco before she started working at Neely; later, Neely became the exclusive sales and service division for Hewlett-Packard. My auntie then worked for Hewlett Packard in Palo Alto, and she moved to an apartment near us on Alma Street.

Auntie Jan worked for Norm Neely, and then later worked with David Packard in the Neely Division.

Auntie Jan was almost 5' 4", but always seemed taller because she wore such high heels. Those high heels had such a tall, skinny heel that it was amazing that anyone could walk in them! But she did. She always had many and things to look at in her apartment; in her travels she had visited the Tiger Balm's Palace in Singapore in the 1950s, when few American women had ever done so. Auntie Jan would always bring back exotic things from her trips, and her apartment had drawings of Thailand dancers, framed and protected with non-glare glass. She had the most exquisite black lacquered desk in the entire world, with abalone inlays and tassels hanging from the many drawer handles.

Everything in her apartment looked Oriental, and she even had two Siamese cats, May Li and May Lin. Those cats were so spoiled! Auntie Jan was the only person we knew who had a litter box inside their house. Most people just put their cats outside during the day and let them in to eat at night, or had them eat outside and let them in sometimes. But May Li and May Lin stayed in the apartment all the time; that was where they lived. Those cats were like kids, only worse.

One time when Auntie Jan was late coming home from work, she opened up her apartment front door and she could see right out the sliding glass door to her balcony, because her drapes were gone! They weren't really gone, but it looked like it because the drapes were all on the floor. The two cats were mad that she was home late and they had climbed the drapes and crawled along the curtain rod and flicked the drapes off the rod with their paws! The same evening Auntie Jan saw that those cats had opened her kitchen cupboard and gotten a pack of dried spaghetti, torn it open and spread it all over. Those cats just sat there washing their faces with their paws, looking at Auntie Jan, acting as if they were innocent and knew nothing about the trouble they had caused. Auntie Jan also had a Pekinese dog named Missy Dog, but her apartment wouldn't allow anyone who lived there have a dog, so Missy Dog lived with Grandpa Bob and Gramma Gigi.

Auntie Jan could speak six languages: Spanish, English, French, German, Italian, Dutch, and she also knew Latin. Because she had a photographic memory it seemed that languages and music were both things that were easy to her, and she played the piano beautifully. But her brains and her beauty and glamour would have been nothing without her laugh. She could make everyone in the whole room laugh and be happy by her just smiling and laughing. She would sit down in a chair and cross her legs like a fashion model, take a long slow draw of her cigarette, and smile at someone, and people felt like they had been blessed.

The first time that Auntie Jan was married it only lasted one year. She went to a place called Milwaukee, but came back when the marriage was over. There were whispers and low conversations in the family, and what I finally understood was that the man had married Auntie Jan because he wanted to be seen with a beautiful woman but that he really didn't want to have a wife. I wasn't sure what that meant, but when Auntie Jan came back to Gramma Gigi's house we were all glad.

One time she drove over to our house in a Cadillac, and we got to go for a ride. That car was amazing, because when Auntie Jan pressed a certain button, the entire hard top would slide down into slots on the car, and then we were in a Cadillac Convertible! Auntie Jan wore a silk scarf to keep her hair from getting wild in the wind, big dark sun glasses, bright red lipstick, held her cigarette to her lips and blew the smoke out just like a movie star...driving that Cadillac down the street with us girls jumping up and down in the back seat, we felt like movie stars!

Her regular car was an M.G. from England, and it was bright blue. There was room for one passenger in the passenger seat, but two kids could squash up there if they tried, plus one more kid on the shelf under the back window if that kid really wanted to go. Auntie Jan would come over on some Sunday afternoons to our house, and she would go to the liquor store or to the regular store, or both stores to get food and drinks. The liquor store was where the corner market had been, and now it was Freeman's Liquor Store.

When Auntie Jan was there everyone would laugh and talk, and the grown-ups would drink, and we would get to stay up late. Everyone would talk and have fun. One time Auntie Jan had a story about a trick that the guys at her work had played on her: She usually parked her car at the same place every day, and because her car was so little, a bunch of the men had picked up her car and moved it around the corner, so that when she came out from work her car was gone! But she saw that they were all watching her, and when she found her car it was wedged tightly between two other cars. The guys were laughing, and then they all picked up her car and moved it out to the street where she could drive it. I laughed and laughed over that story!

On one of her trips to another country, Auntie Jan went to Lucerne, Switzerland, and brought us girls back charm bracelets. Mine was gold, and had a tiny cow bell with a cross on it, the cross of the Swiss flag. It had some other charms on it too, and when I wore it to Sunday School all the little girls came around and looked at it, because no one else had a bracelet that was even similar to that one!

Auntie Jan got married another time, and everyone went to Gramma Gigi's house after the wedding. I had on a brown sweater that had a white cloth poodle sewed on the sweater, with some sequins on the fur of the poodle. Auntie Jan's new mother-in-law started talking to me about my sweater, and on impulse I started talking baby talk to her. We talked for a long time, and a few days later Gramma Gigi was telling everyone about how I had charmed that lady when no one else could even talk to her. The joke was that maybe I had talked, but not to her, because I talked baby talk and she was probably just trying to figure out if I was an idiot or what.

Gramma Gigi and Auntie Jan liked to ride horses, and sometimes we would go over the hill to Half Moon Bay where there was a stable that rented out horses. I was the kid, so I should have been able to ride a horse, but Gramma Gigi seemed like the kid when she rode a horse. She would ride the horse like a person who fit onto a horse perfectly, and she loved to ride along the edge of the beach, right along the water, and ride the horse as fast as she could, and Auntie Jan and she would ride together really fast and when they finished they would be laughing, and I would be sitting on my horse, hopefully Dumb Blind Sam who didn't care if he ran or not, and would watch them having fun and I was just glad I didn't have to race my horse because horses seemed big and scary to me.

We would go back into the woods on the horses and ride on little horse trails, and I liked that a lot because it was really quiet and up on a horse you could see a lot of things, and go a long ways and on those trails it was as if I were a different person, like maybe an explorer or a little girl from history or maybe a time traveler.

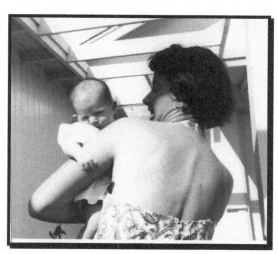

With Auntie Jan around it was fun and she always made me feel like I was the most important person around. She and Gramma Gigi both were like that.

Auntie Jan holding Baby Jennifer

Avocados and Artichokes

Growing up in the Bay Area we took for granted a lot of foods and cooking styles. Gramma Gigi told us a funny story about how when Auntie Jan was a little kid Jan had been eating artichokes and tossing the leaves over her shoulder after she scraped off the good part, and Grandpa Bob had come into the kitchen to see all those leaves stuck to the wallpaper!

We grew up eating artichokes, and on some Sunday afternoons we would drive to Castroville, "The Artichoke Center of the World," and buy bags of artichokes and come home and have them for dinner. We might go to Half Moon Bay and then go down the coast and get fresh brussel sprouts or strawberries and then fresh fish for dinner. There was so much good fresh food, food picked the same day, and food that was available only during the season that it grew around here. We didn't expect to get fresh tomatoes in the winter, or peaches in January, or oranges in the winter...that would be crazy! We ate seasonal food that grew nearby, except for a few things like bananas.

My mom said that when she and Daddy got married that he didn't know how to eat an artichoke, and had never seen an avocado or eaten Mexican food. My dad said that the morning after their honeymoon my mom was eating horse radish on her bacon and he wondered what he had gotten himself in to!

One of our favorite breakfasts was toast with avocado on it. We would cut open an avocado and scoop out the insides, spread in on the warm toast, squirt a little lemon juice and sprinkle a bit of salt and there was nothing that tasted so good! Gramma Gigi told us that during WWII many foods were rationed, so that the American soldiers got foods first before the civilians did, so people learned to make do without a lot of things, and that is when they learned to put avocado on toast, because it tasted like the butter that no one could get.

When my mom was growing up in Oakland, her family had a big avocado tree with hundred of avocados on it each year, and most of the people in their neighborhood did as well. The avocados that you buy in the stores taste nothing like the ones that grow on an old East-Bay tree. Gramma Gigi said that during WWII the rationing was pretty severe, with coupons given out for food like butter and bananas and meat. She told how one day people heard that bananas had just arrived at the Port of Oakland, so she stood in line for half a day to get four bananas. When my mom was growing up they took their wagon down to the wharves in Oakland and would get salmon at the end of the day. The Bay had so much salmon; it was cheap, and that's what people ate if they didn't have a lot of money.

In those days people just had ice boxes, where the ice man delivered ice to them, not refrigerators, so Gramma Gigi would walk to the shops to get food for just that same day.

But when we were growing up in Palo Alto, we had a *Frigidaire* refrigerator with a little freezer on the top, which had to be defrosted every week. When my parents would get home from the grocery store they would defrost the freezer by putting a pot of boiling water inside it until all the frost melted. If it wasn't defrosted it would completely fill up with frost. It held about one carton of ice cream and two packs of frozen peas, so it was small enough that it defrosted pretty quickly.

For Sunday lunch my mom would usually make Sloppy Joes, tacos, or pizza. The pizza would be made with dough that had been rising while we were at church. My daddy never had pizza or tacos until he came to California.

My mom would make tacos with corn tortillas that we bought, but no one bought bottled salsa in those days, just taco sauce that was like Tabasco, and it took my daddy a long time to learn to like the taste of spicy foods. But we girls grew up eating Mexican food, spicy food, horse radish, pickles, bleu cheeses and Italian food. The Bay Area had people from many cultures, and we could buy all sorts of exotic ingredients and spices.

I remember one time when my mom was making chicken for dinner. People always bought their chickens whole and cut them up themselves, and the extra pieces went into a pot to make broth to use for other things like gravy. My parents were laughing about how a lady at the market had asked the butcher to cut up the chicken for her because she didn't know how! They couldn't imagine such a thing! My mom said how her Aunt Gilberta could kill a chicken, pluck it, cut it up and have it in the pan in less than five minutes, and the fact that a woman would ask someone else to cut up a chicken left them shaking their heads in disbelief. Aunt Gilberta was Grandpa Bob's sister and she lived in Southern California, and like many people in those days she had always raised her own chickens for eggs and for meat.

Daddy learned to like many new foods, but when his family came to visit from Kansas they didn't know what to think about a lot of the foods that we took for granted, so we were polite and my mother cooked boring food when the Kansas relatives came to visit. It would have been rude to expect them to eat the more interesting food that we were used to having.

Usually on Sunday morning before church we would have waffles. My daddy hardly ever cooked, but one Mother's Day he decided he would cook the waffles!

When we sat down to eat, my waffle tasted weird, and as each of us took a bite we started to make funny faces. My daddy was all excited and waiting for us to tell him how good the waffles tasted, but as we took our second bite we all were getting stranger and stranger looks on our faces. Then my dad started saying, "I followed the recipe **exactly**! You are teasing....aren't you?" Then he tasted a waffle and got a funny look too.

Then my mom asked him, "What butter did you use?" and Daddy showed her, and she said no wonder, Daddy had made the waffles with the garlic butter that was left over from the night before! She had made garlic bread for dinner, and Daddy hadn't known that my mom had added garlic powder to a certain cube of butter and Daddy had melted that butter and added it to the waffles, and then had buttered our waffles with it before he put on the syrup! We didn't buy store-bought syrup, we added brown sugar to water and added maple flavoring, heating it up in a tiny bent up saucepan that had been around forever. So we had syrup on our garlic waffles.

From that day onward, my mom added paprika, parsley and black pepper to the garlic butter so anyone could see that the garlic butter was different than the regular butter!

When my parents made coffee, they would buy coffee in a metal coffee can. To open the can there was a little metal "key" glued to the bottom of the can. The key was like a sewing needle, because it was metal and had an eye in it, but it was also flat. You always had to check and make sure the coffee can had that key, because without it, you could not open the can. We all liked to watch the new can get opened. There was a piece of metal all the way around the can just below the lid, and at the end of the metal strip a small piece of metal stuck out and it fit in the slit in the key. Then it was my daddy's job to turn the key slowly, holding it straight and next to the can, and as he twisted the key it wound up the metal strip that held the lid on. At the very end there would be a whooshing noise as the vacuum seal was broken, and the smell of the fresh ground coffee was really, really good!

If we ever got to have canned peanuts, they came inside the same kind of can; a metal can with a key. Grown-ups **had** to open all of those kinds of cans because usually the person opening the can got at least one cut. The metal strip **had** to stay exactly right on the key or by the time the person opening the can got to the end of the strip it would no longer be wrapping around the key, it would just be twisting up in a big mess. When you got to the end of the metal strip then the end that was still fastened to the can had to be snapped off, and that was not easy. Then the key with all the metal on it had to be thrown away so that no one got hurt on it.

When we got the coffee open, my parents would get the coffee scoop from the old can and put it in the new can. There was no such thing as coffee filters in those days, or if there was, we never bought them. We made our coffee in a percolator, and we girls took turns on who got to go get exactly one sheet of toilet paper, peel it apart so it was one layer thick, and then put the toilet paper in the bottom of the percolator basket. The toilet paper was the coffee filter, and then the scoops of coffee went in the coffee basket. The basket was metal with a lot of holes on the bottom, and a bigger hole in the middle that a metal tube went through. The lid went on the top of the percolator, and the top of the percolator had a *Pyrex* dome. We could watch as the water started to boil how it came up through the tube and changed color from clear to brown as the coffee got stronger. My parents would use the coffee grounds for two days in a row because coffee was expensive and that worked out just fine.

Then the coffee grounds went into the garden to make compost.

We never threw out the empty coffee cans! Coffee cans could be used for everything. We had one on the stove to save our grease in, because we saved bacon grease to cook with. We used a different coffee can to melt paraffin, and Daddy saved cans to put nails and screws into. Coffee cans could be decorated and given as presents for button collections or other collections of things that needed to be kept safe and dry. A person would never have too many coffee cans, but you had to be careful when you took the lid off or put it on, because the edges of the lid were still very sharp.

Sometimes people used empty coffee cans as cookie jars, but that would be if you were giving away some cookies as a present, because everyone already had a cookie jar in their kitchen, and moms would bake cookies on Sunday afternoons.

At our house we alternated our cookie-making: One week we would make chocolate chip cookies, measuring out the butter and the flour and the sugar and adding in the ingredients and putting the dough on the cookie sheets. We would use three cookie sheets. A sheet would go in the oven with the raw cookie dough on it, and then the next would have the raw dough on it in just the right spots. After five minutes the second sheet went into the oven, then after six more minutes the first sheet came out, was set on the counter on clean tea towels, and the third sheet went in the oven. The finished cookies were taken off and put on a clean tea towel to cool off, and more dough put on that cookie sheet. That way we would make six dozen cookies in a very short time, and when they were cool we would have cookies and milk and fill up the cookie jar.

The next week we would make oatmeal raisin cookies, or peanut butter cookies. Peanut butter cookies took longer because you had to refrigerate the dough, but they were fun because the dough got rolled up quickly into little balls, and then we got to dip a fork in water and press it in the top of the cookie, then change to the other direction and press it again, so that the finished cookies had a criss-crossed pattern on their tops. Every weekend we usually made cookies, unless it was too hot outside, and then we were making jams and jellies and canning food anyway.

When I started to bake I made a cake. It turned out as hard as a rock. Exactly as hard as a rock. Just like cement, and it was only about one inch tall instead of about three inches tall. It was a sheet cake and I couldn't even cut it with a knife. I was hitting it with the edge of the knife until I broke off a chunk, and with a straight face my daddy tasted it and said it tasted all right.

I kept looking and looking at the recipe trying to figure out what I had done wrong. Judy was making faces at me and sticking out her tongue when no one was looking, but I was busy thinking. I finally figured it out: The recipe said to add one cup **plus** two tablespoons water and I had only added the two tablespoons of water!

We used to eat a lot of spaghetti. I got so sick of eating spaghetti. My mom would make the sauce with hamburger meat and garlic and tomato sauce and tomato paste and pepper and onions, but I still got sick of it. Jennifer would only eat "twice-cooked" spaghetti, and she got away with not eating it the first night and only eating it the next day, but she was the baby so that was okay.

The only times I didn't have to eat it was if I was sick, or if I had been hurt. And I seemed to have a habit of walking into poles at school...I would be thinking about something else and turn around when the bell rang and **smash** right into a pole, and my upper teeth would go through my lower lip and swell up and hurt, but then I had an excuse to not eat spaghetti!

When I was in elementary school it seemed like I alternated between split lips and bandaged knees, but I also had been in quite a few automobile accidents by the time elementary school was over. Parents often drove on school field trips, but sometimes we took a school bus rented specially for a field trip. One year when we were on a bus, the bus brakes failed on Fell Street and the bus went backwards and crashed, and I was the only kid hurt badly. Another year the car I was in on 19th Avenue in San Francisco crashed into another car and I had a bad cut on my leg.

My mom started saying that when there was a field trip she would wait until the end of the day and go to school and sure enough the car I had been in was the last one back because it seemed like I was always in the car that got in a wreck. That was kind of weird.

One meal that we always had was potato soup on Christmas Eve. I don't know why, but we did. On Christmas Eve my mom would peel and thinly slice up a whole lot of potatoes and yellow onions, which are really only yellow on the outside. Then she would put some oil in the bottom of a big pot and gently sauté the onions, and when the onions were soft she added all the sliced potatoes and when covered them with water. When the potatoes got soft she would add a lot of milk, and stir it in until the milk was hot. Lastly, she added a bit of butter and parsley and that was it. The soup was hot and good, and the yellow butter would float in tiny puddles on top of the soup.

Sitting in the kitchen opposite the kitchen window I would see my reflection, but usually the window would have condensation from the hot steam of the soup and the cold air outside. Maybe it might be raining. But eating potato soup that was oniony and salty and warm felt good.

Judy 7, Great Grandpa "Grandpa Frenchy," my mom, me 4, & Baby Jennifer

Southern California

During the summers that we did not go to Kansas, we went to Southern California to visit my mom's family. Southern California was like a different state than Northern California. My mom used to say that when she was elected governor of California she would first of all ban all the Volkswagens from the State, and second of all she would cut California off at the Tehachapi Mountains and let Southern California float out to sea because they always stole our water. When I saw the *Dr. Doolittle* movie I could visualize how a floating Southern California would look. When we visited Southern California we stayed with Maude and Ernie and their dog, Gordo. I would get confused if it was Aunt Maude or Aunt Ernie, or Uncle Maude or Uncle Ernie, because I was not used to those names in the first place.

Aunt Maude and Uncle Ernie had a house in San Bernardino. Ernie was Grandpa Bob's younger brother. Grandpa Bob was born in France in 1898, but came to America through Ellis Island when Grandpa Bob was just a baby and before Ernie was born. Their family settled in the Riverside area after a failed attempt at homesteading in the Southwest. Their last name was Houplin, the same as Gramma Gigi's last name and my mom's last name before she was married. We had a whole bunch of relatives in Southern California: My mom's cousins and their families, plus my mom's aunts and uncles. When we visited Southern California, we went to Disneyland, or Sea World, or Santa's Village, Knottsberry Farm or Lake Arrowhead.

Disneyland was overwhelming. I really liked the Jungle Ride, because you felt like you were really on a boat in the jungle. I didn't like scary rides or roller coaster rides because they made me feel like throwing-up, but I loved getting a Mouseketeer hat, just like the kids on the TV show *Mickey Mouse Club!* Southern California was ten days of relatives, theme parks and going places to visit.

Disneyland! Me 7, Daddy, Jennifer 3 & Judy 9

There was a Santa's Village in the Bay Area at Scott's Valley near Santa Cruz, but our family never went there, we went to the Santa's Village in Southern California in the San Bernardino Mountains at Lake Arrowhead.

My mom's Aunt Gilberta, who was Uncle Ernie and Grandpa Bob's sister, was married to Lee Kemp. Uncle Lee worked for the fire department at Lake Arrowhead, working there for more than forty years. Visiting their cabin was always very interesting because he was an inventor and a ham radio operator and the cabin was full of clever inventions. The cabin was on a steep mountainside, surrounded by tall pine trees. One of Uncle Lee's inventions was that he had hidden flexible tubes throughout the cabin walls; when he was in one part of the cabin, like the basement, he would speak into a funnel at the end of a tube and wherever my Aunt Gilberta was in the cabin, she could hear him!

Grandpa Bob and Uncle Ernie's dad "Grandpa Frenchy" never learned English very well, but he had Frenchy's Store at Lake Arrowhead for more than 40 years. Lake Arrowhead was a resort town, and when they started Frenchy's Store the road up the mountain side was made of railroad ties put one next to the other. Frenchy's Store is still at Lake Arrowhead, but was sold and has a different name now.

Jane 7, Jennifer 3, Judy 9, & my mom at Santa's Village in the San Bernardino Mountains

The other name that everyone in the whole family called Grandpa Frenchy was "Little Grandpa," because he was very short. It seemed like whenever we visited and Little Grandpa was there, someone insisted that I read out loud to him. I didn't like to, because he was scary to me; I couldn't understand a word that he said because of his accent plus it just sounded like growling to me. It felt like he was sitting on the chair behind me looking over my shoulder, leaning on his cane and growling. But I did like his big fluffy white mustache.

There were a lot of cousins in Southern California. They were all related to my mom. Gramma Gigi's mom and some of her family lived there too, because Gramma Gigi's parents, my great grandmother and great grandfather Emmert, had moved from the farm in Washington State to Riverside. When I was little only my great grandmother Emmert was still alive.

We had a cousin named Little Louie, his dad was Bob, not Grandpa Bob but a different Bob, and there was also a different cousin named Big Louie, but Big Louie's name really was Armand. There was a heck of a lot of names to remember.

One time we all went to the Salton Sea. It was a weird place because it was desert, and then there was a lake...just like that. Desert. Lake. No trees around the shoreline, so everyone just drove their cars right up to the very edges and made shady areas with umbrellas and blankets. It was fun to go in that lake, but there were a lot of dead fish everywhere and we kids all picked them up and held them like we had just caught them, and got our pictures taken in our bathing suits holding dead fish.

At Salton Sea – right by the edge of the water!

The Southern California families were more like the part of the French family. Uncle Ernie would go down to the Italian part of town twice a year and get a big barrel of wine, because he really liked the wine that one family made. And the barrel was used to fill the wine jugs if there was a big dinner or party. Otherwise Uncle Ernie just filled a glass...one for breakfast, one for lunch, and one for dinner, because that was how people were supposed to drink wine. But when all the cousins and family went to the Salton Sea, we took a big picnic with lots of food and beer and wine, and we kids could have some too. We kids were allowed small glasses of wine mixed with water at dinner time at the Southern California relatives or a Gramma Gigi's on special occasions, but I don't think the relatives in Kansas ever drank wine. They usually had Coca-Cola or iced tea or coffee with their lunch and dinner.

The other thing that the Southern California cousins did was have talent shows. You would go to their house for dinner, and they had a big swimming pool and before dinner all the kids would do a skit, or sing, or dance, or do something in front of everyone else. It was crazy! But because they lived near Hollywood, everyone acted like they were movie stars too, and they just thought that having a little talent show before dinner was normal. Judy and Jennifer and I had to think of a performance without much time to prepare, so we decided to sing a TV ad that we liked: At home there was an ad on the TV and on the radio where an actress named Dinah Shore would sing about Ellis Brooks Chevrolet. The camera would show the real man, Ellis Brooks, sitting behind a desk with five coffee cans stacked on it, and he would say, "I'll give you five pounds of Hills Brother's Coffee just for coming in and taking a look." Then Dinah Shore would sing the ad. We girls decided that we would do that ad for our performance. "See the U.S.A. in your Chevrolet" went like this:

"See Ellis Brookes today, for your Chevrolet,

Corner of Bush and Van Ness.

He's got a deal for you, oh what a deal for you,

The kind of deal you'll like the best.

See the U...S...A...in your Chev...ro...let

At 48th and Van Ness..."

When Dinah Shore sung the jingle she rocked back a forth and sung her arm out when she said "U.S.A." and then again when she said "Chevrolet" and we girls always practiced imitating her at home because we liked that song. We girls thought we were pretty good at imitating Dinah Shore in her Chevrolet ad, but I don't think the cousins were impressed. .Southern California cousins wanted a bit more than a San Francisco Chevy ad in their talent show, but hey, **we** weren't actresses!

Aunt Maude's parents had been in Vaudeville, which meant that her parents had traveled around a lot and that they both acted for a living. Aunt Maude and her brother grew up in boarding schools because their parents traveled too much to take their children with them. Aunt Maude had a scrap book that was filled with many photos of her parents: Her dad with Will Rogers and other famous silent-movie actors, and her mom in beautiful costumes. The scrap book was like an advertisement for an actor, and each photo was a snapshot of them dressed differently and posed differently so that an agent could see all the characters they could play.

This meant that much of the conversation was about movie stars. When we visited Aunt Maude and Uncle Ernie and all the Southern California relatives much of what they spoke about was movie stars and what the movie stars were doing. Because Aunt Maude had grown up around acting, she always went to the beauty parlor and had her nails done and thought about fashion all the time. And Uncle Ernie called her "Maudie" and would do anything in the world for her.

When they were talking about movie stars or the family, there would be a lot of conversation about "wet backs," and braceros, gun control and politicians. The braceros were Mexicans that came legally into the United States, and they harvested the crops up and down the State of California. I learned later that "wet backs" was what many people called the Mexicans who came here illegally. People thought that the illegals swam across the river to get into the United States.

When our family visited Southern California, Grandpa Bob and Uncle Ernie would get together, their glasses of wine in hand, and talk and laugh and tell stories about Riverside when they were kids, and what it was like growing up for them. Riverside had many orange and avocado orchards, and Grandpa Bob said that they used to get a nickel from the farmer nearby for every gopher tail that they brought the farmer, because there were so many gophers that the gophers would eat everything that was planted, so the farmers wanted the gophers killed.

Their family came to America not knowing any English, just French, and when Grandpa Bob and Uncle Ernie started school they knew no English, but they just stayed in the classroom until they learned English. They would speak French at home, but English at school.

They told a funny story of how young Ernie wanted to learn to ride a bicycle, and young Bob was sick and tired of teaching him, so Bob took Ernie to the top of a hill and tied his feet to the bicycle and gave him a push, and by the time he got to the bottom of the hill, Ernie darn well knew how to ride the bicycle! Ernie said he remembered looking over his shoulder and seeing Bob at the top of the hill and Ernie knew he darned better learn how to ride that bike in a very short time!

One other funny story was how young Bob would trick Ernie by telling him to put his head under the covers in the bed where they both slept together, and Ernie said he would always say, "No," because he knew his brother would fart, but Bob would trick him each time until Ernie put his head under the covers and then young Bob would fart! And what was so funny was that this was my grandpa and my uncle and they laughed and laughed about that story, but it was so silly and I could imagine how it was when they were kids! Uncle Ernie would tell the story, and he would stand up and wave his hand behind his butt and squeeze his nose shut with his fingers and he and Grandpa Bob would laugh and laugh about it! We kids we not allowed to say "fart," so it was twice as funny to hear Grandpa Bob and Uncle Ernie tell their story and hear them say "fart!"

Aunt Maude and Uncle Ernie had a long, shiny, aluminum *Airstream* trailer that they traveled in. Their two kids, Diane and Armand, were grown up, and Aunt Maude and Uncle Ernie had both retired early from their jobs so that they could travel around the country and into Canada in their *Airstream*. They might stay at a trailer camp for a few months and be the people in charge there, and then move onto a different place and do the same thing, so they traveled and saw all sorts of places and met a lot of new friends.

Maude and Ernie had a little black Spaniel dog named Gordo. I thought the dog's name was "Gardol" because there was an ad for Colgate toothpaste where Gardol formed a shield around your teeth and it sounded like that's what they said when they called the dog.

One time when we were visiting them, Gordo got hit by a car. His nose had all this bloody froth coming out of it, and then he quit breathing. Everyone was crying, because Aunt Maude and Uncle Ernie really loved that little doggy. So Uncle Ernie and Daddy dug a grave in the backyard to bury Gordo, and put him in the grave. People were looking at Gordo and crying when Gordo started to move! He wasn't dead after all, so Uncle Ernie got him out of the grave and Gordo lived a long time after that!

Judy and I would share a bed when we visited Aunt Maude and Uncle Ernie. One summer the bed sheet had a little hole in it, and my toe got stuck in the hole, and when I moved my foot the sheet got a big tear in it. I was horrified, and Judy said she was going to tell on me and that I would get in a bunch of trouble. So when Judy wasn't watching I looked around all the closets and drawers until I found where Aunt Maude kept the sheets and I took out a new, clean sheet and traded it for the torn sheet. Then I folded up the torn sheet and put it back in the closet, because I didn't want to get in trouble. Then when Judy came to bed that night and started to tell me how I was going to get it for tearing the sheet, I told her I didn't know what she was talking about! Judy looked and looked at the sheet on the bed and couldn't find the tear, and I just lay there with a smug smile thinking "hardy ha ha ha!"

As we got older, Daddy got three weeks vacation, and we started going camping for one of the vacation weeks, while still keeping the schedule of family visits.

Cowgirls at Knottsberry Farm – Judy 6 & Jane 4

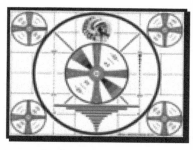

A television test pattern

Television

Our next-door neighbors, the Jensens, had a television before we did. It was a black and white TV. No one knew anybody who had a color TV. Their TV was part of a cabinet, and the TV turned on with a knob. People had to turn the knob slowly to find the television station. Between the stations there was just fuzziness. Sometimes stations didn't come in, and sometimes they did. In our neighborhood we received Channel 4, Channel 5, and Channel 7, and after ten o'clock at night all three channels would play the National Anthem while a movie of the American Flag was on the screen, and then there would be the test pattern, and then the picture would go fuzzy and sparkly, because no more TV was on until the next morning.

In the afternoon on school days the neighborhood kids went over to the Jensen's to watch the *Mickey Mouse Club*. At the beginning of the show there would be a roll call, when each Mouseketeer had the camera show just them and they would say their name out loud. They wore their Mouseketeer hats and sweaters. All of us kids copied them: We would stand up at the same time as a Mouseketeer, and point to ourselves and say the Mouseketeer's name. It was pretty complicated, because all of the girls wanted to be Annette, and all of the boys wanted to be

Cubby, so we had to take turns! When it was my turn to be Annette, I would stand up and say "Annette" with a really big smile and pretend that I was on television. It was amazing that we remembered when our turn was; there were only a few fights about someone calling out, "Annette" or "Cubby" when it wasn't their turn, and then the person whose turn it was supposed to be got to take an extra turn.

We would watch the *Mickey Mouse Club* religiously, trying to guess the outcome of the episodes of "The Hardy Boy's Mystery," or "Nancy Drew," or "Spin and Marty." Episodes meant that they just showed a little bit every day and would stop at the most scary or exciting part. We laughed at the jokes, and tried to copy how the TV kids danced and sung. At the end of each show, the Mouseketeers would sing a song: "Now it's time...to say goodbye.....to all our family..." All of us kids would sing the song with them, because we didn't want the show to end. We would talk about the episodes after the show was over, and discuss how we thought it might end... then the next day they would have a little review of the day before and continue the story. Usually one story would last one week, because they would finish it on Friday.

The TV show that was really funny was *I Love Lucy*. We would watch that once a week at night, and Lucy was always doing something that got her in a terrible situation that was also very funny. Then she would have to get out of it....we would laugh and laugh at Lucy because she always tried to trick her husband Ricky, and she never could. Ricky was a Cuban band leader, and was handsome like Dean Martin, Perry Como, and my daddy. Lucy and her friend Ethel would make up all sorts of ways to get out of trouble and they always got in worse trouble, but their husbands, Ricky and Fred, would end up laughing with them at the end of every show.

I was in second grade and sitting in the big green chair watching *I Love Lucy* when my first baby tooth came out. It had been quite loose for a few weeks and my mom kept saying she was going to pull it, but now it came out by itself! The place where my tooth had been felt funny, and tasted weird when I put my tongue there.

That night when I went to sleep I put my tooth in a little envelope under my pillow. The tooth fairy would come and take my tooth away and leave me something it its place, because tooth fairies lived in houses made from teeth and were always needing more teeth to finish their houses. I tried and tried to stay awake, but I must have fallen asleep because all of a sudden it was morning! And guess what? Somehow the tooth fairy had traded my tooth for fifty cents in two shiny brand new quarters in the **same** envelope that my tooth had been in! Fifty cents was a lot of money, and it was exciting to get that money and know that the tooth fairy was real. The envelope didn't even look opened, so I knew there was tooth fairy magic, and that magic had been at my house!

On Saturday night there was a show called *Victory at Sea* that was all about war ships and Daddy would watch it and always say, "Look at that! Would you look at that?" It did not seem interesting to me. The next year there was a show called *The Jack Benny Show.* Jack Benny was funny because he was really stingy, but what I really liked on that show were the ads. My favorite ad was a cigarette ad for Lucky Strikes Cigarettes. It went: "**L S M F T**.....Lucky **S**trikes **M**eans **F**ine **T**obacco!" The Lucky Strikes ads were great, and all of us kids had them memorized. It felt like a secret code: L S M F T. The kids in the neighborhood knew what L S M F T meant, and we would practice the movie star pose and pretend that we were smoking, and then say to each other, "L S M F T...Lucky Strikes Means Fine Tobacco." We were very accomplished marketers of smoking, that's for sure, and we would pose like models with our heads thrown back and our hands on our hips, while we spoke the cigarette slogan as if we would gain wealth and fortune with our sultry imitation. And even though no one in our house ever used Alka-Seltzer, we loved to watch the Speedy Alka-Seltzer character and the amazing Colgate Dental Cream with Gardol ads. The highlight of the Colgate ads was the invisible shield, and we were astounded about how that ad worked, because a baseball player would throw a 90-mile-an-hour baseball at a person, and it would stop in mid-air, just like Gardol would stop the germs that were after your teeth!

After school there was another show, *The Mayor Art Show*. This was a Bay Area show. Mayor Art dressed in a high hat and tails, and the kids on the show pretended to be the city council, and each kid got their own gray high hat with their first names written on the front of the hat! Mayor Art also had a hand puppet, a bird named Ring-a-Ding who lived in a cuckoo clock, and had a tendency to bite Mayor Art on his nose. Mayor Art would have the city council on some bleachers and talk to them and ask questions and tell jokes, and then the *Popeye the Sailorman* cartoon would come on. Talk about confusing! Sometimes the bully was Brutus and sometime he was Bluto, but they looked like the same person, and Popeye would eat canned spinach to make him strong. In real life canned spinach tasted horrible, but Popeye must have liked it. And he had a girlfriend, Olive Oyl, who had a baby already, and the baby always crawled away when Olive Oyl wasn't watching, and Popeye would have to rescue the baby. The baby was named Sweet Pea. Olive Oyl was stupid because she always would believe Bluto and then Popeye would have to rescue her, because Bluto was a bully and always mean to Olive Oyl. Sometimes they repeated cartoons, and my favorite one was about Goon Island, where Popeye was undressed like a caveman and pulled his face down and looked like a Goon, and he rescued his pappy, who was named Poopdeck Pappy.

We got our own TV when I was in second grade. The TV had rabbit ears that we kids were not allowed to touch.

When the TV blew a tube...well, there often was an exploding sound and then no more pictures. The TV repairman had to come out to the house and put in a new tube, so most people were happy to have neighbors with a TV because tubes were always blowing and then you would go to some other kids house to watch TV. In the winter time if it was raining and our chores were done we could watch TV on Saturday morning. Saturday morning had the *Little Rascals* and westerns with Roy Rogers and Dale Evans and *The Lone Ranger*, and then *Lassie* and *Rin Tin Tin* and *Sky King*. If a kid sneaked in and turned on the TV too early, there would just be a test pattern, because TV was only on during the day time and went off at ten o'clock at night. The test pattern looked kind of like a bull's eye.

There was a show called the *Honeymooners* but that was on after our bedtime, so we didn't watch that. But whatever show we were watching I sat really close to the television, because I could hear it better that way. And it also turned out that in addition to having the hearing loss from scarlet fever I could not see very well, so that was the second reason to sit so close to the TV. Otherwise there was no point if I had to sit far away because I could not understand the sound or see the picture.

I had to go to bed at seven-thirty at night until I was seven years old, and then my bedtime changed to eight o'clock. In the summer that was the worse thing in the world because I could hear all the other kids in the neighborhood outside playing and I had to go to bed. No one could go to sleep when it was still light out except for Jennifer, but it gave me a lot of time to think about things. I would lie in bed and wonder how it could be that there were millions and millions of people in the world and that I was the only me. It seemed like there must be someone in another country far away who looked exactly like me, because there were only so many ways to make a face: There were eyes, nose and a mouth. How many combinations were possible before a face would be duplicated? And besides, no one had ever seen all of the faces in the world at the same time, so how did anybody really know that each face was unique? I would wonder how it felt to be someone else, and what I must look like to other people, and what it would be like to travel in space, and how my eye could see. I wondered what I sounded like to other people when I talked; I wondered what it was like in Africa or in Russia, and if there was another little girl somewhere in the world at bed at the same time thinking thoughts like I was. How did people who lived in the desert go to the bathroom, and where did they get water? Did their feet hurt from walking on the desert? There was so much that I didn't know, and I wanted to know it all, and wanted to know why I was born and what life meant.

The hour or so I lay in bed before sleep during the summer gave me time to devise plans of how to dig a tunnel if the Nazis came and took over, and to review in my mind the *Reader's Digest* articles about staying afloat on a sinking boat surrounded by sharks and all the many other survival stories they would feature. So it was not really time wasted, but as a girl who could imagine and visualize so many things I had plenty of time to grow my vivid imagination.

More School and Other Things

In the mornings before school I had to have my hair braided. I hated having my hair braided; I had to sit on the floor in the living room while my mom sat in a chair, and she would undo my braids and then brush my hair, and then redo my braids. It always hurt because she would pull my hair so tight. I would say, "That hurts, don't make them so tight!" and my mom would always look at me and say, "They are not too tight. If they were too tight your eyes would slant up like a Japanese person." I would always run to look in the bathroom mirror and pull my eyes up at the corners and see if my braids were so tight that my eyes stayed that way. They were tight, but never that tight.

The only tolerable thing about having my hair braided was watching the dust in the air sparkle in the sunlight. I had to sit very still while my hair was braided, and in the morning sun there would always be tiny specks of dust that I could see. I didn't understand how those specks could be floating in the air, and what were they and why were they there? If I blew gently I could see the dust move in patterns. It was weird to sit there and know that I was surrounded by dust in the air.

Usually every morning my daddy and I sneezed a **lot**. No one talked about "allergies" in those days, but both my daddy and I would sneeze and sneeze every morning. I never was able to breathe through my nose for as long as I could remember. When my mom braided my hair she would tell me to close my mouth and breathe through my nose! Sometimes she would get mad at me and pinch my mouth shut with her fingers to try and make me breathe through my nose, but that just made me gasp for air when she was done. And the funniest thing was that she would always say, "Breathe through your nose, Dammit! Do you want people to think you have the slack jaw of poverty because we can't afford Kleenex?!"

Kleenex was the paper tissues that people used instead of handkerchiefs, but most men, including my daddy, used handkerchiefs. They thought Kleenex was for sissies. I would imagine all these terribly poor people breathing through their mouths with snotty noses all plugged up, wearing rags and probably their mothers never even thought to yell at them about breathing through their mouths! Maybe the poor kids' moms yelled the opposite: "Dammit, don't breathe through your nose! Don't be putting on airs like you have the shut jaw of richness, acting like you can afford Kleenex!"

A few years later the doctor prescribed some medicine called Novahistine to control my daily intense morning sneezing. My daddy and I would each get a spoonful every morning. It was a bright green liquid with a minty-alcohol flavor, and it did help stop the sneezing. Unfortunately it made me sleepy at school until I got used to it, but it sure was better than all that sneezing. I still couldn't breathe through my nose though.

I loved tomato juice with breakfast, but we usually had orange juice, and I was sick of orange juice every day. I would time my leaving for school so that I didn't have time to finish my orange juice. Then my mom started saving it for me to drink after school. One morning my mom stopped me at the door and said, "If you don't drink this goddamn orange juice, I will get on the bicycle with the big balloon tires and ride up and down Louis Road with your glass of orange juice, and then I will come to your classroom and knock on the door and have your teacher make you drink it, and I will be wearing my bathrobe!"

My classroom was on the front of the school, so that we could see Louis Road outside our classroom windows. After that, even if I had eaten all my breakfast and drank all my juice, I frequently checked out the window. I could imagine my mother on the balloon-tire bicycle in her bathrobe riding back and forth in front of my classroom window while holding a glass and yelling, "Janey did **not** finish her breakfast!"

We hardly ever had homework in elementary school except for big reports that we had a long time to work on. The only time a kid would get homework was if they had been sick for a day or two or if they had been bad in class and had to make up some work, or if they asked for it because they just liked doing homework. If a kid was sick for more than a few days, then all the kids in the class would write something nice to them, and another kid would bring all their messages to their house on the way home from school.

I got sick a lot, so at least three or four times a year I would get a packet from school. There would be knocking at the door, and then my mom would bring a folder to me, and inside the folder would be homework and lots of notes from the kids. They would write things like, "Sorry you are sick. Get well soon." There would be notes from kids that never talked to me when I was at school, but missed me and wanted me to get well. And when I got well and went to school, they seemed to forget that they had wanted me to feel better and go back to school.

If we had a new subject at school, we might have a workbook page to do at home, or a ditto to take home and do. A ditto was a paper that had been ran through a ditto machine. The teacher would draw or write or type on the ditto master, which had a special ink on the second layer. The top layer was white, and had tissue paper underneath it, so the teacher would remove the tissue paper before she made the ditto master. When she was done, she went to the teachers' work room, put the ditto master in the ditto machine, loaded paper into the tray, and turned the machine handle. She had to put fluid into the drum of the machine, and be really careful not to spill it. The fluid smelled pretty bad. Turning the handle was a lot of work. There was no such thing as a copy machine at the schools...no one had ever heard of a copy machine or a *Xerox* machine.

The school kids could go to their friend's houses after school or watch the *Mickey Mouse Club*, or play at school, because we didn't have to run home and start homework. But we always had to change from our school clothes and school shoes into our play clothes and play shoes. We could go to our friend's house, or just walk around or ride our bikes.

There were a lot of new houses being built in our area of South Palo Alto, and it was fun to go and watch the changes that happened every day. One day my friends Marie and Christine went with me a few streets over to where some houses were being built. We started daring each other to climb up on the wooden frame of the house, which was just like a house skeleton made of wood. They said they would climb up if I did, so I decided to prove that I could climb all the way to the top of the frame. I climbed and climbed; it was a lot of hard work, but I finally made it to the top! I could see forever! I could see to

Hoover Tower at Stanford, and I could see the salt pile in Redwood City, the tall pile of salt that was right next to the Bay.

Marie and Christine started to climb, but they got scared and could hardly get half way up. They said that I should come on down, because it was getting dark and we were all supposed to be home between 5:00 and 5:30 on school days. Even though we didn't have any watches, we had the sense of time. But unfortunately I didn't have good sense that day, because I couldn't climb down. It had been hard to climb up, but when I went to climb down off that roof, it seemed like my feet couldn't find any place to go and that the ground was really far away. Plus the ground was covered with sharp things, like metal spikes that were sticking up, and a lot of boards that had nails in them. I hadn't noticed those things when I was climbing up. Christine and Marie stayed until it was just about dark, and then they had to go home. They said they would call my house and ask my family to come help me, but I said, "No!" I was already in trouble and I didn't want to be in more trouble. It was as if my two good friends were giving me my last farewell, as if they knew I would be dead in the morning, perhaps a still and wax-like body impaled below on the ground…a tragic figure, really.

Two of the boys from my school rode their bikes by and saw my bike there next to the framework of the house. They got off, and started looking around, and then they saw me up on the top of the wooden frame. My stomach sunk down to the bottom of my feet; I didn't want the trouble of dealing with boys that were probably just going to make fun of me. But it turned out that the boys were pretty nice, and thought that I was brave to have climbed there all by myself, and they helped me get down. By this time it was dark. I knew I was going to get it. I made up a whole story about a flat bicycle tire, and how I had to go to the gas station to get air in my tire. In those days no one ever thought of charging people for air at the gas station; imagine that, charging someone for air! I thought it was a pretty good story. When I got home, filled with dread, it was as if no one even noticed that I had been gone! That was one of those things; you got in trouble sometimes for things you couldn't even figure out, and then, when you really expected to get a beating, nothing happened!

When I was a kid, when you drove into a gas station, the car drove over a rubber tube on the ground, and that made a bell ring inside the gas station. Then whoever was working, usually a man and a few teenaged boys, would come out and politely wait until the driver would ask for the car to be filled up.

Then they unscrewed the gas cap; no one had a locking gas cap, and not only did they fill up the gas tank, they would wash the car windows all the way around. We kids would stick our faces up to the part of the window that the teenager was squirting with soapy water and stick out our tongues at him, and if no one was looking he would stick out his tongue back at us. Usually we always went to the same gas station and everyone knew each other and trusted the people to do all the work on the car just right.

They would open up your car hood and check your oil, and then they would walk around your car and check the air in the tires. Cars didn't have windshield washer fluid that squirted out onto the windshields, so there was no windshield wiper fluid to check, but I bet if there had been that the teenaged boys would have checked that too! Everyone who worked at the gas station wore a white shirt and a special hat, and looked nice and clean in their uniform.

Usually there was something free that they gave away at the gas station. One time we got a whole set of six Howdy Doody drinking glasses. They would have a new glass each week, and when they gave us the first glass they said to be sure and come back next week because there would be a glass with a different picture on it the following week. The glasses must have been made by Welch's juice, because each glass would have a rhyme printed on it like: "Hey kids! Hip Hip hooray, Welch's leads the parade each day," or, "Hey kids! Ding Dong Dell, Ring for Welch's, you'll like it swell."

We would also get S&H Green Stamps just before we left the gas station. All the stores would give out trading stamps when they gave the customer their change. And because no one had ever heard of using a credit card, everyone usually got change because people paid with cash when they bought things.

Stores and gas stations gave out either S&H Green trading stamps or Blue Chip trading stamps. These were little stamps that came in sheets, and the goal was to collect enough stamps to fill up a book. The empty books were free and had blank pages in them with little printed rectangles to show people where to glue in the stamps. You got stamps based on how much money you had spent.

We collected Green Stamps, and the Jensens next door collected Blue Chip Stamps, so it worked out really well because we would give each other the stamps we didn't collect. Often people picked the store they shopped at depending on if they gave out Green Stamps or Blue Chip Stamps. Every time we got home from the grocery store or from the gas station it was fun to get the saver stamp book out of the kitchen drawer and find the page that was either blank or partly filled and lick the stamps and put them in the book.

Sometimes we had so many stamps that we would get a wet sponge to dampen the stamps instead of licking them.

During the 1960s, the S&H rewards catalog was the largest publication in the United States and S&H issued three times as many stamps as the U.S. Postal Service. The catalog showed all the things that could be traded for the stamps. When we had enough stamps we would take them all to the S&H Stamp Redemption Center and get the thing we had been planning on and saving up for. One time we got a card table and four chairs! We got all of our sleeping bags for camping by saving up those stamps and trading them for the sleeping bags. We got our camp stove from S&H too, and our *Melmac* set of dishes. It was fun to save for things with Green Stamps

Sometimes when we were at the grocery store there would be a customer who would get stamps but didn't want them, like if they were visiting from some place. One time the man in line in front of us got almost a whole book's worth of stamps and asked us if we wanted them and we all said, "Sure!"

At the Stamp Redemption Center people stood in one line with their bags of full booklets, and there were no products to see. We would go to the counter and tell the lady what we wanted, and she would flip through all the books to make sure they were full, and then yell to a teenage boy to bring up what it was that we had saved for. Then the boy would come from the back with our new item! Then it was fun to look in the newest catalog to plan what we wanted to get next.

In second grade we studied farming. We built a model of a farm that covered a really big table, and had little wooden trucks and tractors that we could pretend to drive on the roads of the model. We learned about silos and different crops and grains, and had little farm animals in the model. It was wonderful to make and to play with!

One time our regular teacher was gone for a while. Our regular teacher's name was Mrs. Johnson and she was young and pretty and had blond hair and smelled really nice. We had a substitute teacher who was old and did not smell good at all. One day the substitute teacher was talking about silage. She kept saying that word over and over... "silage, silage, silage" and when she said it her teeth clicked together in a peculiar way, and she almost sounded like she was hissing. She explained about how the silage at the bottom of the silo could smell really bad, and that if you fell into the silage it could kill you. Oh great! I hadn't read a *Reader's Digest* story about escaping from silage, so now I had one more scenario in my mind to worry about. A few months earlier some boys had been playing on the salt pile in Redwood City and had disappeared and when they were finally found they were dead, buried in the salt, and I could imagine the same thing in a silo of grain or of silage. Perhaps one could escape using the same techniques as the breast stroke across quicksand, I wasn't sure, but used that technique in my imaginary falls into silos.

The substitute teacher was the kind of old lady that would grab onto a kid when they walked past, and sit them on her knee when she was teaching, and she caught me and I was on her knee when she talked about silage and her teeth were clicking together and her breath was so bad that I thought silage could not smell as bad as her breath, and I didn't want to look at her because she was so stinky. I learned about silage, believe me! I will always remember that awful stinky breath that smelled like rotten garbage and how bad silage must smell.

We went on a field trip to a dairy farm with our regular teacher, and we got to watch how the cows were milked. The dairy farm was on Mountain View-Alviso road, and there were hundreds and hundreds of dairy cows there.

It was really weird because inside the big milking shed the farmers hooked up machines to the things that hung down from the cows big milk bag. The milk bags were really big and pink and looked like they might burst. I knew the word nipple, but those didn't really look like nipples, but what else could they be? Then the farmer kept talking about "udders" and I figured out he was talking about those long things hanging from the cow. Who ever heard of or made up a word like that? I couldn't believe that was a real word! It didn't even sound nasty...most of the words that had to do with body parts sounded nasty, and udders just sounded silly. The next time I heard someone say the word "utterly" I just couldn't stop laughing, because it sounded like "udderly."

I thought that those machines must hurt the cows, but the farmer said it didn't. The cows were all lined up in a row and we could see their backsides all lined up too. We saw cows go to the bathroom, and that was also weird, because they would just be standing any place and their tail would lift up and they would go! When we went to the other side we saw all of their beautiful faces. The cows were very tame, not like the cows that had been down the street from our house. Those cows were wild looking and could chase a little kid as fast as that kid could run!

The milk would go to a dairy in a big truck, and at the dairy it would get heated up to kill germs and then put in clean bottles. I knew all about this, because right down the street from our house was Pier's Dairy on Louis Road, right next to the creek. Pier's Dairy was named after the Pier's family, and they didn't have cows on Louis Road any more, but the milk would come there and you could walk inside the store part and see through a window the glass milk bottles going down rollers to another door where the milk got put into the bottles.

There were always Pier's Dairy milk trucks in the parking lot, and that is where the milkmen got their milk to deliver. We didn't get our milk from Pier's; our milkman was from Borden's Milk. My mom said that sometimes the Pier's Dairy cows would escape to a tomato field and eat tomatoes, and then their milk tasted bad. My mom thought that Borden's milk tasted better that Pier's Dairy milk.

The Borden's milkman would come six days a week, but not on Sunday. It was exciting like when the mailman came to the door or the Fuller Brush Man or when we got a delivery from our Sear-Roebuck's Catalog order. The Fuller Brush Man was a salesman who had a route of houses that he would always go to, so every few months he would return to our street and bring a suitcase with all sorts of brushes for sale! He had brushes and cleaning supplies, and would always have some small gift for us kids if my mom bought something.

The milkman's truck had a refrigerator inside of it to keep things cold, and he would leave what ever a person had ordered right on their porch and then knock or ring a bell if they had a door bell; most people we knew did not have a door bell, and we sure didn't.

Sometimes there were specials. There was one special when my mom ordered cottage cheese that it came in an aluminum Davy Crocket glass, and when the cottage cheese was gone, we had the glass to keep. Each week the glass would be a different color, so after six weeks we had six new, shiny glasses. Jennifer liked the dark blue one best because it looked like grape juice, but we had red, blue, green, orange, pink and gray. We had two sets of glasses, one from the gas station, the Howdy Doody glasses, and the Davy Crockett glasses from the milkman. My mom would write a note for the milkman for what we needed the next day and how much we needed, and then we would get it, just from the handwritten note. People didn't need a special form, they could just write a note on any old piece of paper telling the milkman what they needed the next day, and the milkman would bring it. At the end of the month the milkman would deliver a bill showing everything that had been delivered for the month, plus the milkman would leave notes about the specials whenever there was a special. When my mom paid the milkman she would write a check and leave it in an envelope on the front porch. Most people in the neighborhood liked Pier's milk, but my mom was loyal to Borden, with Bessie the Cow on their milk trucks.

I liked to walk down to Pier's Dairy and go into their little store, which was in the lobby. From there you could look through the window. They had the little store where they sold popsicles and juice bars, milk and other dairy products. I wasn't allowed to buy popsicles, but I could buy juice bars. Their freezer was so cold that I could buy four juice bars on a hot day and walk home with them in a little box, and by the time I got home the juice bars would still be frozen hard as a rock. My favorite was lemon juice bars, but they also sold lime and orange and grape. Yuck, I hated grape juice bars, but Jennifer loved them; that was the only kind she ever wanted, plus she loved grape juice. Jennifer loved grape juice so much and drank so much grape juice that one day I looked at her and saw that she had a grape juice smile! She had been drinking so much grape juice that the edges of the glass had left a stain on her face that made it look like she had a bigger smile! She was just this little tiny kid with a big grape juice smile. So from then on everyone in the family had to help make sure her face was wiped off after she drank grape juice.

We always had frozen juice that you added water to in order to make the juice. It was pretty neat the way it happened: All you had to do was get a can opener, open the metal juice can and dump the frozen juice into a pitcher, then read how much water to add, add the water and stir it up and like magic you had juice! Orange juice, orange-pineapple juice, or grape juice!

On the night of our field trip to the farm I was talking about the cows and the farm. Then Daddy told about how he milked the cows by hand every morning at five o'clock from the time he was a little boy until he was twelve years old. He didn't use a machine, he just used his hands. I thought that sounded kind of weird but my daddy said he just did it, that it was just one of his jobs on the farm.

There were a few weeks when my daddy was fifteen when we didn't do any of the chores at the farm, and that was when he went to Union Town, Pennsylvania, with the town sheriff as a deputy to help bring back a criminal.

Daddy's Trip as a Deputy

My daddy was born in a town of 200 people in Kansas. The name of the town was Green, Kansas. My daddy wasn't living there when he was fifteen; he lived in a bigger town. The sheriff of the bigger town needed a deputy to go with him to pick up an escaped criminal who had been captured in Pennsylvania. The sheriff thought that my daddy was old enough to go with him. They swore my daddy in as a deputy and gave him a special gun to take with him, and they drove to Pennsylvania! My daddy and the sheriff stayed at motels and ate at restaurants and crossed the Mississippi River and saw a lot of things on the way.

The car was a special car with no door handles in the backseat. There was a big ring fastened to the floor of the car. When they got to Union Town and picked up the criminal, he was put in the back seat and his leg irons were fastened to the big ring on the floor.

The three of them stayed in motels on the way back, and the criminal would be handcuffed to the metal parts of the bed, and the sheriff and Daddy took turns guarding him. My daddy remembered that the criminal had escaped from Kansas and they were taking him back there for justice. He was a big man, but they safely got him back to Kansas for him to go back to jail and await his trial.

My daddy said there were a lot of Klu Klux Klan people in his little town when he grew up. One time he and another boy were playing in the attic at the boy's house, and they opened a trunk and found Klan uniforms, plus a list of all the people in the town and around town who were in the Klan. The boys recognized the names of the doctor and the dentist and the sheriff and the mayor and many of the men in town. They were scared and closed up the trunk and got out of the attic as fast as they could, because they were afraid that the mayor might find out they knew about those robes. They were afraid because sometimes if people found out who was in the Klan then those people might disappear and then later be found dead.

My daddy said he felt sick and afraid, and he and the mayor's son never talked about what happened. Even though Kansas was part of the Union in the Civil War, there were still a lot of small towns that were suspicious of changes. My daddy told about how his German ancestors had moved to Kansas in the 1800s, and after WWI they were very careful to never speak German any more. When WWI was happening, people who had done business with those German farmers and had been their friends quit trading with them and wouldn't do business with them, because they thought they might be German spies! This was after five generations in the United States and yet the small-town people in Kansas were very suspicious about any one who might be different, black or white!

The Variety Store

There was a dime store in our neighborhood, down at Midtown, on Colorado Avenue near Middlefield. We could walk there, and I loved to go inside and look at all the things. There were shiny glass dishes and vases and plates, and a few clothes and lots of toys. They had a whole section of miniature toys, as if they were made to be toys that somebody's dolls could play with. I would walk up and down the aisles looking at the toys, and one day my hand just took on a life of its own, and took one of the little toys and put it in my pocket. My heart was pounding. Once it was in my pocket I couldn't dare to take it back out again. I left the store and went home and put the toy on my doll shelf. I looked and looked at that toy, and decided that I really wanted to keep it, because my friend Sara Jean Byrnes had a toy just like it, plus a whole lot more, and just maybe I deserved that toy as much as Sara Jean did.

I knew that I was supposed to feel guilty. Some of the time I felt really guilty because the lady that owned the store trusted me and I was nothing but a common thief. And then sometimes I felt like I would never get those little toys for my dolls or little presents for Jennifer unless I took them. The lady at the store had so many things; she probably wouldn't even notice one was gone. And then I would almost die of fear because what if my mom found out that I had stolen that toy? I wanted to be good. I wanted to be honest, but I wished that I could go in there and take all the stuff anyway.

The next time I went to Sara Jean's house, I told her I had a little tiny toy just like she did. She said that she didn't really need that toy, and if I liked it so much, she would give me one that was similar. I couldn't decide what to say. I really liked the toy and wanted it, but it was kind of like charity taking something when you didn't give something back. And then it hit me: I would say, "Yes" and then take back **both** toys to the dime store.

I felt better already, so I was really excited and Sara Jean gave me the toy. My plan was to take both the toys back to the store and sneak them back onto the shelf. But I didn't. Every time I went to the store I felt that everyone in the store was watching me. What if they thought that I was stealing when I was really putting it back? Now whenever I was on an aisle that blocked the view of the counter, it seemed that the lady who owned the store would come around the corner and ask me if I wanted something. I was jumpy and skittish, and I finally decided that she must know and that was why she must be watching me. So I decided that I would tell her, and give her back the toy I took plus the other toy. But then I could never find a time when she was by herself, and it seemed like she never came around the corner of the aisle by herself anymore.

The days went by, and I was going every day to the dime store to try and give the toy back. I was imagining all night long what would happen when she found out that I was a thief. I had heard about reform school, and figured that I was headed for reform school. As long as I was going to reform school, maybe I should steal more things, but I was afraid to go to reform school and didn't steal any more things.

I never did give the toys back. I didn't go back to the store for a long time.

The Holidays

Valentines

We made valentines in school from scratch; no one bought a store-bought valentine's card except a husband for his wife. During the week before Valentine's Day, our teachers at Palo Verde let us use our daily art time to make valentines. We had to make a valentine for everyone in our class, plus for our teacher, our principal, and for all our family. I loved to make the valentines! We would have red, pink, Manila and white construction paper; pink, white and red heart-shaped paper doilies, and heart-shaped patterns to trace around if we needed to. Sometimes we had ready-made paper silhouettes of cupid, the little angel that shot an arrow that made people fall in love. We had glue, tape and scissors, and glitter, crepe paper, sequins, and yarn!

Cutting out a heart shape was really fun, because all you had to do was fold the piece of paper in half, draw one half of a heart on it, cut on the line, and when you opened it up you would have two hearts, one the shape of a heart, and the other would be the hole in the paper that was also shaped like a heart.

The tricky part was that we had to make a valentine for everyone in the class. So for the stupid boys that I didn't like, I would make a plain white heart and usually write "Happy

Valentine's Day" in pencil. That was the least I could get by with and still have it be a valentine. But for best friends and boyfriends...boy oh boy, could those cards ever get fancy!

We kids would layer paper heart cutouts, one on top of the next, all different colors and sizes, using the white *Elmer's Glue* to stick them all together. You could take a strip of crepe paper and crinkle it up to look like fabric, and fold it in pleats and glue it all around the edge of the valentine, and then glue a heart-shaped doily in the middle. Sometimes it would take the whole art period to make just one or two valentines.

Writing on the valentines that I gave to my girlfriends was pretty easy: "You are my best friend in the world, valentine!" or "True friends like you are the best valentine that there is!" It was trickier writing to the boys that I liked, because all the kids ended up showing each other their valentines, so I would maybe write, "Be my Valentine!" in my best writing, and then draw hearts and use glitter and make it look really fancy. Giving and getting a fancy valentine meant that person really liked you, but most of the boys were not that good at making valentines. Then for our family we had to make nice cards, and also a nice card for our teacher. I always really liked my teachers, so it was fun to make their cards, and all the kids competed to make the best card for the teacher.

We also would make a valentine "mailbox" to hold our valentine cards. One year we all made a heart-shaped big envelope from woven-together strips of pink and red paper. Each envelope had a paper handle and hung on the back of each student's chair. Another year  we all decorated boxes that we placed on top of our desk.

The idea was that no one would see each other's valentines; that it was a secret, but usually all the girls shared with each other and showed each other and compared what we got.

At home on Valentine's Day when we girls got up and went to the breakfast table, there would be a big box of candy on the table for my mom, and three small heart-shaped boxes of candy on the table, one at each plate for us girls.

We were all Daddy's Valentines!

Then we would go to school, and in the afternoon we would have a classroom valentine's party, usually with cup cakes to eat, and we would all walk around the classroom and put our valentine cards into everyone's envelope or box, and then we would sit down at our chair and look to see what we had gotten.

We all knew each other's names, we knew where everyone lived because we all walked to school, and as we went from kindergarten to first grade, first grade to second grade and advanced on up in the grades, we would get valentines from many of the same children from one year to the next. We felt like a community, and making the cards for each other was part of that community feeling. When I got home at the end of Valentine's Day I would look at the cards over and over again to figure out which boys liked me and which girls said I was their best friend. Then the cards got put in my desk. I could take them out and read them again whenever I wanted.

In third grade on Valentine's Day morning there was a mystery chocolate heart that had frosting writing on it: "Jane - Be my Valentine" and it was in a beautiful box with a see-through panel. My boyfriend David Trainer had sneaked it on to my front porch while everyone was asleep.

St. Patrick's Day Saint Patrick's Day was important because we were supposed to wear green so that we would not get pinched. When I first started elementary school, my mom would tell us, "Just tell people that you are **not** Catholic and you are **not** Irish! Tell them **not** to pinch you!" She said we did not have to wear green because of those two things, and I would tell people that I had green eyes so they could not pinch me. Then we girls would pick grass and put it in our pocket so that we had some green. After a few years of us coming home all pinched, my mom understood that we needed to wear green on Saint Patrick's Day. All the kids would look for four-leaf clovers on St. Patrick's Day because it was supposed to be lucky; I actually did find one once, and put it in a box that had cotton in it and kept it for a long, long time. Usually on Saint Patrick's Day people talked about rainbows and pots of gold and leprechauns, and it was kind of confusing because it seemed like Rip Van Winkle had something to do with it as well.

People liked this holiday because usually in San Francisco there was at least one big Saint Patrick's Day parade, and everyone liked going to a parade.

But the most interesting thing about this holiday was hearing that Patrick was a Saint who drove all of the snakes out of Ireland, and that because of him, Ireland has no snakes! I wasn't quite sure what driving snakes out looked like…what was this Saint driving and how did it work? But I had seen drawings of him in a book, and it looked like he used a big stick to do the driving. I was amazed that something like that could happen, and thought that Saint Patrick must know Jesus or God, but I couldn't really figure out the green part and the pinching part of it. Plus the grownups would drink a lot of beer to celebrate, and one time Auntie Jan put some green food coloring into some beer for Saint Patrick's Day!

 April Fool's Day April Fool's Day was my favorite holiday. It had taken me a while to catch on, but once I did it was the best holiday to plan for. At first, Daddy was always the one who had the best tricks, and they were very simple: I would come out to the kitchen and Daddy would shout, "Stop! Don't move! You have a big spider on your shoulder!" I would stand there, petrified with fear, and my daddy would walk over with a look on his face that said if you were a spider you were about to die, and then he would flick the imaginary spider off my shoulder and calmly say, "April Fool's!"

Wow, a whole day to play tricks on people and not get in trouble. For the first few years all we could think of was the "Oh look you have a spider on your shoulder" trick, and my daddy would pretend to be tricked, but as time went by we had to come up with some better tricks.

I tried the newspapers tricks, running into the room and announcing things like: "Did you see in the paper today that there is no school because of a bunch of poisonous snakes let loose at the school!?" "Wow, did you see in the paper that all candy bars are free today at the liquor store. You can just go in and take them without paying!?"

It was really, really hard to think of a joke that didn't scare everybody to death and was therefore mean, or a joke that was too easy to guess. So I started thinking of the jokes ahead of time, trying to make them funny.

I found that if I saved my allowance long enough, and if Judy and I went in together to buy something for a trick, then we could get a good trick going. One time we went to Bergman's and bought some fake barf. That's right, they made some really gross fake throw-up that was plastic but it looked real. We put it on the floor behind the toilet and then I went in to the bathroom and made throw-up noises. I got sick pretty often, so I was the best person to make the noises. Then Judy and I hid and watched my mom find the fake barf. It was funny! Well, my mom didn't think so, but Judy and I jumped out and yelled "April Fool's!" so my mom had to think that it was funny!

Another time we did a similar trick, only it wasn't fake barf, it was worse than that, it looked like a cat or a dog had gone to the bathroom in the corner of the living room. It was fun to hide and see which grown-up found it first.

At school you had to be careful, because most of the jokes could get you in trouble, so practically all of the kids spent the day saying thing like, "No, I am not kidding you, you better hold really still, because there is the biggest spider I have ever seen going up the back of your shirt... let me knock it off...I am not kidding..." and jokes like that. Or they would try and put a "Kick Me" sign on someone's back as a trick.

 **May Day** May Day was another name for the first day of May, and Palo Alto always had a May Day Parade! It was fun, because pretty much anyone could be in the parade, so when we were little we decorated up our tricycles and went in the parade dressed as cowgirls! The parade went down University Avenue, the main street in Palo Alto. University Avenue went from East Palo Alto all the way to Stanford University. When the parade was finished there was a May Fete Dance at the Community Center on Middlefield, but it wasn't for everyone to dance in, only for the dancers who had practiced. There was a tall pole with big ribbons hanging down from the top, and all the dancers would circle around the pole, dressed in pretty outfits, winding the long ribbons around the May Pole.

In forth grade I marched in the parade with the Traffic Patrol, and Judy and my friend Linda marched inside of a Purple People Eater costume. There was a really popular song about a "One-eyed-one-horned-flying-purple-people-eater" and that is where they got the idea. Together they were a one-eyed-one-horned-flying-purple-people-eater. My mom had taken a box

Judy, the Purple-People-Eater

big enough for both of their heads when they walked side-by-side, and covered the box with a sheet she had dyed purple, and then they made a horn from a cardboard tube and sewed an alien face on the sheet. It looked really cool!

A few days later Linda came down with the mumps, so everyone was worried that Judy would get the mumps, but she didn't, even after sharing a box over her head with Linda for the whole parade! However, I got the mumps, and they hurt and made my face swell up, and I missed the three weeks of school being sick with the mumps.

May Day was also a day to surprise someone with a little basket of flowers. At school each kid would make a little woven basket out of paper, and the basket would have a little handle on it. The basket was big enough to slip the handle over a door knob so the basket could hang there. On the first day of May we were supposed to pick some flowers and put them inside our basket and sneak the basket of flowers on to somebody's front door knob while they were still sleeping. When they opened their door that morning they would have a nice surprise of a basket of flowers and wonder who had left it there.

We were supposed to look around the neighborhood for someone who looked lonely or didn't have a family, and then get up real early and hang that little basket of flowers on their front door as a happy surprise for them to find when they opened their door.

A few times I hid and waited to see what happened when the person opened the door. But if I had to go to school that same day I didn't get to see. What was really sad was to see a basket hanging on a front door knob at the end of the day…that meant that the person hadn't even opened their door that whole day, or that they were so unhappy they didn't even want flowers!

I liked May Day because it made me look in my neighborhood to see who might be lonely and who might like some flowers as a surprise when they opened their door.

Mother's Day and Father's Day We would make cards for both of these holidays during our art time at school. Father's Day was the week after school got out for the summer, but we still would make Father's Day cards. Mother's Day was a bigger deal, because it happened while school was still in session, so there was more time to talk about it. We made fancy cards with lots of colored construction paper and streamers and crepe paper folded up to look like paper flowers.

For Mother's Day, Daddy would take us shopping at Fremont's Pharmacy, where we girls would go up and down the perfume aisle, spraying our wrists with perfume from the sample bottles, sniffing, and then doing it again. By the time we had decided which perfume to buy, we all stunk up to high heaven!

We would then sneak the present back home and wrap it and give it to my mom on Mother's Day, along with the cards we had made.

For Father's Day it was similar, except that we always got Daddy cufflinks or a tie. Because my mom didn't drive, we would have to be sneaky and plan a trip to the Emporium and then send Daddy off on a fake errand while my mom and we three girls picked out a pair of cufflinks. Those would get hidden until we got home, and then my mom would wrap them, and Daddy got the cards from us girls along with the present.

We knew that all the other kids were doing the same things on Mother's Day and Father's Day. Usually all the kids at school had both their parents living in the same house with them. Divorce was a word that we mostly heard in discussions about movie stars, and if it was about someone we knew, it was usually whispered or talked about after we kids went to bed. Divorce was not a suitable topic of conversation: People got married and stuck to it and that was that!

Halloween For Halloween we were usually gypsies; we would dress up in long dress-up skirts and scarves, lots of jewelry and wear make-up. We had really good dress-up clothes anyway, so we could take those clothes and make them fancier.

My mom had bracelets that she used to wear in college; lots of thin sparkly bracelets and she would let us wear those with our gypsy outfits. Kids didn't buy Halloween outfits in those days; I don't even think that they sold ready-made costumes. Every kid made their own costume with the help of their parents or the help of their friends, or both. All the kids wore their costumes to school all day long on Halloween, and then as soon as it started to get dark kids and one of their parents would walk around their neighborhood with their kids and the kids would go Trick-or-Treating.

Only little kids went. Big kids would have been embarrassed to go Trick-or-Treating and would only go to hold their younger brother's or sister's hand if no adult could take out the little kids. My daddy always took us out while my mom stayed home to give out candy to Trick-or-Treaters. And at each house the person who opened the door would be polite and ask about kids' costumes and what they were, and then give them candy or money for UNICEF or both.

All the teachers at school asked the kids to Trick-or-Treat for UNICEF, and people were used to keeping pennies next to the candy and were happy to donate it along with the treats. Then the next day all the kids would take the little UNICEF container back to school and all the pennies would get counted up and sent to children who needed a whole lot of things way more than we did, and UNICEF would buy those things for them.

Halloween night when we got home we usually spread our candy out all over the floor and counted it, sorted it, looked at it, and would be amazed at how much stuff we had gotten. But after a few months most of the candy would still be there because we were not used to eating candy very often.

*First grade Halloween – Jane a witch at age 6, and Judy
a pirate at age 9*

Second grade Halloween — Jennifer a witch age 3, Jane a dancer age 7, and Judy a gypsy age 10

Fourth grade Halloween — Judy a glamorous person age 12, Jane a gypsy age 9, and Jennifer a fairy princess with a gargoyle mask, age 5

Thanksgiving I think we spent the whole month of November studying about the Pilgrims and Thanksgiving, and Christopher Columbus and the three ships. We heard about the Indians who had helped the Pilgrims and showed them how to plant corn. It was hard to imagine how people had come across the ocean in those ships, and to imagine how it was starting in a new country without even knowing how big the country was or what it was shaped like. I was glad I wasn't alive then because all of the pictures of the clothes those Pilgrims wore looked really uncomfortable and looked hard to wash and iron, and the Pilgrims looked really uncomfortable and weird in those clothes. At least the Indians did not have to wear lots of layers or weird hats; the Indians were just about naked!

At school we made Pilgrim hats from black and white construction paper. We also made placemats, sandwiching autumn leaves and color crayon shavings between two layers on wax paper and then ironing them so that we had a see-through placemat that looked like stained glass!

We made turkey decorations out of pine cones with colorful cut-out paper feathers stuck into the gaps in the pine cones...one end of the cone with the tail feathers and the other end with a cut-out red paper turkey head. We traced around our hand on Manila paper and colored in our handprint drawing, our fingers like feathers with our thumb for the turkey head.

By the time Thanksgiving came around we had made enough decorations to cover the long table at Gramma Gigi's house with our home-made autumn-colored Thanksgiving decorations. Gramma Gigi and Grandpa Bob and Auntie Jan would "Ohh and Ahhh" at how pretty everything looked.

There would be so much food to eat, and the kitchen in San Carlos would almost burst with turkey, mashed potatoes, gravy, green bean casserole, sweet potatoes, and rolls, peas with mushrooms, brussel sprouts, cranberry sauce and pies. My mom would make two mincemeat pies with the homemade mincemeat she had made from green tomatoes, and Gramma Gigi would make the pumpkin pie.

Gramma Gigi was really happy that there was a new kind of turkey; in the olden days all the women had to pull the pinfeathers out of the turkey. The pinfeathers were the new feathers and they were very difficult to pull out; people actually needed pliers. So when stores started selling turkeys that were guaranteed to have all the feathers removed Gramma Gigi said she was the first in line to get one of those turkeys! The first year that those turkeys came out Gramma Gigi was very disappointed. They were advertised as having no pinfeathers, but Gramma Gigi still had to remove many pinfeathers. She wrote a letter to the president of the company, and a few weeks later a car pulled up in front of her house, a man got out, and he came to the door carrying a big turkey! He told Gramma Gigi that he represented the turkey company, and he apologized for the pinfeathers in the turkey she had purchased, and asked if she would accept the turkey that he had brought as a way of the company apologizing. So Gramma Gigi got a free turkey, and it had no pinfeathers! After that, Gramma Gigi was always loyal to that company and never bought a different brand of turkey.

Gramma Gigi would tell us that story and used it as an example for us: Don't complain about something unless you are planning to get it changed! Write the person in charge if you want something fixed and don't give up.

One year Gramma Gigi made a pumpkin chiffon pie at Thanksgiving, and everyone said that it was the best pumpkin pie we had ever eaten, and we wanted that same pie every year. After we had all eaten, Gramma Gigi went back into the kitchen and we all heard her laughing. Gramma Gigi then walked into the dining room holding up the can of pumpkin! She told us she had forgotten to put the pumpkin in the pumpkin chiffon pie! The pumpkin chiffon pie had beaten egg whites, sugar, cinnamon, nutmeg, vanilla and brown sugar, so with all those good flavors we hadn't missed the flavor of the pumpkin!

Every year after that Gramma Gigi would make the pumpkin-chiffon-pie-without-the-pumpkin because we like it so much, but we would also have a regular pumpkin pie as well.

Christmas All the kids made Christmas presents and decorations at school, and for our Christmas party we would bring "white elephant" gifts to exchange. A white elephant gift was something that was already at your house; you didn't go out and buy it, but were not using it any more. It had to be good as new, and the gift would get wrapped up and brought to school without any "to" or "from" with the gift. On the day of our party this is how it worked: All the kids sat in a circle on the floor with a basket of all the white elephant presents in the middle of the circle. The teacher would randomly select a student to pick the first present, and the kid sitting next to them would be the second kid to select a present from the basket. The first kid would go to a big basket that had all the gifts and take one gift out of the basket and unwrap it in front of everyone. Then the next kid had the choice of picking a wrapped up gift or taking the gift that other person had. As more and more people unwrapped their gifts it became more fun and interesting. The very last person had the choice of selecting from all of the gifts!

One year the whole class got to decorate plain glass ornaments with glitter, and the resulting ornaments were beautiful. We selected either a red or green or blue shiny glass ornament, then wrote on it with glue, and then covered the glue with glitter. When the glue dried we had our glitter-writing stuck to the ornament forever. We wrapped our ornament presents up in newsprint that we had decorated with potato prints.

Potato prints were really fun. If you wanted to make a candy cane print, for example, then you drew a candy cane on a piece of paper, and then cut your potato in half and put the paper on the cut potato and pressed with your pencil really hard on the outline of the candy cane. When you lifted up the paper, the outline was on the potato. Then you would carefully use a table knife to remove everything from around the outline, leaving the candy cane shape. The shape would be sticking up taller that the rest of the potato.

Then you could dip the potato in paint and stamp it over and over again on the newsprint paper, making a beautiful design on your own wrapping paper! When that was dry, if you liked someone else's stamp, you could trade and use each other's. That way your paper might have a green Christmas tree and a red candy cane all on the same piece of paper!

One really fun thing that we got to make was Christmas trees that were made from upside-down pointy ice cream cones, the kind called a "sugar cone." We took the sugar cone and put it upside down on a piece of wax paper, and spread green frosting all over the sugar cone. Then we took red cinnamon candies and pressed them into the frosting to look like Christmas ornaments. There was another kind of candy decoration that was little shiny silver balls, balls that looked like tiny bullets, and we got to press those into the frosting so it looked like there were sparkly lights on our tree. We used all sorts of beautiful cookie and cake decorations made from sugar to press onto our frosting, and when we finished our classroom had a forest of frosting-covered ice cream cone trees.

One year when I was sick in December, there was a knock at the front door at the end of the day. My mom came into my room shortly afterwards; not only had the kids in my classroom sent home notes that they were sorry I was sick, they had also made me a frosting covered ice cream cone tree, and it made me feel so good to know my classmates had thought about me and made that tree for me.

Decorating the Christmas tree at home was a ritual. Daddy would go into the attic and bring out boxes and boxes of ornaments that had been carefully packed the year before. The tree would have sat on the back porch in a tub of water for the previous several days, and would have been brought in and positioned correctly in front of the living room window. Everyone would watch Daddy put the tree in the right place, and tell him when it was standing straight so he could tighten the big screws on the Christmas tree stand. Then my mom would open the first box of ornaments, and while we girls sat on the couch we would watch her decorate the tree, and listen about each box of ornaments. Some of the ornaments were very old; they were all special in some way. My mom would hold each one up and tell a story: One ornament was from her grandmother, another was from when my parents were first married; a different ornament was bought at the corner store in Kansas when they lived in the trailer park. Each story was the same year-after-year, and I loved looking at each beautiful ornament and feeling the continuity of life with the stories linked to the ornaments.

Every year my mom would put twelve aluminum multi-colored bells on the bottom branches of the tree. That way she would hear if Baby Jennifer was touching the tree or if Bootsie Cat had snuck into the living room and was trying to climb the tree. It was like an alarm system on the Christmas tree!

When we decorated our tree we never put Christmas lights on it. Instead of lights, my mom had sheets of cotton that she used year after year to place on the branches of the tree so that it looked like snow. Daddy hung a spotlight with a blue light bulb in it above the tree, and at night we turned off all the lights in the living room except for the spotlight, and it really looked like a snowy tree. At least I believed that it did, from what I had seen in books and on TV and what I could imagine.

The other things that Daddy brought down from the attic were two giant candy canes. They were taller that I was, and each candy cane was hung up on one side of the living room window, inside of the house. Every year I would look at those candy canes and want to take a bite from them. It was like they were taunting me. I watched and waited, and one time when my parents went to the store I snuck between the drapes and the window to where the candy canes hung and I took a bite from the corner of one of the candy canes. Yuck! It was plastic, just like my daddy had said! I had a mouth full of plastic and now there was a piece missing from the corner of the candy cane. I hoped and hoped that no one would notice. Why did they make those candy canes look so good anyway? And guess what? No one did notice, or if they did they didn't realize that it was a bite, they must have thought the candy cane corner had gotten smashed some how.

We also had a very small red chair that my mother's Santa doll sat in; a Santa rag doll that was about a foot tall that had its own chair that was from when my mother was a little girl. Every year that chair and doll were taken from the attic to sit right next to the tree. And on Christmas morning Daddy always wore his red socks that had Santa's face in white ink on the sides of the socks!

We didn't have snowball fights on Christmas; we would jump in the leaf pile instead! This is California, and from Thanksgiving time until long past Christmas there are always tons of leaves to rake up. Daddy would rake up leaves, and we were not supposed to scatter them, but it was really fun to fall onto a leaf pile, pick up handfuls of leaves and throw them and toss them and watch how they fell. Many Christmases found us in the backyard in the afternoon having leaf-pile fights; some Christmas Days had the sultry feeling of impending rain, sometimes Christmas was clear and bright and sunny, and sometimes we had a foggy or raining Christmas. Often it was so warm that we would go to Palo Verde and play in the afternoon after we changed into our play clothes.

Third Grade

When I was in third grade, we studied Indians! I loved studying Indians. Lying in bed at night I would think about how it would be to grow up a little Indian girl, and live in a teepee and ride a horse and go to the creek to gather food. I already had braided hair, so I thought that I kind of looked like an Indian. My daddy looked more like an Indian. He had shiny black hair and got really tan in the summer, but he had green eyes like Jennifer and me. My hair was brownish-reddish-blond, not black like Judy's and Daddy's.

I loved to skate. The skates clamped onto our shoes. You had to have leather shoes on or the skates would slide off. There was a skate key that you wore on a shoelace around your neck, and this is how it worked: You would sit on the sidewalk and use the skate key to turn a little gear on the bottom of your skate. The gear would make the part of the skate that clamped to your shoe widen out, and then you could put your shoe in the skate. Then you would turn the skate key the other way until the skate was tight. The key also could be used to make the skate longer or shorter, so skates could fit a lot of different shoe sizes, and one pair of skates would last a long time, longer that a pair of shoes!

So I was skating around the block, faster and faster, when I saw a dead bird on the grass next to the side walk. It was a black bird, with shiny feathers and a shiny beak and beautiful feet. It must have been dead for just a short while; there were no ants on it and it was still clean. I decided to take it home to make an Indian necklace, because many of the pictures of Indians showed them with necklaces of bear claws or bird feet, and I didn't figure that I was going to find any bear claws lying around, so bird feet were pretty great! I tied the dead bird to my skate key shoe lace, and sped around the rest of the block, braids flying behind me, skating like the wind. I imagined that I already looked like an Indian! I thought maybe I might just keep the whole bird, but I didn't think I had seen any pictures of that.

When I got home I went into the garage and found a knife and was sitting at the picnic table on the back porch busy cutting off the feet of the bird when I heard my mom scream! I ran inside, bird in hand, to see what was the matter. She was still screaming, so I also started screaming, "What's wrong?! What's the matter?!"

Well, she was pointing at me and then my daddy came running in to see what was going on, and there I was, partly mangled bird in one hand and a knife in the other, with my mom pointing at me and screaming. Apparently she had been screaming because she saw me out the window cutting the legs off the bird!

They didn't let me make a necklace with the bird feet hanging from it. I couldn't believe it! I wanted that necklace so bad; why study the Indians at all if I couldn't make a necklace just like them. They made me throw out the bird and I couldn't even keep the feet. "What in the hell do you think the neighbors thought when they saw you skating down the street like a wild banshee out of hell and a dead bird hanging from your neck?!" Sheesh, I bet the neighbors wished they had a necklace like me.

I learned the Indian rain dance, and I made it rain.

I knew how the dance went, with stomping my feet and moving up and down, stooped over some of the time and then standing up. I knew how to make the sound…to yell a certain way from the back of my throat and then clap my open hand over and over again on my open mouth, so that the sound had great power. I knew how to raise and lower my head with the rhythm of the stomping and the power noise.

So when Gramma Gigi asked me if I could do a rain dance, I did the dance. It was hot outside, and no clouds were in sight. Yet I poured my heart and soul into that dance, dancing on her red-painted back porch at her house in San Carlos. I whooped and hollered, jumped up and down, and in my mind I was transformed to another age and to another body, the body of a powerful warrior, until, after almost two hours and near-exhaustion, the big rain drops came down faster and faster and there were an incredible downpour. I had danced all by myself and believed that I could do it, and the rain had come.

Exhausted, I went inside, and asked Gramma Gigi to keep it a secret that I had the power. I didn't want anyone to know that I had the power.

In April of that year, storms caused a levee failure downstream of Highway 101, flooding the Palo Alto Airport, the city landfill, and the golf course to a depth of nearly four feet. I decided that I would never do a rain dance again. That flood was scary. When that flood happened, my daddy had called Gramma Gigi from his work and asked her to come pick us all up from our house in Palo Alto and take us to Gramma Gigi's house. Her house was high enough that no flood could reach it. Gramma Gigi drove through the hard rain and came and got us.

My mom hadn't finished laundry that day, but Gramma Gigi said, "Just put it in the back seat!" The laundry basket was in the back seat, and the inside of the car kept fogging up so badly that Gramma Gigi couldn't even see out the windows, so she told us to grab a piece of laundry and wipe off the windows. There I was on my knees in the back seat wiping off the rear window when I look down and I was wiping off the window with my daddy's shorts! His shorts were his underwear, and I started laughing, and told everyone that I was wiping the window with Daddy's shorts, and pretty soon we were all laughing, my mom, Gramma Gigi, Judy, Jennifer and I, while Gramma Gigi drove us through the foot-high flood waters to get to the safety of her house.

We spent about a week there or more, because my mom and my sisters got the measles and Gramma Gigi had to help everyone get well. I had had the measles a few weeks before and got to stay at Gramma Gigi's house then, because you had to keep people with the measles away from babies, and even though Jennifer was almost 4 now, she was still very tiny. But with my mom sick we all stayed at Gramma Gigi's. Having the measles meant you had to stay in a dark room because you could become permanently blind if you looked at light, and you also had a really sore throat and a rash and a fever and felt awful and it was miserable to lie in the dark for days and days.

Years later when my beloved Gramma Gigi knew that she was dying, she told me that she had read the weather report every day until she was pretty certain that it was going to rain, and then she had asked me to do the rain dance. She said she never forgot how serious I was when I came to her and asked her to swear to secrecy that I had the power. I guess she understood how important to me it was that I had Indian powers. She had never told me until then that I had not caused that miracle of rain, and that in itself was a gift and a miracle.

I still wanted an Indian necklace with bird feet or bear claws. Then one time when we were at Gramma Gigi's house, she asked everyone one if they wanted bear claws for breakfast the next day, because she was going to the store. Even though I wanted bear claws for my necklace, I could not imagine eating a bear claw! Everyone else said, "Yes," but I said, "No." The next morning Gramma Gigi brought out store-bought pastries for everyone but me, and I couldn't figure out why. I asked where my pastry was, and everyone said that I had been asked but didn't want one. I was so confused, why would they say that? Then someone said that I had said I didn't want a bear claw, and I said they were right, I didn't want a bear claw, so then they said why in the hell was I belly-aching about it then?

One thing that we had to do each week at school was to bring in a newspaper clipping from home and stand in front of the class and read it, so that we shared news about what was going on and became good newspaper readers. One week I found a photo of a girl in the newspaper with a short article below her photo, so I cut it out to take to school, because the girl looked like she might be in third grade too. The headline below her photo was "Local Girl Succumbs." Well, the photo was smiling, and when I looked up "succumb" in the dictionary it had something to do with yielding or giving in, so when I read the article and it told about how this little girl had succumbed, I thought that it was a good thing, and that the girl had won something or perhaps had gotten a prize, because the article talked about what time this had happened and how her family was all there.

So I got up in front of the class and read the article. I think the rest of the class didn't realize either that I was actually reading an obituary about someone who had died! When I was done and there were no questions from the class, the teacher pulled me over and asked if I understood what "succumb" meant. "Win a prize?" I answered. "No, it means to die," said my teacher. How could I have read such an article to the class?

On the weekend when I was at Gramma Gigi's house, I showed her the article and asked her if that was really true, and she said yes, it was. Then I asked her the question that had been bothering me all week long: How did they get the photo of the girl with her eyes open and smiling if she was dead? Did they glue her dead eyes open and glue her face so that she was smiling? Her photo looked alive, and if she was dead why didn't the newspaper have a photo of a dead person so that people would know that they were dead?

Well, Gramma Gigi told me that the photo was probably the girls school photo, and that when someone died the family would give the newspaper a photo of when that person was alive to put in the paper, that they didn't take a picture of the person when they were dead to put in the newspaper.

How was a kid ever supposed to learn all this stuff about how things worked and why would they put an alive photo in the newspaper with words that were hard to figure out, when they should have just said "Little Girl Dies" so that it made sense? And then I started thinking about my school photo for that year, and oh, great! If I was going to die and a school photo was used, I sure hoped it could wait until another year, because the night before my photo this year, I had my hair washed and braided, but it was still wet, and I fell asleep on my stomach so that the wet bangs were not lying down flat like they should have been, only half of my bangs were flat and the other half stuck straight up, plus I had been bitten by a mosquito on my eyelid in the middle of the night, so I also had one eye that was swollen shut. I hoped that if I died it would wait until I had a better school picture, not one with a swollen-shut eye and half my bangs sticking straight up!

I had been going to the Palo Alto Clinic about my hearing and they sent me to a special hearing loss clinic. There was no way I was going to wear hearing aides because I had seen them before and they looked horrible and I knew all the kids would stare at me if I wore those. But then the doctor told my mom that the way my ears were damaged that a hearing aide wouldn't help anyway. So for a while I would go on the bus after school with my mom to a place where a lady showed me how to watch people's lips when they talked to that I could see what they were saying by looking at their lips. I hated all those hearing tests and the way it made me feel, but it did make sense to watch people's lips.

Me in my Brownie uniform

I went to Brownies. Brownies were like Girl Scouts, only the younger version. My sister Judy was a Girl Scout, and my mom was one of the leaders in Judy's troop. On the day that we had our Brownie meeting, all the Brownies would wear their uniforms to school, and then the meeting would usually be after school in the multipurpose room. If it was near to Christmas time we would make presents for our family and cards for old people, and then we would go sing Christmas carols at the convalescent homes and give the old people who lived there the Christmas cards that we had made for them.

We sold Girl Scout Cookies by walking with another Brownie around our neighborhood, and carrying the boxes of cookies with us in special cartons that had handles on them. We would go to the door, knock, and then when the person opened the door we would smile and be very polite and ask them if they wanted to buy a box of Girl Scout Cookies. Usually they said, "Yes," and we would take their money and make change if we needed to. A box of cookies cost fifty cents in those days. Then we put the money in a special envelope that had a thermometer printed on the outside, and every time we sold a box, we used

 our pencil to color in one of the "degrees" on the thermometer…each degree stood for a box of cookies, and if you sold 20 boxes you filled up the thermometer, sealed up the envelope, and then started a new envelope. The envelope had each Brownie's name on it, and when we went to door we took turns until someone bought a box, and then we would trade.

There were no Blue Birds at our school. Blue Birds were the little Camp Fire girls, and it seemed that all the kids at a school would either be Scouts or Camp Fire, but not usually both at one school.

In third grade a student who was doing well and got recommended by the teacher could be on Traffic Patrol. All the kids wanted to be on Traffic Patrol. The Traffic Patrol stopped the traffic on Louis Road at the crosswalk so that the students could cross the street safely. The patrols were made up of third, fourth, fifth and sixth graders, but only a few third graders. There were three shifts of patrols: One before school, one at lunch, and one at the end of the school day. There would be four students on each patrol, two who carried the signs, one who told the patrol what to do, and one who made sure the kids who were crossing the street obeyed the Traffic Patrol. Students on Traffic Patrol each wore a special red sweater, yellow hat, a sash, and the leader had a whistle. The signs were stop signs on a round pole about four and a half feet tall, and they had to be carried just right. The Traffic Patrol would start outside the school office, the leader would blow the whistle, and then the patrol would march to the crosswalk… "left, left, left, right, left…left, left, left, right, left" the leader would chant, and the patrol marched along with their feet all together with the chant.

When the patrol got to the crosswalk, the leader would say, "Attention!" and the marchers would stop. Then the leader would bark out the command to ready the signs, and then the two sign-bearers would hold their signs upright, and one of them would cross the street. When they crossed the street, that person held the sign out straight, perfectly, so that all cars would see it and stop. If it was morning before school, then the patrol leader who was watching the kids would cross the street as well. The leader would blow a whistle, and the sign-bearers would spin the stop signs around, twirling them, and then stand at attention with the signs at their sides! The next time the leader blew the whistle, it meant for the sign-bearers to pivot their bodies and face the traffic while holding out the stop signs, so the cars would know to stop.

When kids or adults were crossing the street, they had to wait for the whistle to blow and the signs to stop the cars. The student who was telling the pedestrians what to do would stop people crossing once there were three or four cars lined up and waiting. Then when everyone had crossed safely, the leader would blow the whistle again, but this time there would be two whistle blows. That meant to take the signs back, and the sign holders again got to twirl the signs and pivot their bodies so that they stood at attention at the curbside.

Everyone liked to watch the Traffic Patrol. It was a little bit like the guards at Buckingham Palace, because the kids waiting to cross the street would sometimes tease or try to get the sign holders to laugh or to mess up. But the students on the Traffic Patrol took it pretty seriously, believe you me!

Before a student could be on the Traffic Patrol they had to practice in front of the policeman who was in charge of all the Traffic Patrols at all the schools in Palo Alto. The policeman made sure that he knew who the students were and that they were taking their position seriously. The policeman would watch the patrol practice until they performed perfectly. Officer Frank Mashinski was the police department's Safety Patrol Liaison. Traffic Patrols all marched in the May Day Parade, along with any kid who decorated up their bike with crepe paper.

I was selected to be on the patrol when I was in third grade. I liked the lunch time duty the best because that meant leaving class five minutes early, and there was not as much traffic from the cars at lunch time. Twirling the sign and holding it was difficult, because the sign was tall and heavy, and if it was windy it was really hard to hold that sign straight out. If it was raining the Traffic Patrol had shiny yellow raincoats that they got to wear, called "slickers." We had enough Traffic Patrols that we rotated duties; one week we would be on patrol Tuesdays and Thursdays, the next week it would be Monday, Wednesday and Friday. We also had enough people that we had substitutes in case some one got sick or otherwise couldn't make it.

In those days if a teacher had to leave the classroom to make a ditto or to get something, then the teacher just left the class without an adult in charge, because the students were trusted to behave while the teacher was gone. Usually the teacher would select a student to be in charge while the teacher was gone, and that student had the power to write kids' names on the board if kids misbehaved. No one wanted their name on the board, because that meant staying after school as a punishment.

My third grade teacher was a man. I hadn't had a man for a teacher before, but he was a good teacher. His name was Mr. Crick. When we had been in Kansas, instead of saying "creek" like we said it in California, the cousins there would say "crick," like when someone had a crick in their neck, but they were talking about the creek. When I ended up having Mr. Crick as my teacher, I wasn't sure if he was saying his name funny or if he was saying it right until he wrote it on the board; then I could see it was spelled C-R-I-C-K.

Mr. Crick always wore a sport's coat and slacks, a long-sleeved shirt and a tie, dressing like the other men in the community, but more casual than wearing a business suit. The lady teachers always wore dresses or skirts and blouses with high heels or "pumps." Pumps were low-heeled fancy shoes.

One day Mr. Crick left the classroom unsupervised, and all hell broke loose. For some reason, kids started being rowdy, throwing things and yelling and just misbehaving all over the place. At first I tried ignoring everyone, then telling everybody to stop, but after a minute or two a crayon landed on my desk because someone had thrown it, so I decided to throw it back. I was never a good thrower in the first place; there were some girls that could throw a ball as far as a boy could, but that was not me. I would throw as hard as I could and the ball would land about 12 feet away and never land near to what I was aiming.

I pulled my arm back as far as I could, stood up, and flung that piece of dark blue crayon as hard as I could. What happened next was as if it was in slow motion, where everything slowed down and I watched the scene unfold. I threw the crayon as Mr. Crick walked back into the classroom; he turned his head, and the dark blue crayon got nearer and nearer to Mr. Crick until his ear and the crayon were perfectly lined up and then the crayon landed in his ear.

A professional thrower could have probably tried a hundred and fifty times to get a crayon to land in a person's ear, sticking right out from their ear, and not have succeeded. My one throw broke all the odds; my dark blue crayon landed in slow motion right into Mr. Crick's ear, and his face took on a look of rage and he bellowed out, **"Who threw that crayon?!"** I don't know what it was that caused him to zero in on me, but there Mr. Crick was, color crayon sticking out of his ear, while he stared at me and sputtered, "Did you throw that crayon?!"

I think one of the stupid boys tattled on me by pointing, because Mr. Crick looked at me and yelled, "Go to the principal's office now!" This couldn't be happening, I had never been sent to the principal office for being bad, but now I was. As Mr. Crick stared at me with eyes like burning coals, the whole classroom became silent. Students returned to their seats and the crayons, spitballs and paper airplanes mysteriously vanished. Mr. Crick slowly pulled the crayon from his ear, all the while staring at me. I was in a state of disbelief. Of all the kids who threw things, how could my one throw land in his ear and get stuck there...sticking out straight from his ear like a handle.

I controlled my tears, and stoically walked to the office. But my ordeal was just beginning.

I walked into the office and the school secretary smiled at me. She was used to seeing me there, because I often shelved the library books, and the library was in the office. I also took the roll sheet to the office some of the time. She was smiling at me, and then the policemen who were the Traffic Patrol Officers, along with Officer Frank Mashinski, came out of the principal's office. Time stood still. There was no way in hell I was going to confess my crime to the smiling secretary right in front of those policemen. I could only imagine the outcome. The secretary would change her look to a stern reprimand, and the policemen would most likely get out their handcuffs and take me away to the police station where I would live in a jail cell for the rest of my days, turning pale and languishing away, refusing to eat, cock roaches and rats as my only friends.

The policemen were smiling at me along with the secretary when she asked how she could help me. And without batting an eye, I said, "I am done with my work so Mr. Crick sent me down here to see if you needed any help." And I smiled, and they smiled back. The secretary said there was about a half an hour's worth of books to shelve, and if I wanted to shelve books, then she would really appreciate it.

So I did. I shelved books without looking at anyone, and the secretary and the policemen chatted. Finally the policemen left. I finished the shelving, and went back to the classroom. I didn't want to open the classroom door, because whenever a student was late or walked in after the bell, everyone watched to see what was going to happen.

Everything in the classroom seemed normal when I walked it. Mr. Crick was sitting down in the chair at his desk in the front of the classroom. He said to me, "Did everything get taken care of?" "Yes," I replied back. Because after all, everything did get taken care of.

For several weeks I kept waiting for Mr. Crick to find out that I had not gone to see the principal and I had not confessed my crime to the principal. Days passed, and I finally realized that somehow I was not going to have to see the principal and tell her what I had done. And slowly I let my breath out. I had served my time by shelving books.

When I said "stupid boys" I really meant it. One of the kinds of Indians that we studied in third grade was the Aztec Indians. I wasn't really that interested in the Aztecs because they didn't seem close to me or near to me. The American Indians seemed like part of the land here and I felt somehow more connected in my third-grade world to horseback-riding Indians who hugged the horses with their knees with their braids flying behind and watching the sky from one horizon to another. When the boys in my class told me they had something to show me out of the encyclopedia about Aztecs, I wasn't sure if they were teasing or if they were finally interested in school. There were two boys who were always smart-alecs, but I thought maybe they were being serious for once.

The picture in the encyclopedia that the boys showed me changed my life forever. It was awful, and I always regretted that those boys didn't understand or take responsibility for what they had done. The picture they showed me was a drawing of an Aztec priest cutting a beating heart out of a live human sacrifice. There was blood pouring out everywhere in the drawing, and other Aztecs were holding down the man who was being killed.

I felt like crying and fainting at the same time. How could anything like that ever happen? Why would anyone be so cruel to do that to another person, and how could they hurt someone so badly to cut them open while they were alive and kill them like that? The boys were laughing. They said it was funny. But it was not funny, and I wished for an eraser to take the picture out of my mind and to erase the memory of it, and to erase it from the book so that no one would ever look at so much pain and say it was funny.

That night when I was in bed my mind raced with the awfulness of that picture. How had that person felt and how much it must have hurt, and how mean and cruel those Aztecs must have been to ever allow that to happen on purpose and pretend that it was right. It was not right and there was no excuse. I now knew a different kind of pain in **my** heart which was a pain of the meanness of a religion that used cruelty as if God wanted it, and used cruel people to hurt others. I never ever was able to erase that picture, and wondered why an artist who was so gifted in their ability to draw would choose to draw something so gory and full of pain. There was no excuse for that, because the artist must have liked what he knew was happening in order to draw it. I was angry that Mr. Crick had that book in class and that he had allowed those mean boys to show me that picture. I was angry to have a picture in my head that I had never ever wanted.

When I was a kid there was a lot of competition on the playground. Little girls would compete over how long they could jump rope, how many games of tether ball they could win in a row, if they could Double Dutch jump rope, how well they could play hop scotch, how many rings they could skip over on the ring bars, and how high up the jungle gym they could climb and then jump off. All of the play equipment that we used to have, except tether ball, is gone from playgrounds now, judged unsafe and replaced by plastic molded equipment guaranteed to keep children unharmed.

At Palo Verde we had a metal slide. We would climb up to the top of the slide's ladder, and if this was during recess there would be a non-stop line of kids going up the ladder, then we would grab the hand holds at the top and almost fling ourselves down. But kids didn't just sit on their bottoms to go down the slide; we would slide on our bellies head-first, on our bellies feet-first, on our backs head-first or feet-first. There was competition to figure out new ways to go down the slide....sometimes kids would slide down the very edge of the slide, balanced on the lip of the slide side. Or kids could slide down like they were doing the splits… a leg over one side of the slide and the other leg over the other side. And sometimes kids would pack three or four kids on the slide at the same time. The first kid had to be the biggest because they had to hold on really tight to avoid sliding down when there was one kid behind them. Each kid would squash as close as they could to the kid in front of then, and stick their legs out to the side and try to hold on to the edge of the slide until as many kids as possible would all be stacked up. Then it would be: "1, 2, 3, Go!" And all the kids let go at the same time and pushed hard against each other to go down the slide really fast, and everyone would land on top of each other at the bottom. Little kids couldn't do it because they would get hurt. It was so much fun, everyone would be laughing; even if someone did get hurt kids would still laugh. The kindergarten kids had their own playground, so the littlest kids were not in any danger of getting hurt, because they were not allowed to play with the bigger kids.

On a hot day we would often get shocked going down the slide because our clothing would release static electricity. And there were days that it was too hot to go down the slide because we could get burned. On those days some kid would find any container that would hold water; a paper cup was the best if anyone could find it. Then whoever had the cup would fill it with water, climb the ladder, and pour the water down the slide. Usually the first pour of water caused steam to rise off the slide! Then kids kept pouring water down the slide until it was cool enough to slide down. If we had enough containers we could form a water brigade, passing the full cups up the ladder, and then the empty cups back down the ladder for refills. When we got the slide cool enough a pool of water would form at the bottom of the slide, and sliding down the cool slide on a hot day and landing in that puddle made regular sliding extra special.

There were two kinds of bars to cross: The regular bars, and the hanging rings. The regular bars were like a metal ladder at the top of two half-ladders, all smooth and shiny dark metal. A kid would climb up a few ladder rungs and then reach up and grab the metal bar. For kids who were just starting on the bars and weren't very good, one of their friends would hold them from below so if they fell their friend could grab them. What usually happened is that both kids would fall and the bottom kid became the cushion for the top kid, so it was a bad idea if a big kid had a little kid holding him up. There was tanbark underneath all the play equipment to cushion kid's falls anyway.

When you got better on the bars, then you used one hand on each bar, and incorporated a swinging rhythm, so that you quickly went from bar to bar. When you got really good then you skipped bars. Most of the bigger kids always skipped bars when they went across, and some of them could even skip two bars! Some of the crazy kids would shimmy up the ladder and then get on top of the bars and stand up and cross the bars by walking on them! But those were boys, because girls had to wear skirts or dresses to school and if a girl crossed the bars by walking on top of them, then everyone would see her underwear.

The hanging rings were much, much harder than the regular bars. They were also made of metal and were big enough that kids could sit inside of them or hang by their knees from them. To cross those rings you stood on a little step and almost jumped up to grab a ring, then had to swing back and forth by pushing on the pole with your feet until you had enough momentum that you swung far enough to grab the next hanging ring. If you got really good then you might be able skip rings, but you ran the risk of hitting your head on the ring you were trying to skip over.

There were also some bigger metal pieces of equipment that were made for "skinning-the-cat." Skinning-the-cat meant that you hung upside down from the bar, hanging from your knees, and then grabbed the bar and started swinging back and forth, back and forth, until your momentum built up and you could actually swing around completely. Once you got around it the first time, then your momentum would carry you so that you could spin around and around and around. It was really fun and scary at the same time, and there were tricks involved because as you got better and better you could skin-the-cat by hanging from one leg only and using the other leg to kick the ground to make you go faster.

I loved to skin-the-cat, twirling around and around with my braids flying through the air! When I was finished I would just hang upside down, but like all the little girls I had to hold my shirt up instead of letting my arms hang down free. If I came to the playground on the weekend I could wear pants or shorts, so I could do a lot more crazy things on the weekend because I didn't have to worry about the boys seeing my underwear!

There was a metal jungle gym that was shaped kind of like a big dome. It was pretty hard to climb to the top and pretty scary as well. When I was in third grade, and still dreaming about flying, my dreams were so vivid and the feeling of flying so real that I wanted to fly in the daytime world. We kids were talking about Peter Pan and flying and I said that I could fly. Of course the kids didn't believe me, but there was a part of me that really knew I could fly. I climbed to the top of the jungle gym and prepared for take-off. It was double scary to jump from the top of the jungle gym because the bottom was fatter than the top, so if a kid didn't fling themselves out far enough, then they could smash on the metal jungle gym below as they fell. If you were jumping from the jungle gym, you really had to push off hard to miss the rest of the jungle gym below!

There was somewhat of a crowd gathered to watch my flight. I closed my eyes, was ready, and threw in one of those prayers that asked God to help me fly, and then pushed off. As I crashed to the ground not only was all the air knocked out, but I was astounded that I had not flown, because I truly believed that I could. And then I realized that for a split second I kind of had been flying, for that tiny bit of time when I pushed off with all my strength and spread my arms, I had been in the air!

My only broken bones from my flight were my ring and index finger on my right hand, and my pinky finger was sprained. I had to wear a splint for quite a while, and at home I was always knocking over my glass of milk, because the splint extended out beyond my finger and it was easy to knock things over by mistake. At school I got to learn how to write with my left hand. And the funny thing about it was that the kids didn't even make fun of me for trying to fly. I think maybe they all wanted to fly too, and I had at least tried it.

Jumping rope was so much fun. There were thousands of ways to jump rope. You could jump rope all by yourself and go as fast as you wanted. There were all sorts of fancy steps to do: A kid could jump, jump, jump, or jump, hop, jump, hop, jump, hop; or jump, skip, hop, jump, skip, hop...there were endless new patterns when jumping rope. Most of the time we jumped rope with other girls and we used a big long jump rope. There would be a girl at each end of the rope turning the rope over and over, and there would be a line of girls waiting to jump.

For little girls just learning how to jump the long ropes that other girls held, there was a half-turning of the rope called "Bluebells." The girls holding the ends of the rope made sure that the rope would not turn all the way around, and that it was slow and the rope drug on the ground. Bluebells was how the little kids learned.

There was a special jump rope song for bluebells; the rope would slowly swing on the ground until the words "Eevie, ivy, over," and then the rope would go all the way around for just once. Then the rope would again be turned only half-way around and it would be dragged along the ground.

This was the Bluebells song:

"Bluebells, cockle shells,
Eevie, ivy, over;
I like coffee, I like tea;
I like the boys, and the boys like me.
Tell your mother to hold her tongue;
She had a fellow when she was young.
Tell your father to do the same;
He had a girl and he changed her name.

Bluebells, cockle shells,
Eevie, ivy, over;
Mother went to market
To buy some meat;
Baby's in the cradle
Fast asleep.
The old clock on the mantel says
One o'clock, two o'clock ….."

After a girl took her turn jumping, then it would be the next girl's turn to hold and turn the rope, and then the next person would take their turn, taking the rope and turning it. There were no grown-ups around telling us this, we just played that way because it worked and that was how we did it.

Double-Dutch was when each girl turning the rope would turn two ropes, so that the person who was jumping had to jump into the inside of the two turning ropes, and then jump both ropes. Girls were really good at jumping rope and each classroom had plenty of jump ropes so that anyone who wanted to jump rope had a chance. The rope had to be turned around with the right rhythm, because otherwise it might spin crookedly or hit the ground funny, or the "red-hot-peppers" part would not go fast enough. "Red-hot-peppers" were the fastest you could jump and was at the very end of all the jump rope songs.

Sometimes the chant would change at the red-hot-peppers so it made it easier to count how many times a kid was able to jump the rope which would spin faster and faster, going around as fast as the girls on both ends could spin it, and as fast as the girl inside the spinning rope could jump!.

We always jumped rope to songs. We knew a million of them! One of our favorite jump rope songs went like this:

"Doctor Doctor I am ill

Call that doctor over the hill

Here comes the doctor

Here comes the nurse

Here come the lady with the alligator purse

I don't want no doctor

I don't want no nurse

I don't want no lady with the alligator purse!

Out goes the doctor

Out goes the nurse

Out goes the lady with the alligator purse cuz'

Mama don't' want no babies

Wrap 'em up in toilet paper send 'em down the elevator

Mama don't want no babies!

How many babies didn't mama want?"

Then the red-hot-peppers would start, and we had to jump really fast and count each jump. For this song we were counting the babies that mama didn't want.

Years later when I thought more about that song it seemed to me that we might have been jumping rope to a song about abortion. Who actually was the lady with the alligator purse? But we were innocent and loved to jump rope, and no grown ups were listening to censor our songs, or to make sure we didn't throw tanbark or hurt each other. Most of the time the kids just played and took turns and made up their own rules and played by them.

Another jump rope song we loved was this one:

"Not last night but the night before

24 robbers came knocking at my door,

As I ran out to ask them in

They hit me on the head with a bottle of gin

I asked them what they wanted

And this is what they said

'Chinese dancers do the splits,

The kicks,

The turn around,

Touch the ground,

Get out of town!'"

The boys played dodge ball or flag football, and boys and girls both played tether ball or hopscotch. We had a twenty-minute recess in the morning and a whole for hour lunch, and a twenty-minute recess in the afternoon, so we got in a lot of playing each day at school.

In third grade everyone wanted a Hoppy-Top. Hoppy-Tops were made from heavy rubber, and were about the size of a coaster but much thicker than a coaster. The Hoppy-Top was a store-bought token for playing hopscotch.

Until Hoppy-Tops were around we used pieces of tanbark or rocks, or anything that looked unique that could be tossed and was heavy enough to not blow away. Then all of a sudden, everyone had Hoppy-Tops. When we got Hoppy-Tops, then all the little girls were comparing theirs. Mine looked like someone had taken a multi-colored small rubber ball and then squashed it. But each one had a design different than the others, and mine had a really wide blue striped swirled into it next to a really wide yellow swirl. So I could always know which one was mine. When you played hopscotch, you could play on the sidewalk, or you could play it at school where the squares were painted on the blacktop. To play on the sidewalk, a kid would use chalk to draw a pattern of squares on the sidewalk; our mom would not let us draw on the sidewalk in front of our house, so we would play on the sidewalk in front of the Jensen's house, because they were allowed to draw on their sidewalk.

I was really happy to have a Hoppy-Top, because all the girls had one and it made hopscotch more fun than usual. And after recess or lunch you brought it inside and put it in your desk. If you were going to play hopscotch after school then you took it with you at the end of the day.

We also started SMSG Math in third grade. SMSG stood for something like Student Mathematics Study Group, but it was really just called SMSG. I really liked math anyway, and SMSG math was fun because when I finished third-grade math I got to go do math in the fourth grade class, and so on. If you were in sixth grade math and you finished that, then you got to go to a special math class out at Stanford University!

The bad thing about SMSG Math was this: I finished algebra in fifth grade, then had math at Stanford for the next year, but when I started Junior High they did not continue the program, so Junior High started me back in math that I had completed in fifth grade, plus they only had a shop teacher teaching math that year.

My sisters and I were not allowed to read many comic books, except we had a few *Scrooge McDuck* and *Archie* comics, but that was all. The rest of the kids in the neighborhood read a lot of comic books, so comic books seemed like the forbidden fruit from the Bible, something to be coveted. My mom said that trashy people read comic books, people that didn't think with their minds, and that the way kids would get ringworm was to read trash like comic books, and that I better not sneak off and read comic books or I would get ringworm.

The forbidden fruit: The Comic Book! Lulu playing hopscotch

Well, the challenge had been issued, so I spent a lot of time in the Jensen's garage reading comic books. The Jensens didn't have much stuff in their garage except for some shelves and a water softener, and they would let kids sit in their garage and read. It was cool inside there, sitting on the cement floor with the big garage door open, sitting and talking and watching people walk by. The water softener always had these little chunks of salt on the floor underneath it and next to it, and kids liked to pick up the salt chunks and suck on them while we read comic books.

We read *Archie* and *Scrooge McDuck* and *Little Lulu* and *Superman* and *Batman*. There was one family down the street that we weren't supposed to play with because they were always sick and every year their mom had another baby. They didn't really keep as clean as the other families, so that was why my mom said we would get ringworm; she was afraid that if we read their comic books we would catch it from those books. Plus the mom wore too much lipstick. But they had better comic books and more comic books that anyone else, so they would bring their comic books over to the Jensen's garage and we would all read their comic books too.

Then one day in school I noticed this icky round sore on my arm, a perfect circle of a sore, and then I saw some more. My teacher saw them too, and sent me to the school nurse. The nurse wore a nurse's uniform with a nurse's cap, and she looked at my arm and said I had ringworm. I had to get some special medicine and I couldn't come back to school until I had been to the doctor and gotten that medicine, plus I had to have a note from the doctor that said I could come back to school.

Oh shit. I had to walk home from school with that note. And when I gave the note to my mom she said that she knew I had been sneaking looks at comic books, and that was what I got for being such a little sneak, and she was going to get me for it. But she waited until after we went on the bus to the doctor's.

Judy and my mom said that I had worms inside my arm that were from inside of me eating holes in my skin from the inside. But the doctor had said that there were not worms, it was just called that because it was round and people used to think it came from worms. The doctor never said it came from reading comic books; he looked at my arm and called in a prescription for some cream. Later that day Fremont Pharmacy delivered the medicine, because we had an account there and all the doctor had to do was call them and they would bring the medicine right to our house and we didn't even have to pay for it until the bill came. They knew where we lived because Judy used a lot of medicine.

Later that day my mom gave me a spanking with the wooden spoon for being a liar and a sneak and reading comic books.

*Daddy, Jennifer, Judy, my Mom, me, Aunt Bernie, Grandma
Ruth, Cousin Blake, Greg and Rose at Mission San Juan Batista*

Family Visits from Kansas

Daddy's brother was our Uncle Jack, and he was married to Bernie, and we had three cousins: Rose, Greg, and Blake. They came to California one summer to visit us. We didn't have any extra beds, so we bought some chaise lounges that were like patio furniture, and had those in the living room, and made up extra beds on the floor from air mattresses that we blew up each evening.

When they visited it was fun because it filled the house with people and we went to see a lot of places. Uncle Jack had a big station wagon, so when we went to Monterey, San Francisco, Point Lobos, Muir Woods, wherever we would go all of us would pile into that station wagon together. I remember on the way back from Monterey we had folded down the back seat, so we kids were all sitting in the back of the car, and pretty soon we lay down, piled up on each other, and we all fell asleep. When I woke up my head was on my cousin's tummy, and I had drooled on his shirt while I was asleep, and when everyone woke up they started to laugh because Greg's shirt had a big puddle of drool on it.

When the Kansas family came we went all sorts of places. Daddy would take his vacation and all of us would drive together to visit a mission, or the beach, or just drive up to Skyline, going up Page Mill Road. Uncle Jack would ask Daddy to drive that road, because they didn't have roads like that in Kansas, so Uncle Jack had never learned to drive the steep winding roads like we had in the Bay Area.

My "artistic" pose in a meadow in Yosemite

Me visiting Pebble Beach — Hair ribbons on the top of my braids

My J.C. Higgins birthday bike

Fourth Grade

I was used to getting 100% on all my school work, and that was my expectation of myself. Most of the time school work was easy, but I would make it harder by asking for more work or trying to really understand or learn more about what we were studying. We had reading kits at school, the SRA Reading Laboratory Kit. These kits were in most of the classrooms, and they were large boxes filled with color-coded cardboard sheets. Each sheet included a reading exercise, and then there were questions for students. The questions were multiple-choice, and once a kid had passed a certain number of sheets of one color, then the kid could go to the next level.

I did not like multiple choice questions. Sometimes there were two out of four answers that might make sense, especially if you thought long enough, so sometimes I would miss an answer, and get it wrong. I couldn't stand to get a wrong answer, I expected myself to get all the answers right, and felt totally disgusted when I missed anything at school. I thought that the teachers liked me because I was no trouble and that I got all the answers right; if I missed answers, then they wouldn't like me any more. When I missed an answer, I would cheat and erase the wrong answer and put in the right answer. I could do that because we corrected ourselves.

We would read a story from one side of the card, and then turn it over to the other side that had questions. But our teachers had us write the answers on a half-sheet of paper. That way a whole lot of kids could take the test and no one ran out of answer sheets or had to buy more answer sheets. So kids would just write the numbers 1-25 on their half sheets of paper, and then put their letter of their answer on the paper next to the number. Then there was a separate sheet with the correct answers on in, and we would check our own work.

I was in fourth grade, and advancing on to the next colors. The top level in the kits for elementary schools was sixth grade, so once a kid got there, the kit was finished for them until they went to junior high. I was advancing right along, and cheating every now and then so that I had a perfect score, when I got to the story about the army ants. Why in the world they would put this story in a reading kit for kids is a mystery. There I was, intent upon perfect scores and being ahead of everyone in my class, when the reading kit gave me the army ant story. Sitting in a classroom, indoors and safe, I read the story of army ants. Army ants traveled really quickly across the forest floor, and would eat everything in their way. If you were a person in the jungle you could actually hear the army ants coming, because there were so many of them that hundreds of thousands of little ant feet made a pattering sound that people could hear.

Army ants would bring down a big water buffalo by crawling up its legs and chewing its eyes out until it was blind and then they would just eat it alive! And here I wanted to be an entomologist and go to the Amazon jungle and it was full of army ants. And you know, what was to keep those ants there? How could I plan an escape? It was a good thing that I lived in a stucco house, because maybe if the army ants came to Palo Alto, I might have time to climb up to the roof. I would have to figure out something to keep those ants from climbing up the sides of the house. We really had too many trees close to our roof, because when the army ants came, all they had to do was climb up a tree and drop down on to the roof, come down the chimney, and then eat us all alive.

I was busy planning escapes from sharks, quicksand, the Nazis, bad guys, and now I had to figure out what to do about army ants. I thought that they should never have put that story in the reading kit for kids to read. Didn't they know that kids already had too much on their minds and now they had to figure out how to protect themselves against army ants!? When I lay in bed at night and worried about so many things that weighed down my very existence, army ants and their ferocity and callousness caused me great anxiety. I wasn't quite sure what I would do when I lived in the Amazon Basin and had to deal with the prospect of army ants.

I was in moral turmoil over cheating on the tests. But I had gotten myself into a position where I was "the smartest kid in class." I had a fear of missing answers, of losing the status, of letting people down and becoming more invisible than I already felt. The expectation at home was that on my report card I always got the highest possible grades. Then one day when I missed one answer on the SRA test, I didn't agree that my answer was wrong, and I sat there thinking about changing it or not. And then I saw my teacher watching me, and at that moment I knew that my teacher knew I had changed answers.

A few days later Mrs. Sharpe pulled me aside and told me that she was glad that I had decided to turn in the answer sheet without changing anything. She said that no one was ever expected to get all of the answers right all of the time. She had missed the same one on the test that I had missed, and that she thought the answer that they had as right was really a wrong answer! So you could see why I loved my teachers so much!

My most embarrassing oral report was the report that I did on Nigeria. I had my map I had drawn on a big piece of tag board, using colored pencils to color it. I discussed the population, the imports and exports, the languages, the history, the music, all of the typical things that were discussed in an oral report. The problem was that I didn't pronounce it properly. After I had talked about the Niger River, about Nigeria, over and over again, and sat down, my teacher called me to her desk and whispered: "The Niger River rhymes with tiger, not with tigger!" I thought I would die, because I really hated giving that report out loud and saying the "N" word, but I had done what I had been assigned. I was mortified to the bottom of my very feet. Every time I had said the "N" word, not only had I cringed, but so had my classmates and so had my teacher. It was one of those oral reports that it took me a long time to live down.

Sometime during fourth grade I decided that I really needed to learn to do three things: Spit on the sidewalk, say the "F" word, and "flip the bird." It seemed that whenever I went walking around town by myself, there would always be stupid boys walking together or riding their bikes together, and every time they would pass me invariably they would all say, "God, you're ugly!" It was pretty disheartening, but I thought that I needed some new response skills. I determinedly tried spitting on the sidewalk, but that horrible noise that people make just before they spit eluded me. It made me feel like I was getting a sore throat, and beside, it was so disgusting I couldn't follow through with it.

I would practice saying the "F" word under my breath, walking down the street muttering it over and over again, but I could barely whisper it out, and partially believed the swear police would somehow know that I was whispering that word, or someone would be following me and hear it and tell my mom. But that would be a joke! I was sure if my mom heard me swear I would get my mouth washed out with soap, which was a bit ironic as my mom was an artist at swearing, savoring the words as they rolled off her tongue, using swearing as dramatic punctuation with great relish and satisfaction. My daddy used to look at her and say, "Now Louise, cut it out," but that seemed to encourage her. When I was about three years old I guess no one was allowed to play with me because I swore so much. But anyway, as I walked down the street muttering the "F" word and hoping I could say "'F' you!" to the next group of boys who called me "ugly," I had an epiphany about words. And it was then I made it my mission to respond to those boys with words that would astound them in ways that they that they would not understand, and that it would only be later that they would realize that I had powerfully insulted them! That was a much better idea than trying to say the "F" word...I just couldn't make myself do that.

And as for flipping the bird? That whole thing was really confusing. What was the bird and what was the significance of the flipping? I would walk down the street using one hand to hold down all the fingers on my other hand except for the middle one. I was in bird-flipping practice mode. I wondered what it meant. It had to be something really nasty and shocking because it was so powerful. I spent days and days trying to perfect flipping the bird, but I just couldn't seem to master the angst that went with it and make it mean something. I was more like the angel in the school play pointing with her finger dramatically, not like an angry teenage boy. I think my lack of ability to flip the bird later transformed itself into the easiest symbol and prevailing symbol that I made thousands of times…the vee, the sign for peace, the wonderful symbol that had nothing to do with anger or rage or obscenity, but had to do with hope and love and peace and free love. I guess my fingers were not destined to flip the bird, my throat was not designed to spit on the sidewalk, and my voice had a mission different than to shout the "F" word at those boys who called me ugly.

I was now able to yell back at those boys. "Oh yeah? Well, you obtusely epitomize ignorance!" or "You ineffective Cretin!" I felt power in words and now had many responses to those bothersome boys. Unfortunately I couldn't really do anything about being ugly.

I had needed eye glasses for a long time, but I didn't want glasses because hardly any kids wore them and the styles were ugly and the kids who wore glasses all got called "four eyes." I already had a big nose and because of that the boys called me "George Washington," so I really didn't need any more help on detracting from my looks. The school had a nurse who worked there all the time and the nurse had her own office; for kids that were sick or hurt she would help them or take their

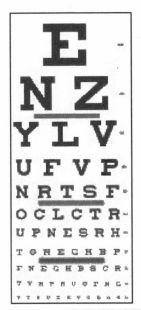

temperature, or let them lie down in her office. She wore a white uniform and a white cap just like the nurses at the doctor's office. The school nurse helped with shots and with eye tests.

Every year the nurse came into the classrooms and each kid had their eyes tested. There was a chart that she put on the blackboard and then she used a pointer to point at the letters and kids would say the letters out loud.

Well, before fourth grade I had just listened to what the kid who went before me said. I could see the biggest letter, and would start there, and then just repeat back what the other kid had said because I was pretty good at memorizing. Fourth grade had been really hard because I was tall and I sat in the back row and in order to see the board I would pull the corners of my eyes up because squinting wasn't good enough to see the board any more. One time I was trying to copy the questions from the kid's paper who sat next to me and he said I was trying to cheat. Like I wanted his stupid answers anyway.

Sheeze!

But this year the nurse started the eye test with the tallest kid instead of the shortest kid. I sat in the back row of tables, which is where the test took place, so all the kids lined up tallest to shortest along the back row. David Trainer was the only person taller than me, but he wasn't there that day so I was first. "Which direction is the big E facing, right or left?" asked the nurse. I took a wild guess; I had a 50/50 chance. "Left," I said. "Very good. Now on the next row, I will point and you tell me which direction the letter E faces each time I point to that letter." Oh great, I couldn't even see the pointer, the chart was a big blur and my eyes had gotten so bad that most people's faces were all blurry too. So I just started saying "left, right, left, right, left…" randomly hoping that I was getting them right.

Well, the room was absolutely silent. I guess the nurse hadn't even started pointing yet. So the nurse said in a very kind and gentle voice, "Just walk a little bit closer to the chart until you can see the second row of letters." I navigated my way up closer and closer, waiting to see the chart clearly. I actually ended up closer than the first row of desks before I could read the second row of letters. She asked me to read the third row, but I couldn't read any more of the chart until I stood about a foot away from it.

The nurse wrote me a note to take home, plus she said that she was going to call my house and tell my mother that I needed to go to an eye doctor because I needed glasses. After the eye test was over for all the kids Mrs. Sharpe, my teacher, switched some students around and put my desk in the front row. When it was time to go home Mrs. Sharpe asked me to stay and said that she wondered why I didn't tell anyone that I couldn't see. I showed her how I could pull the corners of my eyes up to see better and told her that I didn't want glasses anyway. She said that she thought I would be really surprised when I got glasses, that I would like them.

I walked home really slowly that day. I knew I would be in trouble for needing glasses and costing money, but when I got home my mom just said why in the hell didn't I say anything; she thought I was sitting almost under the TV because I couldn't hear, not that I couldn't see, and that probably the scarlet fever had hurt my eyes as well as my ears. I was going to have my eyes tested and then I would have to get glasses. I had never thought about it before, but my mom and all my grammas and my grandpa had glasses too.

I had an eye appointment and we went to the Palo Alto Clinic to get my eyes tested. The clinic was on Homer Avenue in Palo Alto, and was a very old building, Spanish style just like the church out at Stanford University, with a tile roof and archways. There was an entrance to the clinic that was kind of embarrassing, because all around the archway was a painted mural, and it showed a lady at the doctor's office having her lungs listened to,

Section of the Palo Alto Clinic Mural. It was painted by Victor Arnautoff, a student of Diego Rivera

and the doctor had his coat on but the lady was naked from the waist up, just painted there forever sitting on the table in the doctor's office for the entire world to see her without anything covering up her top parts. Why in the heck did they choose that to paint when kids had to walk under it and everyone could see it? They might have just as well have just painted a bare-butted little kid running through the waiting room with a big old doctor chasing after her...it might have been just as embarrassing but a lot more funny!

My mom and I and Jennifer went to the clinic for my eye test. It was in a different part than the kids would usually go, and of course there were *Reader's Digest* to read. Was I ever going to escape reading all those survival stories? But I couldn't read them that day, because after the first eye test I had drops put in my eyes and I had to sit in a dark room without reading for a long time, and then the doctor took me into the eye test room and shone a really bright light into each eye, and said, "Look over in the corner," and it was weird because without ever having seen the back of my eye I could tell that I was seeing a reflection of the back of my eye, and it looked like what I imagined it would if I could see an eye under a microscope.

After that part, the doctor had me wait some more and then I sat in this special chair where I looked through glasses over and over again while the doctor said, "Is this one better....or...is this one better...or....is this one better?" until I had found the best ones. Then he wrote something on a piece of paper and went out and gave the paper to my mom, and gave me a special pair of flexible glasses that looked like they were made of camera film that had not been developed. Those were for me to wear while my eyes were still dilated, to protect my eyes when I went outside, and then he made me promise not to look at the sun or anything bright for the rest of the day because my eyes were dilated. Like I was going to stare at the sun or something! My eyes felt kind of heavy and weird and stingy, but at least the eye test was over.

Then instead of catching the bus at the regular bus-stop corner and going home, we walked over to University Avenue to the Peninsula Optical Company. That was where I was going to get my glasses. I hoped that at least they had something with rhinestones or big wings on them, as long as I was going to wear glasses. But they didn't. The whole store had shelves and shelves of eyeglass frames, just the frames with no lenses. The walls were covered with rows of frames! But they had about four pairs of kid's glasses to choose from and they all looked like boy's glasses: They were squarish and brown or black. Very ugly. But that's what there was. I tried all of them on, and the man there kept asking what did I think about that pair, what did I think about the other pair? Well, first of all my eyes were still dilated, second of all I needed glasses so I couldn't really see what I looked like in the mirror, third of all they were glasses and they all looked ugly! But of course I didn't say that. So my mom and the glasses man selected a frame for me. The man measured my eyes, and the distance that my eyes were apart, and all sorts of other things, and wrote it all down on a card that had my name on it, and said that the glasses would be ready in about a week or less, they would call when they were ready.

We walked over to Woolworth's and got a 1000-piece jigsaw puzzle that was a photograph of the Matterhorn Mountain with a lot of clouds around it and a village with flowers and goats at the base of the Matterhorn. I loved any new puzzle box, how the box was all sealed up tightly and when it was shaken you could hear all of those pieces inside the box just waiting to be put together!

We took the bus home. One thing that Palo Alto had was a bus system; it was the city's system, separate for any county system. And the bus went right down Louis Road. The bus stop was on the corner of Loma Verde and Louis, but all a person had to do was stand on any corner of a street that the bus went down and the bus driver would stop for them. Riding the bus was fun because when you paid your money there was a machine on legs that was fastened to the floor next to where the bus driver sat, almost like a gum-ball machine, and it was see-through, so a person could watch the money go clickety-clack through the machine until all the coins were sorted out and a ticket would come out the bottom of the machine.

Once inside the bus you could see a lot because you were up higher than in a car. And whenever you wanted to stop, there was a rope that hung from the bus ceiling that any person could pull; it would ring a bell and the bus driver would stop at the next corner. Most families only had one car, so even if the mom drove, there was no car around during the week for her to drive, so the buses usually had a lot of people on them. We could go anywhere we wanted to in Palo Alto on the bus: The Clinic, the library, and downtown University Avenue.

My glasses were ready on a Friday, so we picked them up on Saturday on the way to Penny Mayfair, only now it was just called the Mayfair Market. We parked the car on University Avenue and the whole family went in together for me to get my glasses. The man acted like he had never even seen me before, and took the paper receipt from my mom and went into the back and came out like he was an official or something, and had me sit down at a little table with mirror on it and then he opened up the glasses and put them on me.

The whole world changed. I guess I had forgotten what it was like to see clearly. I could read a sign all the way across the room. I didn't even want to look in the mirror. The man finished making adjustment on my glasses, and showed me how to clean them and let me pick out my own glasses case. I picked out one that had a whole bunch of different colors on it. When we left and were walking back to the car my feet looked weird, like I wasn't quite sure where to put them because the ground looked so different than usual. Judy was making faces at me and pretending to laugh, but doing it so she wouldn't get caught. "Four-eyes," she whispered.

The trip to San Carlos was amazing. I had forgotten what it was like to see leaves on the trees and to see blades of grass. I had forgotten how so many things really looked because I was so used to everything being one big smeary blur. I could read store signs and see things far away. But after a while I had seen so many things that I took my glasses off so that I could just see things how I was used to them.

That night when we drove home down El Camino I could read every neon sign and I took my glasses off again. I liked how the signs looked all smeary in the dark, like magical colors with dazzles twinkling around them. I felt sorry for people who could not take off their glasses when it was night time and they were in the car on El Camino Real. I had the better of two worlds now that I had glasses.

One thing that I hated doing every week was cleaning the bird cage. We had a bird named George, who was a blue parakeet who lived in a cage that was in our living room. I don't know how I got nominated, but every week I had to clean that cage, which meant sliding out the bottom tray of the cage, taking out the dirty crappy newspaper from the week before that was on the bottom of the cage and then folding a clean sheet of newspaper so that it fit just right in the cage bottom. Then I had to put in clean water and seed, which I **hated** because that meant opening the cage door and putting in my hand. George would fly around and then bite me. No matter what, I always got bit. And his feet felt creepy when they landed on my finger and he would nibble my finger. Yuck! If I had a hang nail then

George would pull and tug at it and try to tear it off and sometimes he succeeded.

It was also my job to cover up the cage at night with a towel and then uncover it in the morning. One morning when I came down and uncovered the cage, George was hanging upside down from the little swing inside his cage. He had died in the night probably holding onto his perch and just flipped around. I wished that I had gotten to see that happen, and I was kind of glad that George was dead because I would not have to clean his cage any more. I started thinking about how it must have looked when that bird swung down, and wondered did he swing back and forth, back and forth? George had kind of flipped the bird!

I tried to look appropriately distraught when I made the announcement that George had died, even though I was secretly happy. I ran into the kitchen and dramatically yelled, "George is dead, George is dead!" and everyone jumped up to go look. My mom actually started to cry, and then so did Judy, then Jennifer, and pretty soon I did too, just because they were all crying. My daddy took George out of the cage in put him in a paper bag to bury him. I was coveting the feet, wondering how I could sneak the feet off that bird and make a necklace real sneakily without anyone noticing. Bird feet. It was my chance for that Indian necklace that I had wanted so much, but I decided that I hadn't really liked George enough to wear his feet, and my daddy had had a difficult time getting George off the perch because George's little feet had already stiffened up around the perch.

Then my mom announced that because we **all** missed George so much that we would get another bird and that Janey would still have a bird to care for! I didn't want another bird to take care of, but we drove to Monette Pet Shop in Palo Alto and got another stupid bird, another blue parakeet and named it Perky and it was even meaner than George had been!

Mrs. Orris was still the principal at Palo Verde. She had been there ever since the school opened. She looked very old-fashioned, like a Kansas grandmother would look like; she wore the style of shoes that old ladies wore, the brown leather shoes that had laces and a short high heel that was fat, plus she always wore solid-colored dark dresses that were several inches below her knees.

But we all liked Mrs. Orris because she was nice to the students and she liked her job. During the summer between fourth and fifth grades Mrs. Orris told my mom that the teachers were having a summer luncheon. Mrs. Orris asked my mom if I could help clean up after the luncheon, so when my mom told me about it I said, "Sure."

Mrs. Orris said I and a friend would each get paid three dollars for cleaning up after the luncheon! I asked Marie if she wanted to help, so the two of us felt pretty proud that we were trusted enough to help out the principal. It was a big responsibility.

When the day came there was a **humongous** mess to clean up! There must have been 30 people who had eaten in the teacher's lounge and had then moved out to the school library to talk and to plan the next year. The teacher's lounge was very nice; it had a double sink, a refrigerator and a stove, and a big glass window that looked out on to the patio and grass area that was behind the lower-grade wing. There was a door out to the patio, and lots of trees which provided shade.

All of the dirty dishes were in the lounge; all the silverware, and all of the pot-luck leftovers from their meal. We set to work, putting away leftovers, wiping off the tables and washing and drying all the dishes.

Someone had brought red *Jell-O* with canned fruit inside of it, and a can of whipped cream to go with it. Somebody else had brought green *Jell-O* with cottage cheese inside of it and a can of whipped cream to go with it also. The green *Jell-O* salad had a lot left over, and had started to kind of melt, and it looked like something disgusting, like throw-up. Marie and I started teasing each other about the two *Jell-O*s and how disgusting they looked, and then started trying to get each other to clean the *Jell-O*s up. And then one of us grabbed a whipped cream can and started squirting the other one; who knows why, we just started squirting each other with the cans of whipped cream!

When Mrs. Orris walked in, Marie was hunkered down under the big table, alternating standing up and taking whipped cream pot shots at me while hiding under the table, and I was running around squirting the whipped cream at Marie as fast as I could. Whipped cream was everywhere! Marie and I had managed to cover ourselves and a lot of that lounge more than you would think possible!! Maybe they made whipped cream differently in those days; it sure did squirt a long ways.

Jennifer in kindergarten, Jane a fourth-grade Girl Scout

Breathless and laughing, Marie and I looked up, stunned to see Mrs. Orris in the doorway of the lounge. She stood there, slowly looking over the room, taking it all in; whipped cream on the floor, the table, the refrigerator, both of us girls, whipped cream just about every where. Time stood still.

"Well girls," she said. "It looks like you will have quite a bit more cleaning up to do before you earn your three dollars!" And with that she turned around and left the room, but not before Marie and I could see the beginning of a laugh on her face; and then Marie and I were laughing again as soon as Mrs. Orris left the lounge.

I think it took the two of us about four more hours to get the lounge and all the dishes and platters and trays and utensils cleaned up, but we did, and after Mrs. Orris inspected our work we each got the promised three dollars, and I could buy the next book in the *Little House on the Prairie* series!

Jane 9, Jennifer 6 — Weekend cooling off

The Town Changes

Oregon Avenue in Palo Alto was being widened out. It would no longer be an avenue but would become an expressway. That meant all the homes on one side of the street were either being torn down or moved somewhere else.

The first time we saw a house being moved down Louis Road we could not believe our eyes! One kid had seen it from a long ways away, and pretty soon everyone, all the kids and their parents, were outside standing in the street, looking. There was a house coming down the middle of the street! The house was as wide as the whole street, and it was moving really slowly, with two city trucks in front of it with their lights flashing. You can't imagine how weird it looked as the house came up over the creek bridge and got nearer and nearer.

The house was on a special truck and was very low, riding close to the street. The special truck was like a gigantic flatbed truck. It was moving so slowing that if a kid was skipping next to it then they would be going the same speed as that house was moving! A crowd of people were walking next to and behind that house, because it was amazing to see a house come down the street...it took up the whole street.

For the next year there was at least one house a month that came up the street. And some of the houses had been cut in two! You would see one half of the house go by, and be able to look right into the inside of the house, and then there would be a second truck with the other half of the house, and you could see right inside that half too.

And each time a cut-apart house went by we would joke that we hoped there was no one inside the house taking a shower or going to the bathroom. Because everyone could look right into their house, and see the bathroom and the living room!

After about a year we were hardly excited any more when a house went by. But we knew where the houses had gone and after they put them on the ground and fastened the two pieces together and put plants all around, no one would be able to look at one of those houses and know they had been moved, because they just looked like regular houses. Only the people who had watched them going down the street and followed the moving homes knew where they had gone, plus the people who owned the house.

Bloody Fifth Grade

Summer between fourth and fifth grade was almost over. In those days school didn't start until the second week in September, so we really had three full months off for summer, from the middle of June until the middle of September.

My parent's wedding anniversary is September 8th, and that summer we girls decided to bake an anniversary cake and surprise my parents. My parents went out two times a year: The annual Christmas dance held by my daddy's bank, and their anniversary in September. Usually my mom made a new dress for the Christmas dance (and got to wear it unless someone cut the sleeve off) and then she made a new dress for their anniversary date. Because this was such a special day we made some big plans for a surprise.

I went to the market at Middlefield Road and Loma Verde and bought a yellow cake mix and some powdered sugar. Then I went to my girlfriend Christine's house. Christine was in on the whole plan, and we were baking the cake at her house and then sneaking it back to my house.

Baking the cake was successful! It didn't burn, and we had two beautiful round layers of yellow cake. At home we usually made a sheet cake, not round cakes....it was harder to stack the two layers and have it turn out right. So our plan was to ride our bikes back to my house and sneak the cake into my bedroom and then frost it after my parents left for their evening out. I put one cake layer inside a paper bag and put it in my bicycle basket, and Christine took the other inside a paper bag in her basket and off we went.

There was one rough part of sidewalk that I knew to avoid on the way home, and I was so busy avoiding that patch that I didn't see that someone had left their skates on the sidewalk, and in swerving to avoid the skates I tipped my bike over, scraped up the side of my leg, and the cake tumbled out onto the sidewalk. Oh crap. Another moral dilemma. The cake was barely damaged, and if I threw it away then we wouldn't really have an anniversary cake, because we would only have a measly one-layer cake. If I kept the cake and repaired it then I would be living with the fact that I had served up sidewalk cake. Christine had rushed to my aid, and our eyes met. Sidewalk somewhat-damaged cake or not? We picked up the cake and put it back in the paper bag, and back into my bike basket and headed onward to my house.

I didn't feel very good on the bike ride home. I thought that I was just nervous about sneaking the cake in, and I was upset because my leg was all scraped up and bleeding. When we got to my house Christine and I successfully accomplished our mission of getting both cake layers into my room, safely hidden. My leg was all scrapped up; I needed to wash it off and put some gauze pads on it, so while I was in the bathroom I went ahead and used the toilet. When I went to go pee there was all this bloody stuff in my pants. I didn't know what was happening and I didn't know what to do. I thought that I was dying...I was going to die on my parent's anniversary! Judy was talking to my mom, but for once I had to interrupt. "I think I am dying, there is all this blood in my pants." I was almost crying. I forgot that I had a guest over; I could only stand there in fear of death and wait to hear what my mother said.

My mother said, "Come here," and took me into my parent's room and sat me on the bed and got three little booklets out of her drawer. "Read these," she said, and left me in the room alone with the door closed; I had never in my life been alone in my parent's room. The booklets were all about "Becoming a Woman."

I sat there and read for around a half an hour, and I was so confused and horrified that I didn't know what to think. I got to the part where there was this thing inside me like an upside down pear and that I had eggs inside me and that this bleeding would happen once a month for the rest of my life; I couldn't go swimming when it happened and I couldn't even figure out how to pronounce what all this was called! There were a lot of fashion tips thrown in about what to wear when this happened, including a fashion recommendation that chartreuse green did not go well with anything and that a sleeveless white blouse looked good with a summer tan, but only if your bra straps were securely pinned so as to not slide down your shoulder. Bra straps that showed sent the message that you were the wrong kind of girl. There was a lot of other stuff in the booklets about not kissing boys and about how boys would be more interested now that this awful thing happened.

All of that in one half hour. I felt betrayed by my ten-year-old body. Whatever this was, I was not ready for it. The book said that you were not supposed to swim when this happened, and that you couldn't run or do exercise either. And there I was on the Thursday before fifth grade was going to start, and I was reading for the first time about this awful thing that would happen to me forever and it just seemed like some sort of secret nasty trick.

My mom came back into the room and asked me if I had any questions. I was so full of questions that I didn't know where to start, but I just said, "No." Then my mom opened my parent's closet and on the floor of the closet was a cardboard box, and the outside of the box said "sanitary napkins" and my mom reached inside the box and handed me something that was like a long pad with long skinny strips at each end and told me to go change my panties and safety pin that pad into my panties and that I would get a new pad each morning and night and put the used one all rolled up and wrapped in toilet paper into the bathroom trash can. I was supposed to do that until the blood stopped. I recognized the sanitary napkins from Gramma Gigi's house. We sometimes used them to set our hair! We would wrap our hair around these pads and twist them up and tie them, and I suddenly saw with great clarity why Gramma Gigi would get such a kick out of setting hair with those things. Oh, I thought I would die for sure!

I sat in the bathroom shaking my head. Was this a bad dream? Did this happen to everyone? Had this happened to my sister Judy? Did this happen to Auntie Jan and to Gramma Gigi and to my mom? Was this like a secret society that no one knew about until it happened? The whole thing was way too much for me. I didn't want anything to do with it, this awful thing called a "period," especially having read about what was called cramps inside of girls when this all happened. A period was something at the end of a sentence. None of this was remotely understandable. I just wanted the whole day to start all over again and not drop a cake, not scrape my leg, and not come home and have this awful thing happen to me.

Christine was talking to Judy. They looked up when I came into the room. They knew something was wrong, because I had been gone for almost an hour and we were supposed to be planning the anniversary surprise! But I just said that nothing was wrong, how could I tell them about this whole weird thing when I wasn't even sure what it was? Besides, it was embarrassing. If it wasn't embarrassing, then I should have known about this a long, long time ago!

I just acted like nothing had happened. "Let's figure out what we are going to do tonight!" So we planned out making the frosting and that when my parents got home from their dinner out that we would hide behind the couch and jump up and sing "Happy Anniversary" exactly like it was sung on the *Flintstone's* TV Cartoon! On the *Flintstone's* they had an episode where that song was sung soooo funny, going up really, really high at the end, and then it was repeated faster, then repeated faster again, just sung over and over faster and faster until the singers couldn't sing faster, and that was our plan. It was going to be funny!

That night it seemed like my parents would never leave. They had to give us a billion lectures about what and what not to do and what time to go to bed and what to do in an emergency, as if we were stupid. Grandpa Bob was not babysitting because we girls were older now and my parents were not going to be out very late. They finally left, and Christine and I went and got the cakes out of my room.

The one layer was a bit abused, but it was what we had. We made sure we brushed it off, and then went on to do the frosting. We had ingredients for frosting and there was a new can of whipped cream in the frig. We were making this really fancy! Our frosting was a success! All you did was take soft butter, put it in the mixer and add powdered sugar until the beaters mixed it together perfectly into frosting. We put the bottom layer on a plate – it was the kind of beat up layer and that way no one could really tell - and put the frosting on it, and then put the next layer on top. Our plan was to squirt whipped cream on the outside of the cake for the rest of the frosting. We should have known each other better, because all of us, even Jennifer, used to sneak whipped cream right out of the can when no one else was looking and squirt it right into our mouths and my mom was always saying, "What in the hell happened to all the whipped cream?" So that was what **I** was saying when we ran out of whipped cream about a third of the way through squirting it on the cake.

There we were spreading out the cream; Judy was squirting and I was spreading the whipped cream with a knife, when a fly landed on the whipped cream and before my brain could tell my hand to stop, I had frosted that fly right into the whipped cream! Then we had to go on a fly hunt...moving all the whipped cream around trying to find the fly. We couldn't find the fly, and we didn't have any more whipped cream and we were running out of time!

Judy went over to the Jensen's to see if we could borrow some whipped cream. They weren't home! Then I said we should go over to the Thomas' house and ask them if they had any. You could have heard a pin drop. We were forbidden to talk to or be with the Thomas family even though they lived next door. We didn't know what to do. We didn't have any more powdered sugar or cream. This was becoming a disaster! But I said again that one of us should go next door to the Thomas's and see if we could borrow some powdered sugar or some whipped cream, and we would promise a blood oath to not let my parents know. Christine's house was too far away, and besides, she thought if she went home so late at night that they might not let her out again, plus it was dark.

For some reason Judy volunteered to go next door. Jennifer, Christine and I waited and waited for Judy to come back, and nervously looked at each other, listening through the open back door for any sounds of screaming or murder or something like that. And then Judy was back with a pint of whipping cream in a little carton plus some regular sugar. She said Mrs. Thomas had told her how to make whipped cream in the mixer! We washed the mixer really clean and washed the beaters and put in the cream and slowly added the sugar, and we had the best whipped cream we had ever seen in out lives! We still hadn't found the fly that had been frosted in. So we decided to watch really carefully when we ate our cake, and to look really carefully when my parents ate theirs, and if we saw the fly in their frosting, we would just grab their cake and make a joke about grabbing it. We couldn't figure out anything else to do!

We got the cake frosted and we put 14 candles on the cake for the 14 years my parents had been married. We had matches ready to light the cake and we sat behind the couch waiting to hear them walk in the door. And it all went perfectly! My parents came home, and they seemed happy, us four girls jumped up from behind the couch and sang "Happy Anniversary" until we ran out of breath and were laughing so hard, we went into the kitchen and lit the candles, and my parents were so surprised and blew out the candles, and we all had cake!

I don't think my parents realized how closely each bite they took was watched, nor how we girls scrutinized each of our own bites. I just know that I did not eat the fly!

The next day my mom called me into her room again and gave me this weird elastic thing that she said was a sanitary belt and that I was to put each of the long ends of the sanitary napkin into the little clips on the sanitary belt instead of using safety pins...safety pins were only for emergencies. I was to always carry safety pins now in case I needed them. I went into the bathroom and couldn't make heads or tails of how to get that stupid thing on or how to wear it or how it worked. It was supposed to just go inside your panties, but I ended up putting my arms through the loops and then I couldn't stand up straight and had to lean over when I walked, and after a few minutes of that I just gave up for the day because I figured if I was walking around like that, all leaning over with the big elastic loops over my shoulders everyone who saw me would know. When my mom asked if I had figured it out I said, "Kind of" and then she actually showed me, but I hated wearing it because the metal clasps had pointy things on them and it felt like I was being stabbed all the time.

When school started the following Monday I think I was the only fifth-grade girl who started school that day having the awful period. My mother had passed me a note just before I walked out the door. "If your teacher wants you to run around the field, give him this note." I opened the note on the way to school, and written in my mom's beautiful cursive it had the date in the corner, and was addressed to my new teacher, Mr. Andrews: "Please excuse Jane from physical education." And then it was signed by my mom.

So of course when it got to be P.E. time, my new teacher, Mr. Andrews, clapped his hands and told everyone to go run three laps around the field. I hung back until the room was empty of all the students. Mr. Andrews was telling me to go out and hurry up and catch up with the other kids, but instead I handed him my note. He read the note and then asked me "Why can't you do P.E.?" The whole world stood still and I heard a ringing in my ears and felt like I was spinning around. I looked at him and stammered, "I have a note. I have a note; my mother wrote me a note." And that's all I would say. I would have rather walked over hot coals in my bare feet that have said the word "period" to a man. How could he be so stupid and mean, couldn't he just see that I had a note?

Mr. Andrews went outside with the class and I was stuck on the first day of school wearing this thing that was like a diaper only worse and not being able to run, and I loved to run. I was in a combination class, so there were fifth and sixth graders in the same classroom, and I thought that the sixth-grade boys were looking at me funny. I wasn't sure though.

We had a student teacher. She was very young, maybe about 22 or 23, which was still old, but much younger than our teachers. She was very nice, and she told me something that always stuck with me. I was able to talk to her, and told her how much it hurt when boys teased me about being ugly and being skinny. She said that skinny was really the same as slender. Slender. What a beautiful word. She told me if someone commented about being skinny, to just say, "Thank you! I like being slender!" I never thought that I could do that, but I tried it once and after that it was pretty easy to say! "Thank you! I enjoy being slender!" I felt how an English-second-language learner might have felt, repeating the same phrase each time, but I stood even a bit taller every time I said it.

For Halloween in fifth grade I was a cigarette girl! A cigarette girl was a woman who worked at a hotel or a restaurant or the movies, or any place that people might want to buy cigarettes. She would carry a tray of cigarettes around, and people would buy them from her. Christine let me borrow her skating outfit for my costume. She had a reversible skating outfit that was red on one side and gold on the other side, and it was made of satin, with a tight long-sleeved jacket that stopped at the waist and a very short skating skirt that was really full, so that when someone wore it while skating and twirled around the skirt would spin out straight. It included tiny shorts as part of the skirt! So I had the outfit, and we made a tray for carrying cigarettes from a big box lid, and made a strap for the tray with some ribbon, so that the ribbon went around my neck to help hold the tray, which I held with my hands anyway. I had gloves and a little beret hat. And some fancy shoes I borrowed from another friend.

I got candy cigarettes to fill my tray; that was the finishing touch to my costume. In those days all the stores sold candy cigarettes, and they were imitations of the real cigarettes, because the candy box was almost exactly like a real cigarette brand, with maybe one letter that was different. Our favorite candy cigarettes were the ones that made it look like you were really smoking. There were some that had a tiny tube in the middle of the cigarette, and the tube had powdered sugar that was very, very fine, so that instead of sucking on the cigarette when you pretended to smoke, a kid would gently blow into the cigarette, and the fine sugar came out from the end and looked just like smoke! All the kids loved candy cigarettes. They had one end that was a tiny bit red so that it looked like the glowing end of a real cigarette!

When I went to the first house to go trick-or-treating the man that opened the door didn't know what to think. I looked a lot older than a 10-year old anyway, and he looked at me and asked. "Are those **real** cigarettes?!" I said "No, this is my costume!"

Later I wondered what that man had been thinking...did he think I was a real cigarette girl selling real cigarettes, or had he just been trying to be funny?

Candy cigarettes like the ones any kid could buy when I was growing up

One day the student teacher was there, and Mr. Andrews was not. The student teacher was out on the playground with us, actually out on the field, and she was talking to another adult.

I decided to skin-the-cat on the backstop. The backstop was the big chain-link section of fence behind home plate on the baseball part of the field. It kept the ball from going further down the field after the catcher missed catching it. This tall fence was held up at both sides by other pieces of metal that stuck out at an angle, resting on the ground and shaped like the capital letter "A" on its side. There was so much space between the top of the bar and the bottom of the bar that a kid could skin-the-cat on those side supports.

I was doing skin-the-cat, spinning around and around, when I heard the student teacher call my name. I stopped, and she told me that she thought I shouldn't be doing that because I might hurt myself. I had done that a million times before, and wanted to show her it was okay and safe, so I told her, "No, I won't get hurt, watch, you'll see." I don't think she heard me, because she turned around and was taking to the other adult. So I started skinning-the-cat, going around and around the top metal bar. What I didn't know was that the bottom bar, the one resting on the ground, had a screw about 1 ½ inches tall sticking straight up. On what was to be my final spin, I spun around and my head drug over that screw and I cut open an artery in the top of my head.

I stopped spinning around and stood up and put my hand to the top of my head where it felt weird and then pulled my hand back and looked at it. The entire palm of my hand was covered in blood and there was blood dripping down my arm! Already I could feel the blood running down my head and into my ears and it came on my forehead and was running in my eyes and on my glasses. I put my hand up to the top of my head to try and stop it. I didn't know it was an artery and with every heart beat the blood was squirting out.

I kept saying, "Excuse me, Excuse me," to the student teacher because the student teacher was talking to an adult and I wasn't supposed to interrupt, but I finally just took my blood-covered hand and shoved it in the adults' faces! They started screaming, then everyone was screaming, and the student teacher was half-carrying me back to the classroom, and someone yelled for someone to go to the office and call my house.

They half-carried me back to the classroom, and shoved everything off the big table in the back of the classroom near the sink. They helped me get up on the table and had me lay down on my back and stuck a whole pack of paper towels under my head. I saw then that the front of the student teacher's dress was all bloody, there was a trail of blood into the room, and that my sweater sleeve was soaked in blood.

My mom came from home, and she said that all she had to do was follow the trail of blood to find me, and there I was lying on my back on the table with a completely soaked stack of paper towels under my head. My mom didn't drive and the Jensens weren't home, so the school called a taxi to come get us to go to the doctors. They half-carried me to the front of the school, and there was a big crowd of kids, all of them from my classroom and other kids as well, all crowded around.

The first taxi cab driver would not take us. A second driver came, and my mom had to borrow some money from the principal to pay because she didn't have enough money at home. The cab driver drove us to the clinic in downtown Palo Alto, and they took me right away into the doctor's office to stitch me up. I lay down on my stomach on a table that was covered in white wax paper. The doctor had to shave part of the top of my head. My head hurt so bad I thought I would die, and I felt dizzy and sick. I had to lie there really still while my head was stitched up. The doctor tried to give me a shot to take away the pain of the stitches, but he said he couldn't because it was bleeding too much. So I lay still while I got stitched up, and the blood ran into my eyes and my face and my ears.

Finally the bleeding stopped. I lay there in pain. And then I could get up, the nurse was helping me up, and I could see the table where I had been laying. What I saw made me almost faint, because on the white wax paper where my hands had been there were two perfectly white hand prints surrounded by blood that had thickened and molded around my hands, so that when I had picked up my hands there was jelled blood all around where they had been. Never, never, after that was I able to look at tomato aspic salad without thinking of that bloody paper-covered table.

We took another cab home. I didn't feel good. I went in my dark room and lay down, but not before my mom made me take off my sweater. The back of my gray wool sweater was completely red-brown, soaked in blood. I could see the blood where it had ran down my sweater almost completely covering the back. The sleeves were the same. I lay there in the dark, hurting, until I went to sleep with a head throbbing in pain.

I had to be awakened every two hours and my eyes checked to see if the pupils were the same size or not. That lasted for one day of hardly sleeping; getting woken up every two hours and a flashlight shone in my eyes. I didn't have a concussion, because my pupils matched each other in size.

I stayed home for several days. I guess the rumors at school grew and grew until some kids thought I had died. Someone said the janitor had complained about having to clean up that day, because blood was everywhere.

My head hurt for days and I could hardly even stand up. I finally did get to take a bath but I couldn't wash my hair for ten days until I went back to have the stitches taken out.

I had my long hair full of stinky dried blood and I had a circle on the top of my head that was shaved off from when the doctor had made the stitches. Plus it turned out that the stitches on the inside were cat gut and I was allergic to them, so they were getting infected and working their way out through the skin. After ten days I had to go back to the doctor to get my stitches removed, and that hurt and felt weird all at the same time. For many years I had a place on the top of my head where there was a rough bump over an indentation. Finally it became just a bump over an indentation.

Skinning-the-cat had been so much fun. I wasn't used to the big body I had developed, the 5' 3" tall ten-year-old with a 32B bra and size seven shoe all in fifth grade. I was the biggest girl in school but inside I was still a little girl. I had to get my hair cut and styled because of the shaved part on the top of my head. I usually wore my hair parted down the middle and braided into two braids. But now I had this shaved part where the new hair was starting to stick straight up like a little crew cut on the top of my head. There was a beauty shop at Midtown Market where my mom would go a few times a year if my parents were going somewhere special. The shop was called

"John and Reed." Before I went there I had my hair washed and combed at home, and my picture was taken from the back showing my long hair. This was the "before" picture. Then I had my hair braided for the last time.

Me in cut-offs in from of my mom's rose garden – just before my hair cut

Age 10

My mom and I took the bus to the hair stylist. My mom had talked to them when she made the appointment and told them what had happened and what needed to be done. Before I cut my head open I couldn't have short hair because it wasn't really lady-like, even though a lot of the girls were getting short hair. We had a new girl at school named Nancy, and she had short hair in a cut called an "artichoke." The artichoke was a lot of layers and was short, and Nancy was really cute and all the girls wanted their hair cut in an artichoke too.

When we got to the hair salon, I sat down and they cut my braids off as close to my ears as they could while still leaving enough hair that they could style. That was my daddy's request; he wanted to have my braids. They put rubber bands at the top of my cut-off braids and put them in a box, and I took them home with me. My daddy always kept my braids in his drawer.

My new hair style

I got my hair cut in an artichoke. The hair stylist assured my mom that it was appropriate and that all the girls were getting their hair cut like that. I tried to watch in the mirror to see how my hair was being cut, but they made me take off my glasses during the hair cut and I couldn't see a thing! I could feel them cut and cut and comb and spray water, all the while talking and chatting and non-stop discussing everything from Marilyn Monroe to the president to baseball to fashion and nail polish and so many topics it made my head swim! Then they set my hair in rollers when the cutting part was done, and I sat under a hair dryer, which was warm and then pretty hot and noisy and made me feel pretty safe like I could just go to sleep there!

When I look at that "before" picture now, I see a girl in red tennis shoes and shorts with beautiful blondish-reddish-brown hair several inches past her waist; it is hard to believe this is a 10-year old. The "after" photo shows the same girl but in a dress, looking very mature and stylish and uncomfortable.

Our class got to go on a roller-skating party! There was a roller skating rink in Redwood City, and two classrooms from Palo Verde took a school bus there for a party, the sixth-grade class and the fifth-sixth combination class that I was in. We got to rent special roller skates made just for indoor skating, and skated on the smooth wooden floor. There was a man talking on a microphone about what kind of skating to do, music was playing, and everyone was skating around and having fun! Some of the kids could even skate backwards, and the man would stop the music and say things like, "Our next skate is a backwards skate," and then those people who knew how to skate backwards would go out and skate. It was fun to watch, and exciting, and everyone was having a whole lot of fun.

Christine and Marie and I were skating together, just laughing and holding hands and going fast. Then the man with the microphone said it was a "couple's skate" and for the boys to ask a girl to skate. Christine, Marie and I couldn't get off that skating floor fast enough, because we didn't want some creepy boy to ask us to skate, but I guess I wasn't fast enough, because the tallest sixth-grade boy, a boy named Paul that all the girls thought was cute, came and asked me to skate. Before I knew it, he and I were holding hands and skating around to the music and going faster and faster around the skating rink!

Then disaster struck! Somehow our feet got tangled up and we both tripped and fell down. I fell on my back and he fell down on top of me and his face was right over my face! "Please God, Strike me dead right now because if you do not I am going to die of embarrassment anyway…" was my fervent prayer as I lay there, my eyes closed for that seeming eternity when time stood still.

But God did not do me the favor, and as I opened my eyes and struggled to get up, I realized to my absolute and total horror that my skates and Paul's skates had inexplicably become tangled together in a way that made it impossible for either one of us to move, let alone get up!

Everyone in the whole rink stopped skating and started crowding around us, and the man on the microphone stopped the music and said something like, "Well, folks, it looks like we've had an accident on the rink, so please make some room!"

Paul's face was about one inch from my face, and he was in top of me, and every time we struggled our skates got more tangled up. Mr. Andrews came over and tried to pick up Paul, but that didn't help. I recognized many of the faces staring down at us from above as I lay there on my back. The humiliation went from my head to my heart down to my very toes which were trapped in the tangled-up skates.

Finally someone from the skating office came out with a screwdriver and used the screwdriver to separate our skates. I didn't even want to look that horrible boy in the eyes again, but he still asked me to skate and they started the music up again and we skated over to the entrance part and then I told him I didn't want to skate with him any more ever again in my entire life, and with what little dignity I could muster I exited the rink and took off the wretched skates.

On the way home on the bus Marie and Christine and I shared a seat. They kept looking at me strangely and I overheard hear the sixth-grade boys teasing Paul that he had a girlfriend. I felt like crying but didn't. I hated stupid boys.

There were two girls from the sixth-grade class who used to lie in wait for me after school. They were not in my fifth/sixth combination class, so I didn't really know them. They would tease me and follow me and make my walk home miserable. I wasn't sure why they chose me, but when I walked home I knew they would be waiting right behind the multipurpose room to follow me and walk right behind me and call me "ugly" and "four eyes" and one day they beat me up after school just because there were two of them and one of me. I fought back pretty well, but they both were strong and pretty aggressive fighters.

Then the next day they were waiting for me again, and beat me up again. This happened for the whole week, and I was sure that sooner or later they would finish me off. But then the next day when they were waiting, they said they wanted to talk to me, and they handed me a note and went running off.

I opened up the note and read it on the way home:

Dear Jane,

We are sorry we beet you up all the time and promouse not to do it agan. We wood like to be your frends.

Abby and Lorraine

I was astounded, and also baffled. Was this a trick? But the note really bothered me, and I went home, found a red pencil, and corrected all their misspellings. I acted just like a teacher, and circled the mistakes, and wrote "sp" inside a circle and then wrote the correct spelling above the misspelled word.

Dear Jane,

We are sorry we beet you up all the time and promouse not to do it agan. We wood like to be your frends.

Abby and Lorraine

If I was going to get a note of apology, I wanted it right.

The next day both girls were waiting again for me, and when I got near they asked if I had read their note. I said that I had and that I couldn't believe they were in sixth grade and were so stupid that they thought "beat" was spelled "beet" and didn't they know "beet" was a vegetable? And I threw their note back at them and told them I had corrected their mistakes and if they were going to write me a note it should be done right!

Well, that got me another beating, because those two girls couldn't believe that I did that. But they took the note with all my corrections with them after they beat me up.

The next day they were waiting again, only this time they said they were sorry and asked if I would help them with their school work, because they knew I was smart and they had beat me up because I was always showing off how smart I was. I told them if they corrected their note and did it properly then I would help them. Abby was the girl who really meant it, that she wanted to learn, and the next day she brought me a new note that was done perfectly.

That began a friendship with Abby that lasted many years. Her house was much different than ours; there were never any adults around, and her older sister would be on the couch with her boyfriend, and maybe he would be helping Abby's sister shave her legs, and there was a lot of loud music, and a bunch of people helping themselves to what was in the refrigerator and teenage boys were all hanging out and a whole lot of people were being loud and funny and smoking and sometimes drinking beer. They all called me "four-eyes" but when they said it, it wasn't mean; it sounded funny because they liked me. Abby's brother said he was glad that I was helping her study because Abby would be smart if she just had someone explain things to her. I loved being a teacher, and Abby loved being taught. And I was starting to learn a lot of things as well.

Looking for Another House

There were five of us living in our three-bedroom house, which sounds okay, but there were two small bedrooms and one medium-sized bedroom, and my parents got one of the two small bedrooms, and I shared the medium sized bedroom with one sister or the other. That meant ever since Jennifer had been born I had always shared a room. First of all I shared with Judy, but then she and I were too big to share and were fighting all the time, and then Jennifer and I shared a room, and Judy had her own room.

Judy and I would fight like wild animals and were driving my parents crazy. With three girls it was always two against one, and the two would gang up on the third. And the players changed constantly, so it might be Judy and me against Jennifer, or Jennifer and Judy against me, or Jennifer and me against Judy. But unless the three of us had something to unite us, like we were hiding something from our parents or planning a surprise for them, or we had been so bad that we had to unite to hide evidence and get our story straight, business as usual meant two against one. Finally my parents decided that we needed a bigger house, because they did not look forward to three teen-aged girls in our small house.

It had been seven years since my parents bought their house, which was long enough for the trees to grow, a tall fence to be built, and for the rose garden to get established. We had a healthy vegetable garden, beautiful planter boxes and shaded front and back porches. But we were getting cramped in our bungalow that had seemed bigger when we kids were all small.

So we started looking. Looking at houses was interesting; we would find a house for sale that one person liked and one person hated. These were not new houses, but houses that had people living in them that were for sale. There was one two-story house that we all really liked, but it was too expensive. We would go look at houses in the evening after dinner, and on the weekends. Pretty soon it seemed like we had looked at every house in Palo Alto that was for sale, and then my parents decided that it didn't make sense to move us three girls to another school or to get new neighbors, or pack up and move all our stuff; we should just add onto the house that we already had.

My parents started talking about how we would like our house to be. It was exciting, because we got to draw sketches and ideas and share thoughts, and because we had looked at so many other houses, all of us had ideas of what we would like in our remodeled house!

My daddy had gone to college to be an architect when my parents had lived in Kansas. That's when my parents were living in a Masonite trailer in a trailer park that was full of young couples who had gotten married after the war, and all the couples had one or two little babies, and they would hang the clean laundry out in the cold and the laundry would freeze dry and sometimes the water inside of their trailer would freeze! The trailer was eight feet wide and sixteen feet long, and they lived there with Baby Judy, but ended up staying in the Bay Area when they came out to show Baby Judy to Gramma Gigi and Grandpa Bob. So Daddy never finished his architect training, but now that we were remodeling he was excited to be using his architect drawing skills, and all the drawing tools he had kept since college. Even though the city required that a professional architect submit the plans for the remodel, Daddy got to do a lot of the rough drawings, and my parents planned together how they wanted our "new" house to be. They had a friend who was an architect, and their friend did the final plans.

We were going to add a second story to the house! We didn't know any one who had remodeled their house, but we made great plans. We would have the front of the house extended out and make a bigger living room, a bigger kitchen, and upstairs there would be two bedrooms and a bathroom and a bigger attic with a full-sized door at the top of the stairs to enter the attic! This was so exciting! We girls did less fighting and became friendlier with each other, just knowing that we would one day have our own rooms.

The one sad part was that my mom's rose garden in the front of the house was where our new living room would be. My mom grew beautiful roses, and people walking down the street would stop and look at the roses and admire them. You could smell the roses a few houses away. When it was the season for the roses to bloom we always had roses inside the house; I would sneeze my head off because I had so many allergies, but it was nice to have flowers in the house. I would tell my mom that it was my turn to take flowers to school, and she would cut a big bouquet for me to take to school, and then I would tell my teacher that my mom had sent in flowers from her garden, and the teacher would put the flowers in a vase on her desk and everyone liked them. I thought if I just asked for the flowers my mom would say, "No," so I would just tell her that it was my turn.

Then my parents had to hire a contractor. For a few weeks there were a lot of people coming to the house until my parents picked out the people that they liked to work with, and who would let my parents do much of the work themselves, because the more that my parents did of the work, the cheaper the costs would be.

We had so many new things planned: Two more bedrooms and another bathroom, so we would have five bedrooms and two bathrooms and a second story! We would have a dishwasher, and a built-in stove with a built-in fan, and a gas range with a hood over it. The hood would have a light and a fan. And the kitchen would have a lot of cupboards, and would be much bigger, because we were knocking out the wall between the kitchen and dining room and making a big kitchen.

We were even going to have a refrigerator with an ice-maker built right into it! One change would be that we had one less door going outside to the backyard. We had a kitchen door that went out to the patio, and we also had a dining room door that went out to the patio, but combining the two rooms into one big room meant that the dining room door would now be the door for the new kitchen.

We had a cat named Bootsie. He was an old grey tom cat with really long fur. In those days a lot of cats were wild and there used to be a lot of cat fights, like in the cartoons where the cat would howl on the fence at the moon. Bootsie wasn't really allowed into our rooms because he had fleas and it was hell trying to get rid of fleas in the house, but he was allowed to come inside for his dinner. We didn't buy cans of cat food; I don't even know if they sold cans of pet food then. My parents would buy horse meat at the regular grocery store and cut it up and give it to the cat, and no one thought anything about it.

We had this habit that when Bootsie rattled the screen door to come inside that Jennifer had to answer the back door and let Bootsie in. Our screen doors were ones that Daddy had made, and they had a wooden frame with the screen inside of the frame, so when Bootsie wanted his dinner he would start climbing the screen and hang there and shake the door, and my daddy would say, "Let the darn cat inside because he is ripping up the screen and I'm tired of replacing the screen!" Around dinner time, Jennifer would listen for the cat at the kitchen door, and when she heard the screen door rattle she would go to the door and say, "Hello, my name is Jennifer Lee Richter, come in stupid!" And she always said that to the cat because she insisted that if she didn't say it the cat would not come inside!

Well, when we had our remodel in progress we no longer had a front door, because the front of the house was all torn up with plywood and sheets of plastic hanging over the new openings. But we also had a paperboy who would come every month to get paid for delivering the paper.

Paperboys rode their bikes, delivered the paper, and then came around each month to get paid by at each customer on their route. Most people would give them a tip, because they knew the paperboy personally and also because they wanted the paper delivered properly, and tipping the paperboy helped a lot.

One night Jennifer heard Bootsie at the kitchen door, and she opened up the door the way she always did and without really looking outside in the dark she said, "Hello, my name…is…Jennifer…Lee…Richter…come…in…s.t.u.p.i.d…?" Then she screamed and ran into her room, because she saw it was the paperboy!

The paperboy did not know what to think when Jennifer opened the door and said her name, invited him in and then called him stupid! We all laughed and laughed. The only way the paperboy could come to ask for his money was by coming to the kitchen door, and Jennifer had thought he was the cat.

Years later I went to a prom with that same boy; I was in junior high and he was in high school. He still remembered that night; we laughed about how funny that had been.

Sixth Grade

I had a man teacher for my last year in elementary school.

This would be my third time to have a man for a teacher. In sixth grade I had Mr. Burns for my teacher. He had been a summer recreation leader for a long time, he and his family went to the Congregational Church just like our family, plus he rode his bike past our house a lot, so I felt like I already knew him. He had taught for many years in other Palo Alto schools and lived in Palo Alto a few blocks from Palo Verde.

We had (whisper) sex education in sixth grade. The boys went to the office or some other room, and saw a movie, and the girls stayed in our classroom; the school nurse came in and talked to us and then we saw a movie. We big kids couldn't all fit into the Audio Visual Room anymore, and besides, the school now had several projectors on carts with wheels, so we could watch movies right in our classrooms. The movie was in black and white and was so old that it was all scratchy. It was a cartoon version of a sperm and an egg meeting and then a baby growing in nine months, and the word "pregnant" was used as well as "sperm." It showed that pear-like thing inside a woman and called it a uterus, and said the word menstruation. Why did all those words sound so weird? I guess because in real life no one ever said them.

Then the boys came back and we saw a movie with the girls and boys together, and then Mr. Burns did a question-and-answer session. I could answer every question he asked, especially that it took nine months to make a baby, but there was one question that no one asked and that I was afraid to ask: When two people kissed how did the sperm get from the man's lips down to inside the woman's body so that the baby could grow? I was pretty worried about this, because Abby's sister was always kissing her boyfriend.

Mr. Burns then talked about next year when we would be in seventh grade and in junior high school. He said he did not want to hear about any of us making out behind the bleachers, because that would lead to trouble. I couldn't believe that Mr. Burns knew the words "making out," and that he would say them right in school. Making out was what you did to get that sperm stuff ready to make a baby and who did he think we were to want to go behind bleachers and do whatever he was talking about?

My girlfriends and I whispered about it later. One girl said that making out meant kissing, but another girl said that it really meant taking off all your clothes and lying together naked. The whole thing made no sense at all and we didn't know why they were telling us all this embarrassing stuff. The boys were all in groups too, talking with each other, but boys were stupid and when we walked by them they said stupid things like, "Let's go make out, come on..." Fortunately I had practiced my disdainful look for years and it was easy to just walk past the boys and pretend that I didn't see them or hear them. But now I started worrying about what if someone tried to make out with me behind the bleachers. I wasn't sure what it was, so I just figured I better stay away from the bleachers.

I tried asking Abby about all of this stuff, but she just kind of laughed and said not to even think about it. Abby was already in junior high, but she was still my friend. I would help her do her homework...it was really easy and when we did it together, she thought it was easy too. One day at her house a different sister of Abby's was there. This sister was already married, but she had come back to live at the house with her family because her husband beat her up. Abby's sister's face was a real mess, all swollen up and black and blue, and one eye was completely bloodshot. I looked at her and felt sick. I figured it out then, that if you hit someone in the face everyone would be able to see what you had done, but if you hit them other places, no one would know about it.

Christmas in sixth grade was odd. Christmas Eve Day my mom always made a lot of food, because Auntie Jan and Grandpa Bob and Gramma Gigi would come to our house for Christmas and people ate all day long, and in the afternoon we girls might go to our friends house for a while to see what presents they had received, and maybe then our friends might come to our house to see what we got. Christmas Eve Day my mom was making one of the *Jell-O* salads that she would make every year. It had shredded cabbage, lemon *Jell-O*, pimientos and some other stuff. My mom had a machine that she used for shredding vegetables; a different machine than the one she used to grind meat. Both machines were similar in that the food was pushed into the top of a sharp wheel that fastened to a handle that turned with one hand while the food was pushed onto the sharp blades with the other hand. The one my mom used for vegetables was easy to turn by hand and went very fast. She was pushing the chunks of cabbage into the blades when she got her thumb caught in the spinning blades.

She was bleeding like crazy. Fortunately my daddy and Grandpa Bob were both there, so Daddy drove her to the clinic and the doctor needed to sew 22 stitches to close up the bad cut.

My mom had a huge bandage on her thumb, made of gauze that was wrapped around and around, and she had to hold her thumb up all the time.

Grandpa Bob had been at the house that day because he was helping Daddy take stucco off the side of the house; stucco is like cement or concrete that is put on the very outside of the house. The frame of a house would be made of wood, and then there would be tar paper, chicken wire, then the stucco, which would dry hard just like cement. The chicken wire was inside of the layer of stucco and it made it stronger.

To take the stucco off, Daddy and Grandpa Bob would hit and hit the side of the house with a sledge hammer until a crack appeared, and then they would use a crowbar to wedge into that crack until the crack would get big enough that they could use wire cutters inside the crack to cut the chicken wire which was embedded in the stucco. A sheet of stucco could then be wiggled off the outside of the house. The plan that day was to get all the stucco off the part of the house where the addition would go, and to then take all that stucco to the dump.

Grandpa Bob and Daddy had been working all Christmas Eve Day long, except for taking my mom to the clinic for her stitches. And then a piece of stucco came off too early, and my daddy's thumb was in the way of the falling stucco, stucco which had chicken wire hanging from it. The stucco and chicken wire grabbed my daddy's thumb and all of a sudden he was bleeding like crazy! Daddy wrapped his hand up in his t-shirt, which was turning red from blood and he was yelling, "I'm okay, it's all right, just bring me a Band-Aid!"

Grandpa Bob drove Daddy to the clinic. The nurse on duty had to phone the doctor because the doctor was at a Christmas Eve party. When she told him that Mr. Richter was there to have his thumb stitched up, the doctor thought that the nurse was joking. He was the same doctor who had stitched up my mom that morning! The doctor came from his party to stitch up my daddy's thumb, and Daddy and Grandpa Bob said it was the only time they ever saw a doctor wearing a tuxedo stitch someone up!

Daddy had 25 stitches on his left thumb, with a huge gauze bandage all around his thumb, and he had to hold it up all the time too.

Christmas looked like this: I was taking up the entire couch, lying down because I had double pneumonia and had been sick for two weeks already. I felt horrible and it hurt to breathe. Auntie Jan had been in a car wreck and had a cast on her broken leg, so she had crutches and her leg had to rest on the hassock, which was our big, soft foot stool. Auntie Jan was sore all over and had bandages and a lot of bruises all over. My parents were sitting in chairs, holding up opposite thumbs, each thumb with a huge bandage on it.

Then Auntie Jan said that she should have gotten a deck of cards for my parents for Christmas, and we all started laughing! With the two of them having opposite thumbs in big bandages, and having to hold their thumbs up higher than their heart all the time, it would have been impossible for either of them to even try to shuffle a deck of cards. The mental picture of my parents trying to hold cards or shuffle a deck of cards put all of us into fits of laughter, even though with pneumonia I had a hard time laughing.

The remodeling continued, but was delayed a few weeks because of my parents' injuries. When we got to the point that the construction actually started it was very interesting and exciting, because some days we would come home and something big was happening, like when the concrete slab for the living room was poured, or when the frame for the second story stared going up. Our second story was different than anyone else's that we had seen, because above the garage was where the two new bedrooms and the bathroom were going, the stairs were going right next to what now was the garage outside wall, and above the new and old living room was a big new attic, so that the new roof line went to a point above the garage, and then had a really long slant downward across the new attic, so our house would look ultra modern.

Starting to see changes!
The new roof line.

We had the entire front of the house open and the whole second story open with just plastic sheeting to keep out the cold when it snowed. Snow in Palo Alto! We couldn't believe two things: One was that it snowed enough to make a little snowman, and the other was that our house was all opened up when it snowed! It was a Sunday morning and I didn't want to get up for church, so I thought that my family was teasing me when they kept saying that there was snow outside. I thought they were just trying to trick me into getting up out of bed.

It snowed! Daddy waving from the new upstairs. There were icicles on the clothesline!

We still had to go to church that day, but even at church they let us make snowmen on the grass outside of the church. I had never been in the snow before, because it never snowed in Palo Alto and we always saved Daddy's vacation time in the summer to go to Kansas or Southern California or camping, and we never went any place over Christmas school vacation except maybe on a weekend. I think that my parents had gotten so sick of snow in Kansas they couldn't imagine paying money to go somewhere where there was snow! We didn't know anyone who went skiing or to snow places anyway, it just wasn't popular then like it is now, and cars were likely to have radiators freeze up or slide off the roads, because people just put water in their radiators, roads were not routinely plowed, and tires were a lot different. People didn't go to the snow for fun...it would be dangerous, not fun.

As the house progressed, my parents laid the asphalt tile themselves; they put down the mastic, heated the tiles and pressed them down on the concrete slab. Mastic was the sticky glue that held the floor tiles to the concrete. If the mastic didn't hold, you can imagine how awful that would be…tiles would peel off and the floor would be a real mess! They hung the sheetrock, and my mom did the taping of the sheetrock with the paper tape and grout over the seams in the sheetrock. They painted the walls, and laid the tiles in the new bathroom upstairs. My mom sanded and finished all the wood, the stair handholds and all the kitchen cupboards, and that took quite a while, because she would sand, then varnish, then sand with steel wool, then varnish, until she had many, many coats and the wood was a smooth as glass and very well protected.

My parents installed the doorknobs, the faucets, anything that they could do that the contractor said was okay to do. Even though it may have taken longer to do it, they saved money and we all took pride in the jobs that they did.

Then when it was all finished they had the front yard to redo and the entire inside to rearrange. I was excited because I would have a room of my own! I was getting the downstairs room that had been my parent's room, Judy and my parents would be upstairs with one bathroom, and Jennifer and I would be downstairs with the original bathroom, and my mom now

Almost done – Grandpa Bob & Grandma Gigi's car in the driveway with our car

had a sewing room downstairs. She had a room for the ironing board and sewing machine and fabric and yarn and she could spread out her projects and leave them partially done for the first time, instead of the way it had always been, with the sewing machine in my parents bedroom along with all the projects and the ironing board up and down each day instead of being able to leave it up all the time.

We had the only two-story house in the neighborhood.

The remodel is finally done, at least on the outside.

I had new furniture for my room, a beautiful new Danish-style desk with its own matching chair. It was sleek and modern-looking. For the first time I had a store-bought desk! My desk before was very nice; my daddy had made it as part of a bookcase in the corner of the room, and the desk part fastened up and shut when I wasn't using the desk, and when I wanted to use the desk I would unhook it and it folded down as a desk. It had been painted the same pink as the old kitchen table and as Judy's doll closet. Daddy had built both of those things.

But now I had a big desk with a bookcase almost up to the ceiling and two big drawers and one small desk drawer and the surface of the desk had a special shiny coating on it that made it very smooth and impossible to scratch.

The chair matched the wood and had a white cushion that was attached to the chair and wooden back that had a white cushion too. A few weeks after I got my new desk I was standing on the chair while my parents were at the grocery store and the chair broke. The leg just split apart right down the front leg, and I fell over and so did the chair.

I was horrified and couldn't believe it. I hadn't been doing any thing wrong and my new chair was broken. Judy walked by and saw it and said, "Boy oh boy! Are you ever going to get it!" But then we started trying to figure out how to fix it so that I wouldn't get in trouble. We got the *Elmer's Glue* out and put it on the leg and on the broken off part of the leg, and waited a few minutes like the instructions said, and then we pressed it together and held it really tight for about twenty minutes and wiped off the glue that squeezed out and cleaned it all up and put the glue away.

I was afraid to sit in the chair because I thought that the chair would break, so a whole week went by and I hadn't sat in the chair. Daddy came into my room on the next weekend and asked me something and I forgot about the chair and I went to my desk and sat down, and as I sat down the chair broke again at the place where we had glued it together.

I crashed to the floor and my daddy picked me up, and called my mom into the room, and said that they were going back to the store with the chair and make the store give them a replacement chair because all I had done was sit down, that he had seen it, and that the chair was defective.

My parents went to the furniture store with the broken chair. I didn't go; I was nervous to see what would happen, if the store would say that they knew it had already been broken and glued together. But my parents returned a little while later with a brand-new chair! The people at the furniture store told my parents that they were sorry and gave them a whole new chair! I got a replacement chair and everything was okay.

A few weeks later I was at Gramma Gigi's house and she and I were talking about my new room. I had the same old brown rug that had been there forever, and the same old drapes, and Gramma Gigi asked me if I would like new drapes for my birthday, and I said "**Yes!**" Gramma Gigi phoned my mom and asked my mom to measure the drapes and told her that I was getting drapes for my new room for my birthday!

I was so excited; we went to the Emporium department store and there were a lot of ready-made drapes there. My mom had sewn the drapes for most of the house, putting the special pleats on the top of the drapes with the special stiffening that was needed to make the drapes hang properly. However, ready-made drapes could be bought at the Emporium. They had so many to choose from, but most of them I didn't really like, and then I saw the drapes that I wanted: Long enough that when closed they would cover my whole wall down to the floor, gold fabric that was shimmery and shiny and smooth like satin. I fell in love with them that very moment and Gramma Gigi could tell, so she put them on her Emporium department store account, and we got to take them with us that same day and they were ready to go into my room!

Gramma Gigi drove me home on Sunday a little bit earlier than I usually would go home so that we would have time to hang up the drapes and see how they looked.

We were so excited, and went into my room, took down the old drapes and put up the new ones. The drapes looked so beautiful and harmonized with the brown rug. And when my mom came in she took one look at the drapes and started crying because she said she hated that color of gold and of all the colors we could have picked, why had we picked the color that we knew she hated!

I didn't know my mom hated that color. I hadn't thought about it. Even if I had thought about it I don't think I would have known or figured out that she didn't like the color gold. She wouldn't let me wear orange or yellow, but she had said that was because they didn't look good on me, not because she didn't like those colors. And Gramma Gigi and I hadn't picked out those colors on purpose to upset my mother with a color that she hated, but that was what my mom thought. So I felt awful about my mom, but I liked my drapes. I didn't know what to do. It was supposed to be my room, but I had never picked out anything for my own room myself in my whole life, and now I had picked out the first thing and my mom hated it.

If we took back the drapes and got something different maybe my mom wouldn't like those either. Maybe she only liked the things that she picked out herself. Then she said that I could keep them, but that she would never come into my room again because she couldn't stand the color.

That night when I was in my room by myself and I closed the drapes I thought they looked beautiful but I was sad that my mom hated them.

It was difficult for me to be in a room all by myself. I couldn't remember a time that I had slept all by myself in a room. I was used to hearing my sister breathe at night and maybe hearing her talk in her sleep. But now my parents were upstairs and so was Judy, so only Jennifer and I were downstairs. I kept thinking that I was hearing someone breaking into the house, because the noises were different in the remodeled house, and it was quiet in a different way than it had ever been. Before the remodel we had all heard each other, and I had always heard my daddy snore all night long ever since I was born, and all the other night time noises that my family would make, and now the house sounded different in my new room with my new drapes all by myself.

I couldn't decide if I wanted to sleep with my door open or closed, so I decided to sleep with it halfway open. My sister used to say that I walked in my sleep, but I didn't believe her. Then one night I woke up after smashing into the door in my sleep…waking up actually seeing stars and wondering what was happening. Someone had closed my door after I had gone to sleep, and I guess that sleepwalkers walk around fine in their sleep remembering how things were positioned when they went to bed. And in my sleep I thought that the door was part way opened, not closed, so I had walked into the door, and waking up was awful because I smashed my forehead, saw stars, and woke up all at once with no idea of what was happening.

The next morning I had a bump and bruise on my forehead, but my parents wouldn't believe what had happened to me. They just knew that every night I would go to sleep in my bed and then usually wake up on the floor at the foot of my bed.

For a while some of the seventh-grade boys had been coming over to our house. I didn't understand why they were coming over. They would ring our new doorbell, and ask if I was home, and then come inside and we would sit on the couch and pretty much not say anything. It felt awkward and I wasn't sure what I was supposed to do or why the boys came over. One time I asked the boy named Bobby if he wanted to go sit in the backyard, and he said sure, so we went out back and swung on the swings, and finally we started laughing, because swinging was still fun no matter how old a person was!

After a while Bobby got off his swing and was pushing me while I swung. It felt kind of weird, because I certainly didn't need any pushing, but it was nice at the same time. Then all of a sudden the wooden seat of the swing broke! It was as old as our swing set, and later Daddy said it had dry rot, but that was no consolation to me, because I was holding onto the metal chains that fastened to the wooden seat, and as I plunged to the ground the palms of my hands were shredded from trying to hold onto the chain, and then I landed on my butt really hard. My dress flew up into my face and I hoped at that moment to disappear from the face of the Earth, but I was not so lucky.

After that day, whenever the boys would come over I would ask them to wait a minute, and I would go change into play clothes, and then say, "Let's go out front." Once we were out front we could go walking or go to Palo Verde to play on the school equipment, but with Bobby we would run together. I just liked to run, to run for fun, and so did he. For the rest of sixth grade Bobby came over to my house many times and we would go running places together.

In those days people didn't have any kind of fancy running shoes, we just had regular sneakers called "Keds." And there weren't jogging clothes and we never saw grown-ups running around a neighborhood just for the heck of it. Grown-ups were busy doing other things like working and taking care of their houses and their families and we never would have imagined that any grown-up would run around a neighborhood just for the fun of it. Kids usually rode their bikes, but I discovered that if Bobby and I started running together that most of the time a few other kids would yell at us, asking what we were doing, and sometimes they would join us in running. One time I was running on the street with three boys, and people were gawking at us like we were aliens from outer space!

But running with the boys was fun and we didn't really have to talk, and it was hundreds of times better than sitting on the couch not knowing what to say and having Jennifer bring in her little chair and sit right behind the couch and spy on us.

It felt like sixth grade was suddenly going to be over too soon. Marie and Christine and I had been friends for a long time; Marie and me since kindergarten and Christine and me since she had moved to Palo Alto in the third grade. Next year I would go to a different school, to Ray Lyman Wilbur Junior High School. I would not be the tallest girl in school anymore, and I would not know all of my teachers and everyone in my class. I would take a bus to school, and have different teachers and a P.E. uniform and be in seventh grade, the youngest class at junior high. It was scary in a way, but it was time.

I didn't know what things would be like next year. I had finally figured out how some things worked, what the rules were and who were the good and bad guys. But I didn't know if I would ever kiss someone, or fall in love or be an art teacher or have kids or have a boyfriend, or if some day I would be beautiful like my Auntie Jan.

I was thirsty to learn, and the world was so exciting with poetry and writing and ways that I could help other people. Maybe I would be a social worker; maybe I would be an artist. I thought that I would like to live in a helicopter or in a school bus that was all fixed up inside like a house on wheels. Maybe I would live along the Amazon River for part of the year and collect insects, and then maybe I would live in the desert for a while, landing wherever I wanted to in my helicopter.

All I knew was that I had life ahead of me, life that was exciting and amazing and funny. I wanted so much to grab hold of what it was that meant something and made a difference in the world and figure out who I was and why I was on this Earth.

Things were sure to change.

Last day of sixth grade. I had just turned 11 years old.

End of Part One

The first part of the story has been put down on paper. That was the easy part...the part about "The 50/60 Kids," and what it was like growing up in Palo Alto in the 1950s and 1960s.

This next part, part two, is much harder...what to write and what to leave out, how to make sense of those times and tell the vibrancy, the intensity, the hope and the connectedness.

I still had the dreamer inside of me, but my world was expanding, society was exploding; we had sex, drugs, rock n' roll, commitment to social justice and a great faith that society was curing generations of social ills.

Gretchen still said, "Write the next part of your story... I want to know what happened to that little girl."

So I am busy writing the next part of my story; it is also the story of a generation caught up in the sparkling revolution

of the 1960s and 1970s.

Part two will be dedicated to my family and to all my friends, some living and some gone, who remember and were part of

The 60 / 70 Sparkling

A Palo Alto Dreamer

An excerpt from
Part Two – The 60 / 70 Sparkling

Our Junior High had seventh, eighth and ninth grades in it, and was named Ray Lyman Wilbur, "Wilbur" for short. Some years later they changed the name to Jane Lathrup Middle School, and it still is a middle school in Palo Alto.

Junior High was a time of growing up and of the world changing very quickly in a very short time. I was no longer the best in anything, which was a big change for me because I had always been the smartest, the ugliest, the fastest runner, the best drawer, the tallest...there were a lot of "ests" in my life that were gone. And then the reality of "the popular kids" vs. everyone else hit home as well. I think that initially I endeavored to fit in, to copy others, to be like everyone else, but I had what can only be called an epiphany shortly after seventh grade started....